MW01004575

Desire and Duty at Oneida

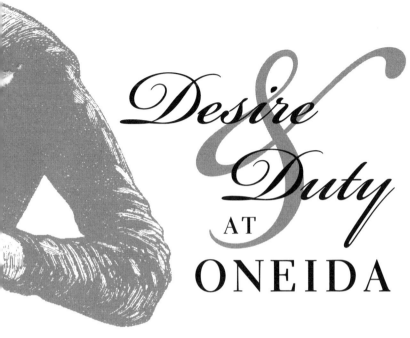

Desire & Duty

AT

ONEIDA

Tirzah Miller's Intimate Memoir

Robert S. Fogarty

Indiana University Press

BLOOMINGTON AND INDIANAPOLIS

This book is a publication of

Indiana University Press
601 North Morton Street
Bloomington, IN 47404-3797 USA
http://www.indiana.edu/~iupress
Telephone orders 800-842-6796
Fax orders 812-855-7931
Orders by e-mail iuporder@indiana.edu

The paper used in this publication meets the minimum
requirements of American National Standard for Information
Sciences—Permanence of Paper for Printed Library Materials,
ANSI Z39.48-1984.

MANUFACTURED IN THE UNITED STATES OF AMERICA

Library of Congress Cataloging-in-Publication Data

Herrick, Tirzah Miller, d. 1902.
    Desire and duty at Oneida : Tirzah Miller's intimate
memoir / [edited by] Robert S. Fogarty.
        p.   cm.
    Includes bibliographical references and index.
    ISBN 0-253-33693-7 (cloth : alk. paper). — ISBN 0-253-
21362-2 (pbk. : alk. paper)
    1. Oneida Community. 2. Free love—United States—
History—19th century Sources.   I. Fogarty, Robert S.
II. Title.
HX656.O5H47   2000
335'.974794—dc21   99-43398

1 2 3 4 5 05 04 03 02 01 00

To my children, David and Suzanne

CONTENTS

PREFACE

Oneida has had a long and complex history and its interpreters have been legion. All have been frustrated by the lack of primary sources about one of America's most daring social, economic, and sexual experiments; only in 1993, when the Oneida Community archives were opened, was it possible to explore a darker side to life at Oneida. By "darker" I mean not only the details of "incestuous" unions, but the complexities of the social and sexual arrangements known formally as "stirpiculture," "complex marriage," and "male continence." I have tried in this volume and in an earlier book, *Special Love/Special Sex* (1994), to give flesh to the desires and aspirations of community members as they struggled to define themselves, to find ways to express their sexual wants and needs, and to bring the kingdom of heaven to central New York.

Oneida was never a single set of ideas but was rather a changing set of assertions and practices dictated by its patriarch, John H. Noyes. Noyes gave life to the community, articulated its vision, and manipulated its membership in the direction of the "New Jerusalem." His niece Tirzah Miller, whose beauty and intelligence created a "magnetic force" that caused many men to love and admire her, also drew her uncle within her orbit. Yet Tirzah doubted her own power, and she sought security in the incestuous love of two uncles. Without doubt, this is the most dramatic account of Oneida to emerge from its recently opened archives. It is a story about sexual communism, about "consanguineous love," about music as it influences intimate relationships, about a community that struggled—in the most intimate ways—to define a social and sexual agenda that honored both community and commitment.

My earlier work focused on the lives of two ordinary members of Oneida, Victor Hawley and Mary Jones, who tried to define their love within the limitations of the colony's eugenics experiment, stirpiculture (from *stirps*, a line of descendants of common ancestry). This volume presents a larger window on that experiment because Tirzah Miller was at the very center of the struggles that led to the dissolution of the community in 1880. Tirzah was a leading member of the society and participated in all the major decisions that shook the society from 1869 to 1880. Her memoir is also deeply personal, reflecting both the turmoil of those years for the membership and her struggle to define her own life in the shadow of her uncle and lover, the colony leader, John H. Noyes. In this memoir we can see her passions, her aspirations, her trust in God's will, and her commitment to the ideals of the Oneida Community, the most radical religious and social experiment in nineteenth-century America.

A Note about the Text

A typescript copy of Tirzah Miller's memoir became available when the Oneida Community archives were formally opened on February 20, 1993. Her memoir had circulated among community descendants for some time prior to its acquisition by the Arents Rare Book Collection in 1983, and Spencer Klaw made partial use of it for his 1993 study, *Without Sin: The Life and Death of the Oneida Community.*

When I arrived at the Arents Rare Book Room the day after the collection opened, I found a faded xerox copy of a typewritten copy of the manuscript on onionskin. Tirzah Miller's 70-page, single-spaced typescript was part of the 2,000 pages of typed manuscript material deposited at Syracuse in 1983 by Imogene Stone. Certain archival material about the community had been burned in the 1920s by Oneida Ltd. executives, but fortunately a large cache of documents had been transcribed by John H. Noyes's nephew and Tirzah Miller's son, George Wallingford Noyes, for a book about the community. That material, including Tirzah Miller's memoir, became a part of the Oneida Community Collection in 1983.

No original copy in Tirzah Miller's hand is available, but the text's internal consistency suggests that it is a fair copy of an original. Had it been edited, certain "explosive" material (to quote a descendant) would have been deleted from the memoir. It was not. Gaps in the memoir may be explained by the details of Tirzah Miller's own life rather than by any effort on the part of her descendants to obscure her history. The few missing words in the manuscript are the result of a badly faded typescript and have been noted in the text. Every effort has been made to verify the details of the memoir by reference to other materials in the collection, including several other contemporary diaries and memoirs cited in the notes. Correspondence between community members confirms many of the details, including material that zealous descendants might have vetted, but apparently did not.

In 1993 a groundbreaking conference took place at Oneida. It brought together scholars and community descendants to discuss a remarkable society. During that conference the discussions were open and frank, and it was out of that meeting that this book emerged. Tirzah's memoir is a memorial to those descendants who believed that an open past might produce an open future.

ACKNOWLEDGMENTS

I am indebted first to my undergraduate teacher, Robert Remini, for encouraging me to work on such an exotic subject and to Allen Breck, my graduate advisor, for giving me the necessary intellectual freedom to work on such a chancy subject. Under both Remini and Breck I came to understand the corporeal nature of ideas, particularly when they involved such a fleshy subject as the Oneida Community.

Over the years the librarians at the Olive Kettering Library at Antioch College have been supportive of my efforts and the Faculty Fund at Antioch College has provided funds for essential research work. Without such institutional support and library assistance this book would never have appeared. An Antioch student, Nova Ren Suma, gave the memoir a close reading and made valuable suggestions about the text. My assistant at the *Antioch Review*, Michelle Giguere, was helpful in getting the memoir on and off the computer. Jane Baker provided superb editorial guidance and help in reshaping the text in its final stages. As a footnote to this institutional history of support it should be noted that Tirzah Miller's niece and namesake, Tirzah Noyes, attended Antioch College in 1923.

The staff at the Arents Rare Book Room of the Syracuse University Library have been unfailingly helpful. Its director, Mark Weimer, has, at every turn, provided advice, assurance, and guidance through a sometimes murky thicket of documents and problems. The Oneida Community Collection has been developed under Weimer's careful direction. He and his staff have been supportive of my work; without Weimer's patient and open collection policy this book could not have been completed. Mary Beth Hinton, editor of the Syracuse University Library Associates journal, *The Courier*, put together a valuable collection of essays about Oneida that highlighted some of the best contemporary scholarship on the subject. Other individuals in and around Sherrill and the Oneida Community Mansion House Association provided, despite certain misgivings about the publication of such an "explosive" memoir, generous hospitality and unfailing courtesy that amounted (in the long run) to essential support for publication of such a controversial document. They are Lang Hatcher, Nini Hatcher, Ed Pitts, Merry Leonard, Betty Wayland-Smith, Giles Wayland-Smith, Jane Rich, Pody Vanderwall, Sally Mandel, Geoff Noyes, Jessie Mayer, Gail Doering, Richard Kathmann, and Bruce Moseley. Joseph Kirschner's work on music-making at Oneida has informed my own interpretation.

And I am indebted to Stephen Stein and Catherine Albanese for their close and critical reading of both the introduction and the memoir.

On a personal note I am continually indebted to Katherine Kadish for her love and encouragement and to my two children, David and Suzanne, to whom this book is dedicated.

Eros

(*Written by twenty-one-year-old Tirzah Miller*
at Wallingford, May 17, 1864)

I

A ride in our graceful boat, & ho!
This lovely evening in May.
We'll skip o'er the waves and toss away woe,
For our hearts are joyous and gay.

II

With Heber for oarsman, and I at the helm
A merry duet are we!
We talk about books and shady nooks,
And the charming sights we see.

III

We leave our brows in the floating stream,
Thus troubling the beautiful river;
Then watch for each others face to gleam
When the waters cease to quiver.

IV

We laugh and talk till the solemn hush
Of deep'ning night falls still,
And stops the liquid songs which gush
From the birds in melting trill.

V

Then feeling and silence and hidden thought
Enhance the charms of the hour;
With magnetic thrills our hearts are fraught—
Subdued by nights strange power.

VI

Thus soft and still we onward glide.
Except we brush the trees
Which droop their graces o'er the tide
And summer in the breezes.

VII

I fancy this a symbol fair
Of the peaceful flow of life,
When doubt, nor pain, nor sorrow, nor care
Disturb with earthly life.

VIII

This is the time 'tween fall of night
And the glim'ring of the stars,
When human eyes are weirdly bright—
The soul throws down its beam.

IX

And lovers look as down deep wells,
In eyes they love to see
And these they read what no tongue tells,
And solve all mystery.

X

Silence oft does tender speak
The thoughts which well in hearts,
Than do the words which vainly seek
Expression's earthly arts.

Introduction

THE ONEIDA COMMUNITY was one of many utopian experiments in the mid-nineteenth century—others were Brook Farm and Fruitlands—but it was by far the best known. It was clearly distinguished by its espousal of "complex marriage" (viewed as free love by those outside the community) and by the only eugenics experiment ever tried in America, which produced fifty-eight children. But Oneida was far more than a sexual experiment: It was a religious colony devoted to exploring the outer reaches of Perfectionism, and it was also a highly successful economic venture.

Tirzah Miller's memoir is the most remarkable document to emerge from the recently opened Oneida archives. Written between 1867 and 1879 by the most prominent figure of the younger generation at Oneida, it gives us a unique perspective on the community and its founder, Tirzah's uncle John H. Noyes. It expresses surprisingly few regrets about either her own life or the life at Oneida. It does contain a great deal of grieving over insults received, slights perceived, injuries done, and losses incurred—all in name of a greater social purpose. Tirzah Miller was at the center of the Oneida Community and her memoir recounts the major traumas that both she and the community went through, including the controversial stirpiculture experiment and the colony's disintegration.

Several key issues emerge in this memoir: spiritual life at Oneida and the religious questions posed by a community in transition from a Bible-based to a scientific society; the nature of the sexual family at Oneida; questions of marriage, incest, and "child love"; eugenics; power as it related to the authority of the elder Noyes and the internal disputes that occurred in the community; and individualism at Oneida, exemplified by the questions of personal choice Tirzah raises in her memoir. Her story both complements and differs radically from the story of Victor Hawley, an ordinary member, who left the community to have children with one woman, Mary Jones.[1] Tirzah, on the other hand, remained faithful to the religious and social dictums of the group.

Social Reform, John H. Noyes, and the Oneida Community

Historically, the creation of social policy alternatives has been the province of small intentional groups, from the first communal group to settle in America, the Labadists, to a controversial contemporary Christian sexual community, the Children of God. Such groups came together in search of practical ways to implement their agenda, whether it was religious freedom or sexual liberation.

In attempting to harmonize man with the moral order, the reform movements of the nineteenth century took on the character of crusades. The spirit of the age demanded a comprehensive effort to shape society along "natural" rather than "artificial" lines. As a result, men and women such as Noyes and Miller examined every institution to determine whether it helped or hindered humanity's "natural" development. As temperance, anti-slavery, anti-tobacco, and scores of other societies came into existence, the eccentric quality of the period was heightened, but its strength was sapped because of overlapping, and sometimes competing, interests. Ralph Waldo Emerson caught the diffuse and comprehensive spirit that attempted to bring together the social and moral orders in his famous essay "Man the Reformer": "We are to revise the whole of the social structure, the state, the school, religion, marriage, trade, science, and explore their foundation in our own nature. . . . What is man born for but to be a reformer, a Re-maker of what man has made; a renouncer of lies, a restorer of truth and good; imitating the great nature which embosoms us all."[2] The search for some unifying principle that could explain the cosmos was characteristic not only of Emerson, but also of the great utopian theorist Charles Fourier, whose American

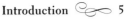

interpreter Albert Brisbane wrote, "There must arise a great genius to discover a theory of Universal Unity, a true theory of the Immortality of the Soul, the laws of Order and Harmony which govern creation."[3]

Would the reformation of society, many asked, come through the application of orderly moral principles, or would a cataclysmic moral revolution forever destroy the vestiges of both feudal aristocracy and Enlightenment infidelity? The reforming spirit of the revivals, which aimed to regenerate the heart of man, opposed both the rational "infidelity" of Unitarianism and the "legalism" of the orthodox churches. The "mind," according to the famous New York revivalist Charles Finney, was limited in its capacity to produce change, but the "heart" could produce a new man capable of moral and spiritual perfection. The evangelical spirit of the heart, begun in the eighteenth century, continued into the nineteenth and helped produce anti-slavery crusades, agitation for women's rights, penal reform, and communal and utopian movements. Perry Miller, examining the native roots of Transcendentalism, found that the suppressed mysticism of Puritan New England was released during the reform period of 1830 to 1860: "But now the restraining hand of Theology was withdrawn, there was nothing to prevent them as there had been everything to prevent Edwards, from identifying their intuitions with the voice of God, or from fusing God and nature into one substance of Transcendental imagination."[4]

The restraining hand of dogma and authority had lost its grip, and the voice of the spirit and the heart was in ascendance. As a result, the spiritual, intuitive side was exalted at the expense of logic and dogma. Mesmerism, Spiritualism, Perfectionism, and Transcendentalism all tended to dissolve the Cartesian dualism of body and mind: "Mystics were no longer inhibited by dogmas. They were free to carry out the ancient New England propensity for reeling and staggering with new opinions. They could give themselves over, unashamedly, to become transparent eyeballs and debauches of dew."[5] John H. Noyes's early career was filled with such "reeling and staggering," as was shown by his rejection of orthodoxy and acceptance of millennial Perfectionism, his rejection of the conventional marriage system and acceptance of complex marriage, and his rejection of piecemeal reform and acceptance of total regeneration as the means of reform, all directed toward the reformation of society. The Oneida Community's growth and development as a spiritual institution was influenced by its constant contact with the new ideas so prevalent at the time. In his history of *Communistic Societies of the United States* Noyes wrote, "As Unitarianism ripened into

Transcendentalism at Boston, and Transcendentalism produced Brook Farm, so Orthodoxy ripened into Perfectionism at New Haven, and Perfectionism produced the Oneida Community."[6]

When one looks at the reform and revival activity of the period, its most striking characteristic is its vibrancy. Western and central New York, where Oneida was located, displayed the same force and vigor. The "burned-over district" of New York was subjected to a series of revivals, beginning in 1825, that upset such orthodox denominations as the Congregationalists and Presbyterians and produced religious and social unrest. Between the opening of the Erie Canal in 1825 and the destructive Panic of 1837, the part of New York State to which Noyes eventually migrated was torn apart by a variety of "isms" but was particularly susceptible to Perfectionism.[7] Oneida was part of this long tradition. Founded in the heady days of reform agitation in the 1840s, it was rooted in a mixture of the charismatic leadership of John Humphrey Noyes, the religious radicalism of the times, and the belief that a "more perfect union" could be created by individuals coming together to form communal alliances.

Both Tirzah Miller's life and the story of the Oneida Community are inextricably bound up in the personal history and theology of John Humphrey Noyes. He was born into a prosperous Vermont family at Brattleboro in 1811; his career up to 1848 (when he established the Oneida Community in central New York) was marked by both dramatic shifts and a growing sense of his mission and importance as a prophetic voice and energetic reformer. His father, a one-term congressman, was a shadowy figure plagued by alcoholism but his mother (the aunt of Rutherford B. Hayes) was a decisive figure and dominant force in his early life. For example, she insisted that he attend Dartmouth College rather than Yale because it would be "a better place for his morals," and she later joined him at both his Putney and Oneida communities.

After graduating from Dartmouth in 1830, Noyes studied law for a year before he was caught up in the tumultuous Finney revivals that swept through New England. The enthusiasm surrounding a revival in New Haven led him to abandon a legal career and turn toward the ministry. He entered Andover Theological Seminary in 1831 but transferred to Yale a year later. There he joined the ranks of avid revivalists and helped form a "free church" in New Haven.

Under the influence of Yale theologian Nathaniel Taylor, Noyes embraced a radical Perfectionist view that rejected the Calvinist doctrine of depravity and asserted that sinless perfection was possible under God's grace. In February 1834 Noyes announced that he had achieved such a state. He also took up certain millennialist notions that fixed the date of Christ's second coming in the past (specifically, A.D. 70), rather than in the future. Noyes and other perfectionists of his ilk argued that this new intermillennial scheme dictated new rules and a new covenant for new men. This heretical theological notion led to his expulsion from Yale in 1834, and for the next few years he moved about New England and New York preaching a doctrine of sanctification and involving himself in anti-slavery work. In 1838 his views on marriage and free love became widely known with the publication of the "Battle-Axe Letters," which consisted of correspondence between Noyes and another Perfectionist. In these letters Noyes condemned marriage and advanced a system of sexual relations that allowed for multiple partners.

In that same year he married Harriet Holton (partly to stem a growing storm of criticism) and gathered about him at Putney, Vermont, a small community of believers, including members of his immediate family (in 1841 they numbered thirteen). Tirzah's father, John H. Miller, joined the Putney Association in 1845 and married Noyes's sister, Charlotte. He was primarily involved with the business affairs at Putney (and later at Oneida and Brooklyn) and he had three children there. In June 1854, while on a trip to Brooklyn, he suddenly fell ill and died. He was only forty. His brother-in-law, John H. Noyes, who was ill at the same time but recovered, became the eleven-year-old Tirzah's surrogate father.

The Putney Society of Inquiry published a periodical (*The Circular*), shared goods and homes, and in 1846 instituted complex marriage, whereby individuals could choose sexual partners based on love and attraction rather than marriage terms. When word of these liaisons became known to the Putney authorities, Noyes was charged with lewd and lascivious behavior and, in order to avoid prosecution, he fled the state. (Noyes's own definition of what was lewd certainly differed from the version of the Vermont authorities. In 1840 he had written, "If God only can properly give a license to copulate, lewdness, fornication, and adultery may take place under the cover of ordinary marriage license from man. Or, on the other hand, it is conceivable that persons may have a license from God who have none from man: but in this case they will be able to prove their license. And, thirdly, God's license and man's may coincide, which is most desirable."[8] (Underlining in original.) (To Noyes, lewd meant "unlicensed" sexual enjoyment; fornication meant "unlicensed" copulation of "unmarried" persons; adultery meant "unlicensed" copulation of "married" persons.) Clearly Noyes felt he had both God's license and a license from his supporters to usher in the kingdom of heaven, even though his behavior seemed "unlicensed" to the authorities.

When Noyes fled Putney in 1847 he went to central New York, a hotbed of radical Perfectionist sentiment, and to the farm of one of his disciples, Abram Burt. The next year he was joined there by his family and followers from Vermont (fifty-one in all) and the Oneida Community took root as a utopian experiment. About a third of the original members were from Noyes's own family. They included his wife, Harriet Holton; his brother George W. Noyes and his wife; his sister Harriet Skinner and her husband; his mother; and the first woman with whom he had entered into a complex marriage arrangement, Mary Cragin, who bore him twins in 1850.

Oneida was, at its core, a spiritual community that developed out of the theological and social upheavals of the 1830s. It was based on Noyes's theology of "Bible Communism" (a return to the practices of the early Christian church) which he developed between 1837 and 1848 and fully articulated in an 1847 pamphlet, *The Berean*. His theology stressed biblical literalism, security from sin, the possibility of Christian perfection, and the messianic belief that Noyes was a prophetic leader in the Pauline tradition. Although Tirzah's memoir indicates little concern about religious or theological questions, she had grown up in a community of Perfectionists for whom social decisions were always rooted in biblical ethics and justification.

Noyes's theological radicalism had a social counterpart in the sharing of property and persons, a commitment to sexual experimentation, and cooperative child care. Like other reformers of the day who adopted the higher-law position in both theology and politics, Noyes denounced the family as a corrupt institution and emphasized communitarianism as a method of addressing social concerns, including the role of women in society. One astute commentator on Oneida, Louis Kern, has argued persuasively that women were passive in the theological and social scheme at Oneida: "God created woman as a companion to man and so that he might have an erotic relation on the material plane. . . . As nurturer of the seed, woman possessed an enigmatic and ominously passive capacity that had to be carefully superintended."[9]

Tirzah, on the other hand, writing in 1867, felt that under communitarianism women would play an equal role with men and begin to shine in practical affairs: "[M]odern progression in Civilization is giving her a higher position & Communism promises her a destiny consistent with the immortality of her soul, so that her character needs great expansion, there must be even now many pursuits in which men and women can engage irrespective of sex."[10] Among these pursuits she mentioned business and intellectual cultivation.

Lawrence Foster, in his *Religion and Sexuality*, has traced the development of Noyes's thought from his days as a theology student at Yale to his later militant stand on marriage. Foster believes that Noyes was willing to let his followers go through periods of confusion and uncertainty in order to create a new sexual order that destroyed the marital assumptions of the day. Noyes wrote in 1839, "The marriage supper of the Lamb, is a feast at which every dish is free to every guest. Exclusiveness, quarreling, have no place there, for the same reason as that which forbids guests at a thanksgiving dinner to claim each his separate dish, and quarrel with the rest for his rights. . . . The guests of the marriage supper may have each his favourite dish of his own procuring, and that without the jealousy of exclusiveness. I call a certain woman my wife — she is yours, she is Christ's, and in him she is the bride of all saints."[11] When this incendiary article was printed (anonymously) in a Perfectionist paper, a controversy erupted over its implications. Noyes was forced to admit his authorship and from that point on he sought to implement the "marriage feast of the Lord" through several communities.

Of this early period Noyes later confidently wrote: "The churches have been looking for the millennium, and the Adventists have been looking for the coming of the Son of Man, and the Spiritualists for the 'good time coming.' Everybody has been looking for something. There had been great hopes for the end of evil, and the beginning of good in this world. All such people will finally turn their attention to the Oneida Community and make up their minds that what they have been looking for has come."[12]

Noyes's theory of society was rooted in a simple belief that sin was the root cause of all the world's ills. Sin, or selfishness, therefore, had to be attacked and destroyed in individuals. The kingdom of God was in the process of development, and changes in society, although often slow in coming, were examples of God working through history. The existence of the Oneida Community was, for example, proof positive of God's spirit in the world working to restore man to the true faith that the Primitive Church had once held: "[The] general principle [of the men in the Primitive Church] was that of leaving the institutions of the world to pass away by the ultimate effect of the abolition of sin."[13]

According to Noyes, reform would come about only if each individual set himself the task of personal reform and self-betterment. As a result, the Oneida Community stressed individual regeneration as well as corporate salvation. Members were expected to improve their minds and souls through regular reading and classes. Therefore, algebra, Greek, speech, literature, and many other classes abounded at Oneida because the community encouraged practical spiritual uplift. The approach of the community to the problems of the world was radical in that it urged the abolition of marriage and labor systems as then practiced. Oneida was both radical and conservative. The New England mystic and the Yankee merchant came together at Oneida.

Noyes believed, according to Lawrence Foster, that marriage treated "women as a form of property, and thus has the same harmful effects as other types of selfish ownership of property."[14] Noyes sought, therefore, first to effect a true reconciliation with God and with the sexes, and then to reform the industrial order: "Holiness, free love, association in labor, and immortality, constitute the chain of redemption, and must come together in their true order."[15] Complex marriage, according to Noyes, sought to eliminate selfishness and reestablish a moral order that marriage had corrupted. All this was to occur within a society that justified all actions by reference to the Bible and the Epistles of St. Paul. (To extend that point, Tirzah Miller, for example, felt justified by both community practice and biblical texts to accept several men as her sexual partners and to gratify their needs, whether they were close relatives or new members of the community.)

During the early years at Oneida there was disagreement over and practical difficulties surrounding the sexual and social-economic practices of the community. But between July 1851 and October 1852 Noyes was confident enough about the religious and spiritual progress that had been made to set forth sixteen governing religious and social principles, which he eventually presented in an undated "Home Talk" titled "Our Platform":

> Sovereignty of Jesus Christ dating from his resurrection and manifested in his second coming;
> Co-sovereignty of the Primitive Church raised from the dead at the second coming;

Union with Christ and Primitive by faith and love;
Unity of all believers in this world and in Hades with the one kingdom in the Heavens;
Resurrection of the spirit resulting in salvation from sin and selfish habits;
Resurrection of the body preventing or overcoming disease, renewing youth, and resulting in the abolition of death and the loosing of captives in Hades;
Community of property of all kinds with inspiration for distribution;
Abandonment of the entire fashion of the world especially about marriage;
Encouragement of love and limitation of propagation;
Dwelling together in Association or complex families;
Home churches and home schools;
Meetings every evening;
Cultivation of free criticism;
HORTICULTURE the leading business for subsistence;
A daily paper as the gathering point for all separate Association.[16]

The first six principles emphasized a commitment to Bible Communism and the last suggests the importance of the press as a proselytizing vehicle. These principles remained in place for the next twenty years until, in the 1870s, dissension over these bedrock assumptions shook the society to its core.

The community's concerns during the early 1850s were both intimate and public. They were intimate in the sense that Noyes was forging a Perfectionist community based on his own biblical and social theories, yet public in that he wanted his program to be felt in the larger world of New York reformers. Beginning in August 1849 Noyes went to live in Brooklyn, New York, as the head of a radical free love (a term they rejected) group while his followers at Oneida struggled to define their utopia. Marriage had not been entirely abandoned within the fledgling commune, and in an 1850 letter Noyes acknowledged how vexing the problem was, particularly for young men. Some members suffered from the "marriage spirit" and were unable to give up their wives, while others were unable to resist the impulse to marry and form what later would be called "special love" relationships. During 1850 and 1851, while Noyes was in Brooklyn, he was forced to deal with what he called the "transition of the young men from the hot blood of virginity to the quiet freedom which is the essential element of our Society." He was trying to eliminate the "sale and delivery" of women through marriage, but found that jealousies persisted and that some women in the community "lost their equilibrium."[17]

The Brooklyn group saw themselves as a phalanx formed to spread Noyes's brand of Perfectionism in the growing metropolis of New York. They met nightly to talk about their religious life, about free love, about the practical difficulties of living in a communal home at Willow Street in Brooklyn Heights. The results of these meetings were sent to Oneida to further the discussions of members there and to provide guidance to their developing sense of community, their sexual practices, and what it meant to be a Perfectionist. At both sites mutual criticism sessions were conducted. Here is one from Brooklyn: "Mrs. Whitfield revealed a secret of her past life which had kept her from fellowship with God and believers. She repeated the confession to Messrs. Inslee and Thomas, who came Wednesday evening. They joined in bringing in their accounts in love matters. Mr. Noyes talked very plainly to them of avoiding secrecy and the importance of being sincere with him and one another."[18]

Henry James, Sr. was a regular visitor to the Brooklyn group, and the communists followed his writings: "Mr. Noyes discoursed upon Mr. James' article in the *Tribune*, 'Marriage and Divorce,' of which he kept a copy. Next evening he talked about the miseries of riches, and Wednesday upon the first and second growth of love."[19] James's most recent biographer, Alfred Habegger, believes that James encouraged Noyes to be more public about his radical sexual policy in the 1850s: "James wanted to push the most extreme sex radical in the United States out into the mainstream."[20] Noyes was publicly aligned with James in an attack on marriage reformers in a conservative Presbyterian weekly, *New York Observer*, in 1852. James later backtracked from his radical, and essentially philosophical, support of "free love."

By 1854 Noyes was forced to focus on the financial future of the association. He left Brooklyn and consolidated his base at Oneida by bringing in a group of Perfectionists from New Jersey. The economic stability of Oneida was secured by the inventive genius of a single man, Sewell Newhouse, a Vermont-born trapper who, after joining the community in 1848, produced a superior steel trap in the machine shop at Oneida. It prompted large orders from both New York and Chicago, and by 1864 the annual production rate of the Newhouse traps had risen to 275,000. The mechanical process for manufacturing traps was later adapted to the forging of the silverware that became synonymous with Oneida.

Between 1854 and 1868 Noyes consolidated the economic and social position of the group by mechanizing the trap production facilities, by opening the colony to an increasing number of visitors, and by continuing to publish his periodicals. New buildings were erected to accomodate a growing population, and an agency was opened in New York City to handle certain commercial transactions and serve as a base for some young people at school.

The years following the Civil War were the calmest in the history of the society. They had emerged from the war virtually unscathed, for only a few members had joined the Union forces. In 1866 the community membership stood at 300. Prosperity had come about not only by manufacturing traps for the commercial fur trade but also through the sale of silk goods, fruit preserves, and traveling bags. As these industries grew, the community was forced to repudiate its earlier idealistic theory of labor and employ "hirelings" to meet the demand for its products. Essentially Oneida had become a unitary family that combined economic, religious, and educational functions under one roof and under the guidance of John H. Noyes. During these post–Civil War years the community maintained a *Daily Journal* that reported on the comings and goings of members, business matters, and evening meetings. These journals, produced at Oneida, were circulated beyond the community to the membership in Wallingford (a satellite community in Connecticut) and New York City. Reports about production problems, canning quotas, and sales projections fill these volumes. For example, it was noted in late December 1868 that $40,000 in wages were paid and 230 workers employed during the peak month of February. Letters from salesmen indicated that they traveled as far west as St. Louis and were always concerned about their contacts with the outside world.[21]

Daily life at Oneida during this period revolved around business, religious affairs, and "social life." One major facet of life at Oneida was the practice of "mutual criticism" wherein individuals either offered themselves up or were singled out for intense group sessions that probed their conduct within the society. Individuals who volunteered did so as sinners approaching the "anxious bench" prior to witnessing their faith. Such meetings were painful, since people's "faults" were made known to them in the hope that they would reform. Some of the manuscript reports of these sessions were published in the *Daily Journal* for the edification of the entire community. Although criticisms about sexual matters rarely appeared in these published accounts, there were hints (later confirmed in diaries like Tirzah's) of problems: "In criticising individuals, sometimes, we talk about being loose in social matters. I think in this connection we might profitably inquire what constitutes true chastity or what in the kingdom of heaven, is the true standard of morality."[22] One member (Charlotte E. Underwood) wrote in 1866 that she wanted to express her thanks "to the family for the sincere criticism of me in showing me my faults . . . I confess my love for Mr. Noyes, Mr. Hamilton and Mr. Woolworth as inspired men . . . I confess my love for the whole community family, and a spirit of subordination to Christ at all times and under all circumstances."[23]

Evening business meetings, held in the Great Hall (the auditorium), were attended by the entire community. Managers reported from various departments, work assignments were given out, and committees were formed to investigate production problems or to purchase some labor-saving device. Oneida had an elaborate and constantly shifting bureaucracy that was dominated by the senior male leaders, Erastus Hamilton, William Hinds, and William Woolworth.

Throughout the history of the society, work bees were used to bring in crops or respond to large orders. An account of a "Queen Bee" in 1866 is a good example of the spirit generated by such corporate activities. The sudden arrival of 139 crates of peaches from Georgia halted German and theology classes for the day, brought workers from Willow Place (a nearby facility for making traps) to the preserve house, and prompted the hired help to volunteer to get the canning done. Some 171 individuals participated; "[T]he bee [was] a complete success and yielded about 800 quarts of fruit to the preserves. We have never seen anything so brilliant. It was perfectly electric. The condensation of magnetic life produced a general sparkle and flash of mirth throughout the bee."[24]

Music and theater were other important focuses of the community. For many members musical performance was both a social pastime and a statement about corporate life at Oneida. In 1864, for example, the community organized "for the benefit of our workmen and near neighbors" a series of twenty-three free concerts designed to improve relations."[25] The executive committee appointed to organize these events pulled together from the ranks of the community a twenty-two-member orchestra, another eleven-member ensemble used for theatrical performances, a brass band, and a choir of twenty to twenty-five singers. In addition, plays were staged and the community children performed in tableaux as part of the entertainment series, which attracted large audiences: More than 900 people crowded into the community hall for these events.

As long as music was a goad to the spirit or a vehicle for expressing community values, it had a central role at Oneida; but when it served "personal" needs and deflected players from a spirit of corporate life into intimate musical ensembles, it was deemed dangerous. Noyes was quick to rein in such a spirit of individualism, or cliquishness.[26] Tirzah, who had a large "appetite for tune" and was an accomplished pianist, and Frank Wayland-Smith were singled out in 1864 for a criticism session that focused on their bonding for both music and mutual pleasure: "Their musical practice together has proved a snare to them by leading into a false love and disrespect to the criticism of the Community; and rather than have this state of things continue, Mr. N. said he would rather sacrifice their music much as he appreciates it." Wayland-Smith later recorded in his diary that Noyes wanted only "mediocre" playing; "music he says, must always be subordinated to spirituality on the one hand, and to industry on the other. He is evidently quite jealous of the influence of music in the O.C. and does not desire any high development of it." It was not only Noyes's limited view of the value of music (Noyes himself was an indifferent violinist) that irked Wayland-Smith, but his characteristic inconsistencies: "Today one is incited to practice; to-morrow he is exalted to quit it, and criticized for drawing the young into superficialities. Up and down, up and down."[27] In an 1874 criticism session directed at the "prima donna fever" among the young women of the community Noyes said, "The essence of the evil seems to be, that among these persons who are in trouble, music has evidently become a selfish, personal thing; they look on their talents, their reputations, ability and success in music as their own, and are quarreling in their hearts about the matter, just as the world quarrels about money and other selfish rights; music in fact is uncommunized property. I thought that if the strife had become such a nuisance among these young girls, it might be possible that the whole musical body is so affected by the same spirit. It is astonishing what an amount of *discord* the science of *concord* can make."[28]

The community provided other in-house entertainments—for example, during the first phase of the stirpiculture program, *The Circular* described a Sunday evening ceremony called "Weighing the Babies." All the "stirps" were brought into the hall, placed (in order of age) on a commercial scale, and weighed. "After the ceremony of the scales the orchestra with its late addition of kettle drums plays two or three times.

The orchestra is under thorough drill this winter, with a new score, new music etc., and it is all we get from them during the week, so we think a good deal of it."[29]

Oneida defied the stereotype of the isolated communal group by accommodating numerous visitors. By 1866 the community was well connected to the world through commerce, publicity about the colony, and a steady stream of curious visitors. Some 16,000 visitors were counted in a period of five and a half years; it was estimated, however, that three times that number had actually come between 1862 and 1867, since many failed to sign the colony register. Some of the visitors were famous (Susan B. Anthony, Tom Thumb, and former governor William H. Seward), but most were simply the curious on a day's outing from Syracuse or Rochester to sample the community's excellent cooking and stroll around the grounds. Many came for the annual Fourth of July celebration and to enjoy the special strawberry shortcake prepared for the occasion. Visitors were instructed not to smoke, intrude into private rooms, or drive their carriages off the driveways. The members often tired of these visitors and their questions, but realized that they needed to remain on good terms with the outside world and to prove themselves earnest and hardworking Christians.

During this period the community received some fifty inquiries a month from individuals wanting to join. Sorting the true believers from the thrill-seekers was difficult; prospective members were always told to read the Bible, study the community literature and, if their interest continued, to make a short visit. Richard Realf, a poet and member of John Brown's secret "cabinet," expressed interest; Charles Guiteau, Garfield's assassin, stayed briefly in 1866; a contingent of free lovers from a community at Berlin Heights, Ohio, joined in 1868. Inquiries came from members of other groups (most notably the Shakers), and some older communards who had been at Brook Farm or the North American Phalanx dropped in. Charles Meeker, who visited in 1866 to do a story for Horace Greeley's New York Tribune, may have come away with some ideas that took root in his 1868 Union Colony, later to become Greeley, Colorado. David Goodman and Jane Cunningham Croly, a formidable pair of journalists from New York who took an exceptional interest in Oneida, visited in the late 1860s; David G. Croly later extolled the community's efforts in his book Glimpses of the Future.[30]

Among those who expressed a keen interest in Oneida were Charles Nordhoff, a former editor of Harper and Brothers and the New York Evening Post, who visited the community in 1874 and recorded his impressions in *The Communistic Societies of the United States*.[31] William Hepworth Dixon, an English reporter, visited in 1866 and described the leaders as "intelligent" and the women as "attractive"; however, Dixon's books *New America* and *Spiritual Wives* both criticized the community's sexual arrangement and Noyes's leadership.[32]

Certainly some contemporaries in the world outside Oneida considered Noyes a crazy enthusiast. For example, a group of clergymen met in Syracuse in March 1878 to condemn the colony's immoral practices. But this Comstockean "raid of the ministers," as Tirzah characterized it, was nothing "compared to the internal dissension" that was beginning to erode the community. "Evil thinking of the administration and general independence" were by then widespread, and J. H. Noyes admonished Tirzah to become the "mother" of the group in order to "master all these young folks." The younger generation constituted the most problematic element at Oneida because they had drifted away from religious principles and toward exclusive "self-seeking."

Though squarely in the Noyes camp, in December 1878 Tirzah experienced an "agony of doubt" about her uncle: "Oh! *Is* he a crazy enthusiast, who is just experimenting on human beings?" This echoed the sentiments of the dissidents who considered the elder Noyes "a bad sensual man," according to Frank Wayland Smith.[33] Tirzah swept such doubts aside, thinking they must have been "injected" into her mind; voluntarily to hold such thoughts would be a sign of sinfulness and weakness. A new baby and a newfound love (James Herrick, to whom she began referring in the memoir as "Jamie") helped her doubts recede.

Similar struggles and conversations were occurring throughout the community, and other diaries and memoirs, particularly Frank Wayland-Smith's, attest to these divisions. For example, Tirzah was approached by Myron Kinsley to throw her support more assertively behind Noyes in the factional disputes over property, sexual practices, and the leadership. Noyes's son Theodore was unable to exert significant authority. The number of those loyal to his father diminished, and a faction led by James Towner and William Hinds demanded a restructured community. By June 1879 it was obvious that the community could not be held together, particularly since the younger members had gone off on their own. Frank Wayland-Smith wrote, "The young are fast breaking away from all sense of moral accountability, scorning advice (i.e. many of them, not all), and some are really impertinent in their self-assertion. . . . All are waiting for something decisive to happen."[34]

On June 23, 1879 John H. Noyes secretly left Oneida for Canada because he feared prosecution at the hands of the local authorities, who had been stirred up by the ministers at Syracuse. Noyes and Otis Kellogg left the colony after midnight and drove thirty miles to Holland Patent, New York, where they took a train and then crossed to Canada by ferry. Noyes was never to return to Oneida. At Stone Cottage overlooking Niagara Falls he gathered a group of loyal friends and family who ministered to him till his death in 1886. At the time of the breakup 112 members signed a document agreeing to go to Canada to form an alternative community, but in the end only about fifteen stalwarts made the journey.

According to his son Pierrepont Noyes, the leader in exile continued to dominate the development of the new joint stock corporation that had been formed at Oneida in 1881. Noyes also continued to deliver nightly "home talks" at Niagara Falls to an assembly of supporters that consisted of Tirzah, James Herrick, Harriet Skinner, Theodore Pitt, and John Cragin. Eight adults (including his wife, Harriet Holton) resided at the modest cottage. According to Spencer Klaw, Noyes refused to allow Tirzah and James Herrick, who were then married, to live together. Tirzah acquiesced to Noyes's suggestion that she go to stay at Oneida: "I remove a cause of temptation to Mr. Herrick and I retire to a position where you can perhaps get into my life better than him, and at any rate put to the test your work on me."[35]

Concord and Discord:
Sex and Marriage at Oneida

Self-control and a growing sense of religious strength within the community were the keys to Oneida's new sexual kingdom: "As we become mighty in the power of the resurrection we shall be able to hold the passions even of the young men quiet, and introduce them to the freedom of love without danger. Till then we must try experiments and wriggle through our difficulties the best we can; and in this transition period the young must consider the difficulties, be patient, and help as much as they can by self-discipline," Noyes wrote.[36] In 1850 Noyes believed that what he termed a spiritual "ascending fellowship" (members should associate with their spiritual superiors, "who drew them upward") could control free love tendencies by regulating the flow of relationships and that "mating horizontally" (his term for numerous liaisons with different partners) could curb excessive passion or "amativeness."[37] During this early period there were several births within the group, some planned, some accidental, but by the mid-1850s both men and women at Oneida

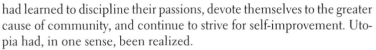

had learned to discipline their passions, devote themselves to the greater cause of community, and continue to strive for self-improvement. Utopia had, in one sense, been realized.

In late 1852 Noyes issued some "Practical Suggestions For Regulating Intercourse of the Sexes" in a "home talk" for the community. His homily emphasized that the sexes should sleep apart, that "love interviews" should go through a third party, that "short interviews" were best, that little talk was necessary between lovers in such an interview, and he advised them "in the midst of passion [to] watch for improvement." Men were expected to take the lead in any arrangement; Noyes distrusted women who made advances because such overtures were, by their nature, reckless and fraught with social danger. However, "a desire to please" others was a major part of a woman's duty—so much so, that when Tirzah was invited by Erastus Hamilton to sleep with him (despite their twenty-two-year difference in age) she did so, and when the seventy-seven-year-old Myron Kinsley asked for a harmless kiss she obliged. In sexual matters at Oneida it was the men who made overtures.

The men also assumed responsibility for birth control. They employed the contraceptive practice long sanctioned by the Christian church, *coitus reservatus* or "male continence," wherein they did not reach a climax but concentrated on enjoying the "amative" stage of their sexual encounter.[38] This method of birth control was, on the whole, successful; few mistakes occurred. "Chivalric" love was the stated norm at Oneida, and a range of partners was available for all, albeit complicated by the ascending/descending fellowship that required individuals to associate with those who could help them "improve" their religious lives. In practice, this led to male authority and sexual arrangements that favored older men having sex with younger women—some as young as fourteen, though Tirzah's diary suggests that John H. Noyes probably had sex with women as young as twelve.[39]

Despite the free love nature of the community some members asserted that the level of sexual activity within the group was undoubtedly less than in the outside world. John L. Skinner, writing to his brother in 1852, said that for the past two or three years their sex lives had been "scarcely one seventh" of what occurred in "ordinary married life in the world."[40] Furthermore, Skinner wrote, those who were addicted to masturbation had found a cure in free love.

In 1868 Noyes advanced an even more revolutionary scheme that was intended to transform the community and promote scientific progress. Drawing on the works of Charles Darwin and Frances Galton, Noyes proposed—in a series of "home talks"—that the community begin to propagate once again by consciously bringing couples together to produce children. Initially Noyes was the sole arbiter of these arrangements, but later he delegated to a committee the responsibility of reviewing the religious and physical characteristics of a pair and deciding on the suitability of a match. Some couples initiated the pairings while others were brought together by Noyes or the committee. The three children born to Tirzah Miller under this regime were the product of both her desire to cohabit with a particular partner and the community's plan to see her superior qualities complement another's strengths. The fact that Tirzah was the only woman who participated in the experiment to have three children indicates her status and desirability.

Several major issues that emerge in the diary are central to our revised understanding of Oneida. First and foremost is the depiction of the character and personality of John H. Noyes; through Tirzah's eyes we see an aging leader concerned about maintaining total control of the society by any means possible, a man obsessed by his plan to produce a race of children in his own image, and a daring sexual experimenter who vigorously promoted incestuous unions as part of his "consanguineous stirpiculture" plan. Miller's memoir makes clear for the first time Noyes's determination to have a child by a natural-born daughter. In 1869 George Washington Noyes wrote to his sister Harriet recounting a "short discourse in whisper" with Noyes after an evening meeting:

> He said: "I have struck on a view of truth in connection with the subject of consanguinity which leads out in many directions. Whether I shall be able to get it all out or not I don't know. For one thing is certain, that the relation of brothers and sisters is the nearest possible one — nearer than that of parents and children or uncles and nephews or husbands and wives. Brothers and sisters have absolutely one and the same blood. These other relationships approximate toward it but there is always in them a fractional quantity of different blood, forming a more or less compound result. The fraternal relation is the true radix of society. . . . Again for the last two years I have been led to teach and practice this doctrine about 'going home.' In the spirit of it I went to Oneida, and set down there in conjunction with Harriet Skinner and she was a helpmeet and wife to me."[41]

"Wife to me" is an ambiguous term. Although there is no evidence in the extant records that they were sexually intimate, Noyes was clearly capable of entering into a relationship with his sister, thinking he was breaching the last bastion of respectability and prudery: "In overthrowing the worldly notion about incest I am conquering the devil's last stronghold. We have routed him on marriage and got our freedom and now remains the last citadel of social falsehood, which forbids the union of brothers and sisters. In setting up this bar the devil bars the possibility of ever founding a new race. It has got to be taken down. The fellowship of brothers and sisters is fundamental and eternal. It is concentration. It approaches nearest to the fashion of God himself whose life ever turns in upon himself."[42] Noyes had constructed at Oneida an intimate biological paradise that he thought was sanctioned by both science and religion. Clearly he tried to hasten the coming of this paradise. An example is the case of Constance, or Consuelo, Bradley (1848–1917), his daughter by Sarah Bradley. Constance was a childhood companion of Tirzah, whose memoir records Noyes's desire to have a child by Constance. Constance, who married secretly at the breakup of the community, denied that Noyes was her biological father; there is, however, compelling evidence that he was, in fact, her father and that he probably had sexual relations with her. Noyes had written in 1869 in *The Circular* about "Consanguineous Stirpiculture" in relation to the controversy stirred up by Harriet Beecher Stowe's attack on Lord Byron because of his alleged incestuous union with his half sister. Noyes said the story raised three questions: whether it was true; whether it was right to publish the allegations; but, most important, "the exact nature and amount of criminality involved in the acts charged."[43]

The question of parentage at Oneida was sometimes vexing even though it was a small, controlled community where the facts of intimate relationships were widely known. Commenting on the birth of a child Fanny Leonard wrote, "There is a Cragin about it. . . . I thought — at first sight — that it resembled John Lord somewhat and said so. But in a day or two afterwards I had doubts about it being John's and thought it resembled L. F. Dunne. I think now that it lies between i.e. that it is either S. Lord's or Leonard Dunne's."[44] Noyes also spoke of Tirzah's being a "true daughter" to him, and George W. Noyes, in an amusing aside in a letter, referred to her as "niece or daughter just which you choose according to the latest doctrine of consanguinity."[45] This was all explosive territory.

Noyes believed, according to the physician and researcher Anita Newcomb McGee, that he had founded a church and a society composed of the "seed of God who are capable of conquering sin and have endeavored to keep themselves pure by shutting out the seed of Satan and all the regenerate. . . . Therefore we must breed these qualities, and especially must we breed to holiness that death may be overcome and the heavenly church firmly established."[46] Though certain members at Oneida might have objected to such terms as "church" and "seed of God" to describe their work, McGee was essentially correct in her assessment of the community's desire to produce spiritual heirs while at the same time improving the physical character of the race. One goal of the stirpiculture experiment was to have the most spiritually inclined parents (which meant, in practice, those who most supported Noyes's own views) cohabit with their near relatives to intensify the breed.

Twenty-four women and twenty men participated in the stirpiculture experiment between 1869 and 1871, and sixteen women were impregnated. On average, sexual liaisons occurred about four times a month for each couple and were usually confined to the two weeks following the cessation of the menstrual flow. Between 1868 and 1879, thirty-five women had children by twenty-eight men, producing a total of fifty-eight offspring. Of these, nineteen were of Noyes's blood if one includes his nephews and nieces, such as Tirzah Miller.

In 1878 Theodore Noyes published a study of the health of the children at Oneida and reported that they were in far better health than the general population and that the infant mortality rate was low. From the 1880s onward a host of studies by outsiders focused on the stirpiculture experiment. Ely Van de Warker's "Gynecological Study of the Oneida Community" appeared in 1884. Medical anthropologist Anita Newcomb McGee, who had in-depth interviews with key players in the experiment (including Tirzah Miller), published her findings in 1891. Two of Tirzah's children published a detailed scientific paper in 1923 that echoed earlier reports: The children at Oneida who were raised in the community or born under the stirpiculture plan had a healthy future. None of these studies, however, attempted to probe the psychological impact of the experiment.[47]

In one brief aside in her memoir in March 1869, Tirzah revealed the startling news that Noyes planned to have couples perform sexual intercourse on the stage at Oneida: "We shall never have heaven till we can conquer shame, and make a beautiful exhibition on the stage." Further details of his plan are found in a letter from Tirzah to George W. Noyes on the day following her memoir entry. In that letter she both reiterates and elaborates on the details in the memoir:

> He [J.H.N.] thinks we are ready for it, says we shall never reach heaven until we have conquered shame and can make it a beautiful ex-

hibition on the stage. He made out quite a program of the performance. He said he would have a man and woman go up upon the stage, unprepared from among the audience, whence a couch being furnished, they should disrobe themselves and dance or perform other evolutions until a man is prepared, when the women should be for a while distractingly coquettish. "It is a sight," he said, "which would purify the whole Community." It would give pleasure to a great many of the older people who now have nothing to do with the matter. There is no reason why it should not be done in public as much as music and dancing. It is the focus of all the fine arts, and singing, music and dancing are only valuable as they cluster around and add charm to that. Then when the Shakers undertake to spring their ways on us we can say, "Yes, brother, we do!" Now that propagation has become such a Community matter why shouldn't children be begotten in this public way? John Lord and Georgia [Sears] might do so.[48]

The Shakers, for whom celibacy was a cause for song and dance, celebrated their aberrant ways before the public. Now Noyes (speaking tongue in cheek?) proposed that Oneidans celebrate their sexuality; their fleshly, yet sublime practices. No evidence in the existing records suggests that such a performance ever took place, but Noyes's remarks indicate his radical frame of mind in 1869 and his willingness to "dare all" at this pivotal juncture in the colony's history. Responding to Tirzah's suggestion about this possible sexual "performance," George Washington Noyes said, "Your note was decidedly piquant. Don't apologize in the least for it. I shall try to keep up with the most advanced ideas, that you and Mr. Noyes may hatch up. Such a Tableau as you describe would carry out the logic of our faith and would be a 'nut' for the Shakers to crack. I hope they will have it."[49]

Such correspondence about sexual matters between aunts, uncles, brothers, sisters, and nieces is often intimate, playful, and full of hints about "consanguinity," the doctrine of breeding "in and in" that Noyes put forward in a "home talk" to the community in 1869 and published in modified fashion in the 1870 pamphlet "Essay on Scientific Propagation." Responding to a note from "Uncle George" in February 1869, Tirzah said, "You can hardly guess what a pleasant 'hum in the tissues' your little note caused me. More than that it made me unscientifically happy. But Uncle George I do know that we do not belong to ourselves, but to the church, and I wouldn't have it otherwise."[50]

Earlier that month she had received a letter from him that emphasized the duties they had to perform in the service of stirpiculture and the need to avoid sentimental feelings for one another: "I am a Randoor and you are a Fille du Regiment, so go along. The Lord will do better for us if we faithfully follow the wars than we could for ourselves. If the programme holds, you have got considerable service to do before you get a discharge, and if in the course of centuries we should ever land on that 'desert island,' why then. . . ."[51] Obviously the community would not tolerate sentiment or idyllic relationships because God's work was being done there and then.

On August 26, 1879 J. H. Noyes announced in a general meeting that complex marriage was abandoned and that members were free to marry, even though celibacy remained the preferable state. This announcement came in response to substantial sentiment within the community (particularly among the younger generation) in favor of marriage and to several impromptu departures without permission. A breakdown of the "ascending-descending" principle, which resulted in a "sexual grab-bag," led to a fear that local authorities might raid the community and that Noyes might be prosecuted. Noyes had tried to stem the tide in favor of marriage by giving several of his male supporters "rovers' licenses" to sleep with whomever they wished in order to reinstate the hierarchical system, but this diversionary tactic failed.

During the forty-eight-hour hiatus between the announcement of the change from complex marriage and the date when it would go into effect, frenzied sexual activity took place at the colony. Tirzah slept with James Herrick and Erastus Hamilton and mused about Homer Barron: "I of course could not help thinking about Homer a little, now that complex marriage is ended perhaps forever." On the very next day she encountered him while getting a lemon for "Jamie": "I can hardly tell how it happened, but there seemed to be a subtle fire between us, and before we barely knew it he hurried me into the inside bath-room, where we—[here the text breaks off]." Presumably they had sex in that moment of passion. Her "off again, on again" relationship with Barron was highly charged. At one point she had given him a nightgown, which she turned into an undergarment for herself after they broke up. Such deeply personal gifts were both unusual at Oneida and reflective of her own erotic needs. Homer Barron once confessed in a criticism session that he kissed the pillowcases she slept on.

From the end of August till the end of December, when the memoir comes to a close, numerous marriages took place at Oneida. Many were presided over by Herrick, who, the community believed, had full

clerical standing even though it had been withdrawn in 1867 by the Anglican bishop of New York after Herrick renounced his orders. The Digest of the Canons for the Protestant Episcopal Church assumed that clerics who renounced their orders would never again officiate at a ceremony, but Herrick did so, and legally. Some married by uttering a simple contract; others were joined by Herrick. All these marriages were legal in the eyes of New York State, regardless of Herrick's canonical status.

Memoir of a Magnetic Force

Michel Foucault noted that "confession was, and still remains, the general standard governing the production of the true discourse on sex. . . . The motivations and effects it is expected to produce have been varied, as have the forms it has taken: interrogations, consultations, autobiographical narratives, letters; they have been recorded, transcribed, assembled into dossiers, published and commented on."[52] Tirzah Miller's memoir is part of that confessional literature. It chronicles her social life, her coming of age within the community, and the struggles she faced over choosing a love mate in a society that spurned special love, or exclusive relationships. The memoir begins when she is twenty-four and ends when she is thirty-six. During that period she had three children as part of the eugenics scheme called stirpiculture, edited the colony newspaper, and was groomed by John H. Noyes to take a prominent place in the Oneida leadership. The memoir is full of her conversations with Noyes—about people and personalities, about her love affairs, her doubts about communism, and her anguish over the loss of two partners. There are several major players in this theatrical memoir (see the "Cast of Characters"), but the star of the show is Tirzah herself: a "magnetic force," to use her own words, who draws a group of persistent admirers.

The term magnetism, as used at Oneida, was taken from the language of mesmerism and phrenology. Mesmerism had come to the United States in two waves, according to Taylor Stoehr, who has explored its substantial influence on reformers. The first wave coincided with the publication of Mesmer's work in the 1790s; the second wave followed the publication of Joseph Deleuze's *Practical Instruction in Animal Magnetism* (1837) and the merger of mesmerism with phrenology ("phrenomagnetism") in the early 1840s. It developed an otherworldly aspect as it gradually melded with spiritualism in the 1850s.[53] Mesmerism assumed that magnetic forces existing in the universe could be channeled and used by "magnetizers" (practitioners endowed with special gifts) to effect cures, read minds, and bring people into contact with the larger spiritual world. Magnetism and sexuality were often linked, particularly when a magnetizer's touch drew a member of the opposite sex within the magnetic orbit. The great phrenologist of the day, Orson S. Fowler, claimed that examination of the lower back portion of the head would reveal the extent to which a person's mental faculty was directed toward love and lovemaking. That portion of the brain produced a feeling he called "amativeness": "Those in whom it is large are splendidly sexed, and well nigh perfect as males and females; literally idealized by the opposite sex; love almost to insanity; cherish for them the most exalted feelings of regard and esteem, and treat them with the utmost consideration, as if they were a superior race of human beings; love with an inexpressible tenderness, and cannot live without sexual sympathy; must love and be loved; are remarkably magnetic and 'captivating,' charming and pleasing in manners, conversation, looks, and all they say and do, and hence are sure to elicit reciprocal affections, and marry."[54] Fowler might have been describing Tirzah, who herself frequently used the word "magnetic" in her memoir. A few examples will suffice. In January 1874 she described a "magnetic talk" with J. H. Noyes. A few days later she wrote that "Mr. H. did not feel magnetic." She described a "wonderful day of magnetism with my beloved" (July 4, 1877) and recorded, "Frank told me yesterday that he felt more of this magnetic, electrical attraction toward me than toward anyone" (June 24, 1877).

Several things should be said about both the scope and the nature of this account. Miller's memoir ranges widely over the history of the society during the controversial phase (1868–1879) when the eugenics experiment—stirpiculture—was being introduced. Miller was representative of the second generation that came not only to maturity but to positions of influence and authority in the 1870s, when the religious assumptions that had guided the group since the 1840s no longer seemed potent. She was an intimate player in the drama that unfolded when the elder Noyes tried to pass on authority to his son Theodore. During these years disagreements erupted under the pressure of establishing the eugenics plan, and cliques formed as the society began to fissure and ultimately break. As this contentious politics of sex and religion emerged, Tirzah Miller sat at the very center of the political discourse as both an auditor and policymaker, as both a woman whom men found desirable and a partner with men she loved. Her memoir is the product of her life of leisure within the community and her journalistic ambitions. She had time to write; she wanted to make her words vivid; she created a persona in the memoir that emphasized her attractiveness to men, her long-suffering dedication to the work of Oneida and the mission of John H. Noyes, and her desire to please both.

The constant struggle for political authority and control was fierce, but no fiercer than the personal struggles Tirzah faced as she tried to negotiate the sometimes murky waters of desire, of need, of passion. At times her memoir becomes an intimate diary, a journal of "self" at Oneida; at other moments it contains mere reportage of events, essays on topics of the moment. The memoir lacks stylistic consistency since she used it as a vehicle to improve her writing and try new approaches; in fact, certain turning points in the story coincide with Tirzah's taking up or leaving journalistic work at Oneida. Elements of the romantic novel enter the memoir as her love life grew more web-like, her dramatic confrontations with Edward Inslee intensified, and her heroic commitment to the community and John H. Noyes took on a melodramatic quality.

The start of her memoir in 1867 coincided with her beginning to work for *The Circular*, the community newspaper. It had a small circulation but was symbolically important to the group since it served as a platform for their ideas and an ideological lure to win over potential members. Although the paper consistently lost money, it was of enormous importance to Noyes, who saw the press as the equivalent of Charles Finney's revivals. *The Circular*, Noyes believed, could regularly reach large numbers of potential converts. When she began writing the memoir Tirzah was being groomed to become its editor (she did, in fact, take charge of the paper in 1872). But although she edited this proselytizing periodical, she expressed surprisingly little religious sentiment in her memoir: Except for occasional references to "doing God's will" or "thanking God," Tirzah dwelt on "self" and her expression of self was secular. Although her letters and occasional writings reflected religious convictions, novels, rather than the Bible, are key texts for understanding her emotional state of mind.

Tirzah Miller began her remarkable and startling memoir with a rather prosaic preface detailing the essential facts of her life and the early involvement of her biological family with the notorious Oneida Community: "I was born September 13, 1843 in Putney, Vermont. My mother was the youngest sister of John H. Noyes, the founder of the famous Oneida Community. At the time of my birth the nucleus of that Association had just started in the Noyes family. Mr. Noyes converted his two younger sisters and brother to his peculiar views of religious and social life, and then having arranged their marriages with persons of similar views, he entered into co-operation with them, having common ownership of this world's goods and forming themselves into one large family with himself at the head." In classic autobiographical fashion she started with self ("I was born"), then moved outward to her immediate family, and then to the larger social "family" in which she would spend her life.

Her life within that "family" was hardly prosaic—quite the reverse. Oneida was over-charged with passion, with conflict, and with contentious politics. Tirzah's life within the group was complicated by her unswerving dedication to the religious ideals of her uncle and lover, John Humphrey Noyes. Not only was he her lover in this community of complex marriage but he was the central driving force in her life, acting as mentor and, on occasion, tormentor. Her first recollection of "Mr. Noyes" came when she was three. Accused of having cut some tassels from drapery in a community sitting room, she was taken in to see him. He regarded her with a "searching glance" and commanded her to "look him in the eye and tell the truth." Later she acknowledged this as her "first experience of fear of a human being," although in the end she remembered being treated with kindness. That early experience of fear and delight with her uncle would be repeated as she grew older.

Tirzah's autobiographical fragment ends with her describing another childhood incident recalled by her mother. When one-year-old Tirzah was struck by another child she responded to the offending infant with a "grieved, reproachful" look. John H. Noyes, who was present, said to his sister, "Charlotte, your little girl has a large heart." Her largeness of heart would be sorely tested in the future, as Tirzah's confessional memoir shows.

The first section of the memoir itself, covering the period from September 1867 to June 1869, might well be titled "Generations." In this period Tirzah both experienced and expressed her love for "Uncle George." John H. Noyes introduced the stirpiculture experiment, thus singling out a group of young men and women for leadership in the community and in the process pitting young adults against their parents. This was a conscious effort by Noyes to shift radically both the direction

and power structure at Oneida. A question central to the entire memoir is introduced in this opening section: namely, the conflict Tirzah felt between romance and duty. Tirzah experienced passion both for individuals ("special love," as the Oneidans termed it) and for music, a passion that put her at odds with her duty toward the community and John H. Noyes. She simultaneously felt an almost religious sense of duty to the community. She was under a scriptural obligation because of her high place in the spiritual order and under a social obligation to conform to the expected practices (for example, no "special love") and to be a "good woman" within the covenanted community.

In this first section we see the beginnings of her intimate relationship with John H. Noyes. He counseled, cajoled, and controlled her; he hinted at her role in the eugenics experiment, going so far as to suggest that he might have a child with her. Tirzah's record of their intimate conversations (both before and after sexual encounters) elucidates his views about sexuality in general and her in particular: "Sleeping with Mr. Noyes the other night he said there was an immense difference in women in regard to the power to please sexually. 'Why, is there?' said I. 'Yes,' he answered. 'There is as much difference between women in respect to ability to make social music as there is between a grand piano and a tenpenny whistle.' Then applying his remarks personally he said: 'I always expect something sublime when I sleep with you.'" Tirzah and another young woman, Charlotte Leonard, who was pregnant with a child by Noyes, compared their sexual experiences with the Oneida leader: "I was thinking the other day, Charlotte, how much of your experience with Mr. Noyes about having a child deepened your character. I believe you got a hold on faith which you will never lose."[55] During the course of her life within the community her own faith was sorely tested, but in the long run Tirzah remained a faithful daughter to Noyes.

Noyes asked Tirzah when they could begin to try to have a child, then suggested that they might have more than one and demanded her allegiance so that she would not be "drawn away again" from him. She felt both attacked and seduced. At the same time that Noyes called her a "man killer" who "liked to be worshipped," he flattered her by alluding to her as the future "mother of the Community," a term usually reserved for his wife, Harriet Holton. Eventually Tirzah broke down under these pressures: "My heart felt soft and broken, and I wept continually, I hardly knew why. His kindness overwhelmed me. I told him that I felt so very sorrowful the night before, but I said to myself I would hold myself at his disposal." Noyes emerges as a manipulative and cruel leader who pitted members against one another, who used spies (like Tirzah) to enforce order, and who was willing to reveal intimate confidences in order to inflict emotional pain.

The death of Tirzah's first significant lover—her uncle George Washington Noyes—is not recorded in the memoir, nor is the birth of the child she bore him—her first—after George's tragic death. This powerful silence is curious and compelling; it suggests a loss so deep Tirzah was unable to give it expression. But although Tirzah's memoir is silent between 1869 and 1872, her state of mind is revealed in an exchange of letters with George W. Noyes between February 1869 and July 1870. The last letters came just eleven days before his death of malaria. The letters reveal a twenty-five-year-old woman who was "delighted" to hold herself "at the disposal of God and the community" and was "free for anything Mr. Noyes wants." When George shared the correspondence with his older brother the eugenicist noted that "two red heads [Tirzah and George] might make a fiery compound—also that my instincts are in favor of crosses between New England and New York."[56]

However, the consanguineous union that produced a child between Tirzah and George W. Noyes came as a surprise to the colony leader, who had not been consulted. Writing in April 1870 in the aftermath of a severe criticism of George Noyes, Charlotte Noyes wrote to "J.H.N." that she knew nothing of her brother's actions in this "vital" matter. George's last letter to Tirzah before his sudden death that year, written at Wallingford, commented on the spawning tendency in the family: "Love to all uncles, aunts, cousins, nephews, nieces, etc., if you can count them up. What a lot we shall have according to present appearances." She replied that the baby had begun to kick "yesterday morning; so I know it is there. . . . I am real well, and considerable of the time full of a new feeling of life and energy."[57] George died of malaria on July 23; on December 13 Tirzah gave birth to their son, George Wallingford Noyes. Her memoir reflects none of this: her deep love for George, his death, the birth of another "G. W.," and her life during that first pregnancy.

When she took up her pen again in December 1872 Tirzah had become "editress" of *The Circular*, but she felt "no confidence" in herself and promised to turn over a new leaf in matters religious and social: "I determined, with God's help, to become more <u>faithful</u>. . . . I resolved, also, to give up H. [Homer Barron, with whom she had a tempestuous relationship] entirely, unreservedly, leaving no thought of future connection with him. . . . Left music for writing. . . . It is like the death of a cherished friend." In short, duty called and romantic notions were set aside. Writing and the success of the community paper were what J. H. Noyes prized, and Tirzah's prescribed role since 1870 had been limited to the literary sphere. She was to become a critic of literature and "have some literary babies." Apparently Noyes had decided Tirzah was to have no more children for at least two years. He was enamored and "bewitched" by her, and he let it be known in the gossipy community, where Chinese whisper games were regularly played, that Tirzah had been a factor in his thinking about consanguinity ever since "God had sprung a trap" on him in the form of Tirzah.

In 1873 the memoir becomes more intimate and diary-like. In sharp contrast to the opening section (pre-1872) is her chronicling of the events and traumas surrounding her relationship with Edward Inslee and the birth of their son, her second child. As Michel Foucault wisely observed, in writing about sex "it is no longer a question simply of saying what was done—the sexual act—and how it was done; but of reconstructing, in and around the act, the thoughts that recapitulate it, the obsessions that accompany it, the images, the desires, modulations, and quality of the pleasure that animated it. For the first time, no doubt, a society has taken upon itself to solicit and hear the imparting of several pleasures."[58] Yet it must also be said, as Thomas Laqueur emphasizes in his *Making Sex: Body and Gender from the Greeks to Freud*, the body is more than an epistemological category and has a destiny of its own.[59]

Tirzah and Inslee, who shared a love of music and played together in a quintet, were united in a ceremony in May 1873 that symbolized the community's effort to breed a new generation. On the evening of the ceremony they tried to conceive a child; Tirzah wondered the very next day if she could possibly feel a sensation in her womb so soon. She was torn by her romantic desire for Homer Barron and a wish to please both the community and Edward Inslee, who had begun to idolize her: "I have been in a struggle for several days between my sense of duty and my natural inclination. . . . God is good to me and I have everything to be thankful for, if I never have what my heart longs for" [underlining in original]. By late July, when she realized that she was pregnant by Inslee—"my death warrant"—she paradoxically felt increasing affection for him, to the degree that they were viewed as "special lovers" and were watched and counseled by the community leaders. Inslee began to rebel against both Noyes and the community decree that he keep away from

Tirzah. Conflict between the elder Noyes and Edward becomes a central drama in the memoir.

To rein her in and make her more compliant to his will, Noyes spoke to Tirzah in January 1874 about her future just as he had done during her first pregnancy: "'How do you know but I shall have a baby by you myself?' . . . . He said he believed it to be his duty, and he had considerable curiosity to see what kind of child we should produce. He said that to combine with me would be intensifying the Noyes blood more than anything else we could do. He was just waking up to the full sense of his duty, which is to pursue stirpiculture in the consanguineous line. *God willing he intends to have a child by Helen, Constance, and me* [emphasis mine]. Ended by lying down." Noyes asserted his dominance over her as a community member and as a woman by claiming his right and duty to have a child with her, then by having sex (albeit consensual by her own account) with her while she was carrying the child of an opponent, a younger man and a talented musician. Noyes punished Inslee for his rebellion by forbidding him to play in the quintet with Tirzah.

Intent on breaking Edward Inslee, Noyes gave him severe criticism sessions designed to bring the increasingly worn-out, yet still rebellious, young man to heel: "Thank God! Thank God!!" Tirzah wrote. "A letter of humble submission from E. to the family." Tirzah had suffered throughout this ordeal; she felt both alienated from Inslee and reproached by Noyes for her feelings of "special love." Her duty pulled her one way, her sentiments another: "O E! If you think I don't love you, how little you know me! You cannot have had a pang that has not struck an answering chord in my heart, and yet I know how this discipline is right, and that we need to be separated."

After one traumatic day when Tirzah had been told that Inslee could not see her, Noyes revealed the contents of a note received from another member, Harriet Worden, "telling of good experience she had last night sleeping with Edward." This revelation produced the desired effect on Tirzah: "It went through my heart like a knife, and it was two hours before I could breathe naturally, there was such pain at the center of my life." In the midst of all this intrigue Noyes told Tirzah that he was involved in an "exquisite little romance" with Lillian Towner, the thirteen-year-old daughter of James Towner, then emerging as the leader of an anti-Noyes faction.

Tirzah vented her jealousy in an unusual passage written two weeks before giving birth to Inslee's child, as she experienced a series of false labor pains that reminded her of her precarious situation. With each pain she thought anew about her condition, her life with Inslee, and her fear of losing him now that they were kept apart by community decree. She wanted to see him before the birth because she had just learned that Noyes intended to keep them separated. Her anger, however, turned against Edward rather than "Father" Noyes, because Inslee had been shown to be stubborn, insufficiently contrite, and, worst of all, associating with a "coarse" woman: "How can you at this serious moment dissipate your time with such a woman as Mary W. [Worden], who is totally incapable of elevating you?" Noyes eventually relented and allowed Tirzah to invite Edward to her room; yet her main concern was the anxiety such a visit would cause Noyes.

She began her labor at three o'clock on the morning of Monday, April 20. Inslee was admitted briefly to the lying-in room: "Edward came in, and clasping me in his arms for a moment kissed me passionately, and then I sent him away. At 10 minutes past 2 the child appeared—a boy weighing just 8 lbs. in a nude condition." Out of this romantic, tortured, and musical relationship came Haydn Inslee, named after the composer. That name would soon become a source of conflict among Tirzah, Edward, and Noyes.

In late September Noyes wrote to Inslee that he should "be weaned from the baby," whom he had taken to his room every evening. Noyes encouraged Tirzah's fear that Edward might love the child more than she, and he attempted to reassert control over Tirzah by suggesting that she refrain from seeing her baby and insisting that the child's name be changed: "He said that the name Haydn was symbolic of Edward's idolatry towards music, and has always been distasteful to him on that account." With much of her life then centered on the baby and Edward Inslee, Tirzah denounced what she calls the "aristocracy of [Noyes] blood" (which included herself, of course) in the community; she feared its negative impact on the colony because it is "contrary to the genius of communism." She perceived an essential conflict between an aristocracy of birth, as represented by an exclusive and familial biological core (Theodore, Joseph Skinner, Constance), and an aristocracy of the spirit that had achieved power through faith. Tirzah mulled over Noyes's demand that the baby's name be changed and then accepted "Paul" as an appropriate substitution since it would help her in "separating both him and me from the associations of spirit connected with his father."

When Edward finally decided to leave the community, Tirzah agreed to release him "from all obligations to myself and the child." His departure, however, left her thunderstruck despite the difficulties his presence had raised: "I thought this would kill me, and I almost drew back; then I did it [signed a legal document freeing him] as I would put my head on the executioners block, or as Queen Elizabeth signed the death warrant of her favorite Leicester." A few days later when the "divorce" document was read in the community meeting, she emotionally collapsed: "I could bear no more, and got out as quickly as I could, and sent for Mr. Herrick. I had an uncontrollable fit of screaming." The queen had abandoned not only her favorite consort, but also the possibility of romance, of music—all for a life of duty. In the midst of this crisis Noyes wrote from Wallingford asking her "to come here as soon as possible. I want you and you want me. Leave all without wasting time to get ready."[60] Inslee's departure and the change of their child's name brought to a close a second phase of her life, which might appropriately be called "Music Lovers."

After Inlee's departure and her breakdown Tirzah went for an extended stay at Wallingford with Noyes and James B. Herrick. Charlotte Leonard, Tirzah's contemporary and the mother of one of John H. Noyes's children, wrote in her journal, "I am glad she can go there, for she needs to get into union with Mr. Noyes and get help out of the state she has been in here. Her relations with Edward have affected her much I think and have made her much trouble. Mr. H [Herrick] was much tried last eve. when Tirzah left at the management of Haydn in the affair. He was with his mother till she went away, and then made a great cry about her going, all of which seemed so unnecessary and unwise."[61]

Though Edward was gone, his child—now Paul—remained as a constant reminder of him. Noyes assigned Paul a new "father," William Towner. But it was Noyes who continued to dominate Tirzah's emotional life: He had sex with her (on November 8) and urged her to have a baby with her cousin Theodore, who did not share his father's views on the importance of consanguineous relationships. During a conversation about consanguinity Noyes asked Tirzah to "lock the door." "When we got up he said: 'There! I didn't!'" Noyes meant that he had withheld his sperm, maintaining his role as prophet and lawgiver. Tirzah, however, had reservations about a third pregnancy because "my past experience had not been such as to make me enthusiastic about having more" children. Nevertheless, Tirzah resolved to be "scientific" and accept the community decision. She revealed her own preference (Homer Barron), while Theodore placed G. D. Allen at the top of a list of possible suitors. Noyes wanted Theodore to approve the arrangement although he himself did not want to be the father: "I don't care a snap which one you have, only I want to have it come entirely from Theodore, and not from your choice or Ann's [Ann Hobart]."[62]

In the midst of her own re-initiation into the stirpiculture scheme Tirzah acted as an intermediary in negotiations for Theodore to introduce Virginia Hinds (about to become thirteen) into the sexual system. She remarked, "He really did it last night, and very wisely and discreetly, too." Few secrets existed about sexuality at Oneida, and although Tirzah's memoir suggests that it was a lively sexual community there were also "platonic" relationships wherein men and women offered calm counsel to one another about matters "social" (the colony term). For example, Tirzah poured out her own "overcharged heart" to George Cragin, who told her that she must be realistic and abandon all hope for reconciliation with Edward or his return to Oneida.

During the winter of 1877 Tirzah was trying for a child with Homer Barron, involved in a new affair with Henry Hunter, and kindling a relationship with Erastus Hamilton. Her affair with Hunter, an eighteen-year-old violinist with whom Tirzah played music, proved the most unsettling and the most romantic, adding freshness and excitement to her life and turning her away from "duty." Hunter was the first suitor since Edward Inslee to capture her so fully; she was intoxicated by the mixture of youth, sexual attraction, and music: "Henry neither eats nor sleeps; neither do I. I hardly understand why the affair should affect my nerves so." But in early May duty won out. Tirzah acquiesced to Noyes's urging that she have a child with James Herrick. Noyes also ordered her to give up music, a notion that "almost paralyzed" her. Clearly Noyes was trying to drive a wedge between Tirzah and her personal passions by turning her back toward a writing career—paradoxically, one for which she feared she had only a modest talent. In Noyes's eyes, Inslee led her astray; now Tirzah "must choose between him [Noyes] and E." Only through Noyes could she learn to suppress her "wicked" romantic impulses and learn to be good.

A concerted effort was made to besmirch Inslee's reputation and to alienate Tirzah. She was told, for example, that Edward was going to marry "a girl of good reputation—a pianist." Not only had he left her behind with a child but he was now contemplating marriage to a woman with a similar passion for music and a "good reputation." A bruising quality characterized these relationships, particularly when intimacy turned toward jealousy and when the passions aroused were channeled and controlled by the leadership. Beneath the romantic intrigue lay rough emotional encounters. Young Paul also needed to be disabused of any affectionate feelings toward his natural father. Yet despite all the efforts to alienate him from Inslee, Paul told Tirzah that he "sees his father in his dreams." And when Tirzah slept with Frank Wayland-Smith (to whom she referred as her "first love") and they spoke of their desire to lead a monogamous life, she confessed that her truest wish was to be reunited with Inslee.

Tirzah's willingness to accept other men as sexual partners despite her yearning for Inslee indicated the degree to which she accepted and internalized community rules and mores. In late 1874, when she was six months pregnant with Inslee's child, James B. Herrick became a significant figure in her life. Like numerous other men, Herrick was smitten with Tirzah.

By June 1877 Tirzah reached a turning point in the memoir. She was aware both of her own attractiveness and the passion she aroused in others: "I should be insincere if I did not admit that I know that I have been one of the most attractive women in the Oneida Community." Yet she felt inadequate to such amorous demands, wistful about her loss of Edward, and indifferent toward her current stirpiculture partner, James Herrick. She asked Ann Hobart who, with Theodore Noyes, was running the community at that juncture, if she "might stop trying with Mr. Herrick, as I have no faith in it." She also confided in John H. Noyes that she had "tried for three months unsuccessfully with Mr. Herrick and if you sympathize I should now like to stop, which I think we ought to be able to do with mutual good feeling."[63]

In fact, she felt old, melancholy, rather useless despite her obvious "majestic force," her political importance, her breeding potential. Her relationship with Herrick floundered and, in an introspective moment in September 1877, she looked at herself in the mirror: "Thirty-four! My weight is 110 lbs., and I do not look as old as I am. My hair is a little gray, though not noticeably so except on close scrutiny; my complexion is still tolerably fair; a few crows' feet have laid their marks about my eyes, and my moustache is becoming quite heavy. How about my heart? I hardly know. I sometimes think I am growing more and more materialistic; then again I revolt against that idea." During a brief illness she reflected on the distance between herself and the younger women: "While I shiver in my woolens, it is almost with a sensation of horror that I observe the girls along in the muslins and fluttering fans." Her age and their vulnerability overwhelmed her in a poignant scene of reflection and consideration.

Eventually Tirzah was swept up in a powerful romantic relationship with Herrick. One night in June they were both "most unexpectedly overcome . . . and [Jamie] ran for a syringe." Both were fearful of such a "calamity" (conception) that they "agreed that we will each speak at such times, so the other can know what is liable to take place." Noyes had, as early as 1852, emphasized that there should be little conversation during an "interview" (sexual encounter) and that it should be brief. In agreeing to speak to one another if Herrick approached a "crisis," he and Tirzah acknowledged a pattern of mutual dependence and growing intimacy; they agreed to rely on their own rules rather than the rules of the community.

Despite their efforts to develop a sexual early warning system, they found that they were easily swept up in passion and went "just too far." Tirzah became pregnant for the third time. Herrick confessed that "he has wanted just such a friend as I am ever since he came to the Community, and that I understand him better than any other woman—even his wife." Tirzah acknowledged that they were both "caught up in special love," but it was not exclusive, meaning that they continued to have other partners although they remained "first" in each other's hearts.

As summer turned into fall her relationship with Herrick matured. She felt more affection for him after becoming pregnant and saw in him many admirable qualities, even while she continued to dream about "E." While Tirzah dreamt about the past, the community was collapsing under the strain of events: young George Cragin died; Ann Hobart left to marry Charles Skinner, abandoning Theodore Noyes; Theodore forfeited his leadership in response to criticism from the community. The elder Noyes resumed the presidency despite poor health. Tirzah, longing for some surcease from the turmoil, had to face certain hard facts about her life at Oneida: "I cannot desert Mr. Noyes and I cannot take George W. [her first child] away from the community." (Underlining in original.)

Shortly after Tirzah gave birth to Herrick's child—a healthy, dark-haired girl weighing seven pounds, nine ounces—on June 8, 1878, she received a note from Edward asking if he could come for a visit. Dutifully she forwarded the letter to "Mr. Noyes." The final phase of her struggle with Inslee mirrored the struggle the community was to go through in 1878 and 1879 as it teetered on the verge of collapse.

Social and personal issues dominate the last two years of the memoir. The Perfectionist, communal, radical free love society, which was devoted to the regeneration of self and society under the leadership of John H. Noyes, moved toward becoming a joint stock company tied together by mutual need and dependence but shorn of all its radical social features. During the final phase certain key questions arose: How would the community manage the economic and political dissolution and restructuring? How would it deal with the sexual system, and how would it be modified after complex marriage had been challenged? Would individuals and couples remain at or leave Oneida? What had the past thirty years meant, and what would the future hold for Tirzah and others? All these questions, which touched every member at Oneida, Tirzah confronted in this closing section of the memoir.

Tirzah's own drift during this period was complex: She still had feelings for Edward, but had now found a soul mate in James Herrick. Yet when he confessed his love for her sister, Helen, she was understandably confused: "I could see how a man might find it difficult to tell between two sisters which he loved best—especially when he had known and loved one a long time before knowing the other; but how it was possible that there should be the same kind of glow, magnetism, and ardent attraction between him and her that there has been between him and me I could not understand. . . . I was sometimes perfectly bewildered, dazed; I was at sea with no compass." In the end she resolved to respect Noyes's judgment since Herrick "loves Mr. Noyes far more than me." She submitted to Noyes, as always at the center of her life, and allowed him to dictate her future.

In a revealing series of conversations with Theodore, Tirzah returned repeatedly to an old theme: the conflict between her duty to J. H. Noyes and her desire for personal happiness. She told the troubled son of the leader that on several occasions she contemplated leaving Oneida to join Edward Inslee; in failing to do so she "sacrificed all hopes of happiness in this life." She concluded that it was "better to sacrifice love than conscience or honor"—in other words, to give up Inslee and stay by her uncle. In April 1878 she confessed to J. H. Noyes her great "temptation" to leave the community. She had remained for two reasons: first, "an inexpungible feeling that my destiny was in some way linked with yours"; second, the "providential trap of having a child by Uncle George." The community's hold on her was enormous; a break with it "can never be done without eternal remorse which would embitter my life."[64]

When Tirzah and Herrick learned that Noyes would not stand in the way of their marrying they applied to do so through the community. Homer Barron announced that he would marry Tirzah's sister, Helen, and the name of Edward Inlsee hung heavy in the air. Inslee still had supporters in the community who believed he should be given a chance to marry Tirzah. Some question surrounded the legality of Herrick's divorce from his wife, and doubt lingered in Tirzah's mind about her proper course. Inslee received permission to visit Oneida. He and Tirzah talked (in Paul's presence), and they played music together. In the end, her decision about whom she would marry turned on a single fact: John H. Noyes disapproved of Inslee.

Herrick's divorce decree arrived from Baltimore, clearing the way for her marriage. It was agreed that they should go to Wallingford to tie the knot. On November 6, 1879 they were married by a justice of the peace and then went immediately to New Haven where they affirmed (before another justice) the legitimacy of their daughter, Hilda.

The affair with Edward Inslee had not quite ended. He wrote that lawyers had advised him that Tirzah was still married to him and that "Mr. Noyes is a fiend." However, she was now Mrs. Herrick. The penultimate entry in the memoir is a legalistic note to Inslee: "Dear E.: I cannot correspond with you while you refuse to acknowledge the legality of my marriage with Mr. Herrick. Your treatment of him and of me is unworthy of you, and not [several words unreadable]. Tirzah C. Herrick." A final entry, dated January 7, 1880, consists of a single sentence, most of it illegible. Here the memoir ends.

After the Memoir

Letters written by Tirzah after she concluded her memoir reveal a woman who, although deeply committed to the community, realized how wrenching the breakup had been for many, including herself. To her close friend Mary Prindle she wrote, "Well, the old community is gone, isn't it? What next? Mr. H. & I don't know yet where we shall live, or how we are to take care of the children."[65] In a letter to Herrick she described a dream in which both J. H. N. and "Uncle George" were "trying to help me and others"; she was deeply touched by "Father saying in his earnest way (gesticulating with his whole arm): 'I tell you ever since the community broke up, this thing has come hardest on the women and children.'"[66] (Underlining in original.) In 1886 she wrote to Victor Noyes, J. H. Noyes's first child by complex marriage, that she had always loved him "as a brother of the true seed, and I pray God to show you the utter uselessness of your running away from the destiny which places you at your father's side."[67]

During the 1880s Inslee tried to see Tirzah on numerous occasions when she visited Oneida, but she rejected his overtures. She grew to despise him for his negative influence over her life. When Inslee asked her to leave Herrick, she replied that she would never "leave Mr. H & Mr. Noyes" and suggested he get married. Inslee complained that "J.H.N. has been governed by personal jealousy in his treatment of me . . . and has treated me meaner than any other man has treated me."[68]

Tirzah's life was a rich one—full of passion, intrigue, and commitment to both the ideals of Oneida and its sometimes harsh realities. When Herrick suffered an emotional breakdown in 1880, she turned once again to Noyes—her confidante, uncle, counsel, and lover—to try to sort out the turmoil that had engulfed her life. In doing so she revealed both her state of mind and her relationship to Oneida: "I remember you told me once that perhaps it would prove that God's treatment of me in taking away Uncle George, the father of my first child, indicated his purpose about me in respect to having husbands; that he did not mean I should have any husband but you. He took away Uncle George; he took away Edward; and now it looks as though he has taken away Jamie, and in a manner which is more terrible than death or desertion. Words cannot begin to convey to you the conflict in my mind between love, respect and trust on the one hand and doubt and amazement and terror on the other."[69]

In a much earlier (undated) letter to Noyes, Tirzah spoke of her "wanton" nature, her need to seek out romantic attachments: "I believe I am a Magdelen. In thinking about going to school to you yesterday afternoon my mind dwelt more than anything on the weakness of my sexual nature. I prayed that somehow you might get possession of it. If you can I believe you will save me and I if you can't I am afraid I am lost. I don't think I ever wanted you should before, but I do now with all my heart and soul."[70]

Noyes died on April 13, 1886. His son Theodore, Tirzah, and James Herrick were present. When Tirzah Miller Herrick died on September 18,1902 she was buried in the community cemetery at Noyes's side. Herrick was buried opposite her.

In death as in life.

Notes

1. For an extended analysis of the Hawley/Smith love relationship and the text of Victor Hawley's diary see my *Special Love/Special Sex* (Syracuse: Syracuse University Press, 1994).

2. Ralph W. Emerson, *Emerson* (New York: Alfred A. Knopf, 1952), 82.

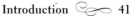

3. Quoted in Sidney Ditzion's *Marriage, Morals, and Sex in America: A History of Ideas* (New York: Bookman Associates, 1953), 139.

4. Perry Miller, "Jonathan Edwards to Emerson," *New England Quarterly* 22, no. 4 (December 1940): 617.

5. Miller, "Edwards to Emerson," 617.

6. John H. Noyes, *History of American Socialisms* (Philadelphia: J.B. Lippincott & Co., 1870), 614.

7. The following definition of "Perfectionism" appeared in Fessenden & Co.'s *Encyclopedia of Religious Knowledge* in 1838 (published at Brattleboro, Vt.) and was one that Noyes thought a fair statement of his beliefs at the time: "Perfectionists: a modern sect in New England who believe that every individual is either wholly sinful, or wholly righteous and that every being in the universe, at any given time, is either entirely holy or entirely wicked. Consequently they unblushingly maintain that they themselves are free from sin. In support of this doctrine they say that Christ dwells in, and controls believers, and thus secures their perfect holiness; that the body of Christ, which is the church, is nourished and guided by the life and wisdom of the head. Hence they condemn the greatest portion of the religion of the world in the world named Christianity, as the work of the Antichrist.

"'All the essential features of Judaism,' they say, 'and its successor, popery, may be distinctly traced in every form of Protestantism; and although we rejoice in the blessings which the Reformation has given us, we regard it as rightly named, the Reformation, it being an improvement of Christianity.' The last opinion, which has some foundation in truth, has long been held, variously modified, in different parts of the Christian world." Quoted in the "Secret History of Perfectionism: No. 4," *The Witness* 1, no. 4 (November 21, 1838).

8. John H. Noyes, "Definitions," in "Scrap by J. H. N." All manuscript materials (unless otherwise noted) can be found at the Oneida Community Collection, Arents Rare Book Collection, Syracuse University Library.

9. Louis Kern, *An Ordered Love: Sex Roles and Sexuality in Victorian Utopias: The Shakers, the Mormons, and the Oneida Community* (Chapel Hill: University of North Carolina Press, 1981), 223–24.

10. Tirzah Miller, "II," August 15, 1867. Unpublished manuscript.

11. Lawrence Foster, *Religion and Sexuality: The Shakers, the Mormons, and the Oneida Community* (New York: Oxford University Press, 1981), 81. Both Foster, in the work cited, and Kern, in *An Ordered Love*, offer distinctive and innovative approaches to the Mormons, Shakers, and Oneida.

12. John H. Noyes, "Kingdom of Heaven," February 2, 1866.

13. John H. Noyes, *The Berean: A Manual for Those Who Seek the Faith of the Primitive Church* (Putney: Office of the Spiritual Magazine, 1847), 335.

14. Foster, *Religion and Sexuality*, 91.

15. Ibid.

16. "Our Platform, July 16, 1851–October 25, 1852," n.d.

17. J. H. Noyes to E. H. Hamilton, March 4, 1850 in "Oneida Journal." Typescript manuscript.

18. "Brooklyn School," February 12–13, 1850.

19. "Brooklyn School," April 1851.

20. Alfred Habegger, *The Father: A Life of Henry James, Sr.* (New York: Farrar, Strauss, and Giroux, 1994), 285.

21. George W. Hamilton reported from Columbus, Ohio, that he had visited with cousin Rutherford B. Hayes, then Governor Hayes: "He [Hayes] spoke of visiting Wallingford some eight years since. Expressed himself as having no prejudice on account of our peculiar religious beliefs, and was well pleased at having a call from one of our people." Rutherford later accepted visits in the White House from members of the community, who were always careful to minimize their relationship with him to avoid embarrassing him. *Daily Journal,* January 16, 1868.

22. *Daily Journal,* February 9, 1863.

23. *Daily Journal,* November 20, 1866.

24. *Daily Journal,* September 14, 1866.

25. *The Circular,* March 24, 1864.

26. Louis Kern quotes from an 1847 talk by Noyes entitled "An Overture" that contrasts the "I spirit" with the "We spirit" and sums up the colony's attitude toward both music and sexuality: "Desire acted on by the *I* spirit is greedy . . . has an unnatural, feverish agitation about it. It has obstinate will, that won't be refused; there is no softness in it—no yielding, no accommodation, no dropping down into another's thoughts and interests, no harmony or communion with other desires. This is a morbid state of the passions. The *we* spirit is gentle and patient; and while at the same time it has a relish for pleasure . . . yet there is no sharp, severe will in it. It is healthful, happy in hope, content in the prospect of enjoyment. It is not greedy of action or of possession, but is made happy by hope. It prefers to wait on the execution of other folk's desires and wills." Kern, *Ordered Love,* 226.

27. Frank Wayland-Smith, "Memoir," December 4, 1878.

28. *The Circular,* January 9, 1871.

29. "Prima Donna Fever," Report of Musical Criticism, August 24, 1874.

30. David G. Croly, *Glimpses of the Future: Suggestions as to the Drift of Things* (New York: G. P. Putnam's Sons, 1888).

31. Charles Nordhoff, *The Communistic Societies of the United States* (1875; reprint, Stockbridge, Mass.: Berkshire House, 1993), 259–301.

32. William H. Dixon, *Spiritual Wives* (London: Hurst and Blackett, 1868) and *New America* (Philadelphia: Lippincott, 1870).

33. "Francis Wayland-Smith Journal," June 25, 1879.

34. Tirzah Miller to John H. Noyes, June 9, 1879.

35. Tirzah Miller to J. H. Noyes, July 9, 1881.

36. J. H. Noyes to E. H. Hamilton, March 4, 1850 in "Oneida Journal."

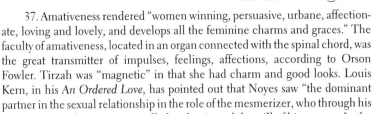

37. Amativeness rendered "women winning, persuasive, urbane, affectionate, loving and lovely, and develops all the feminine charms and graces." The faculty of amativeness, located in an organ connected with the spinal chord, was the great transmitter of impulses, feelings, affections, according to Orson Fowler. Tirzah was "magnetic" in that she had charm and good looks. Louis Kern, in his *An Ordered Love*, has pointed out that Noyes saw "the dominant partner in the sexual relationship in the role of the mesmerizer, who through his vigor and sexual potency controlled or dominated the will of his partner. In the sexual act, the passage of nervous fluid from one person to another followed the same essential laws of physics that required all fluids to seek a state of equilibrium." Women were "weaker vessels," according to Noyes, and Tirzah's magnetic power upset the usual balance: She was able to bewitch men and hold them in her orbit, she drew men toward her and took them in, she had a kind of animal magnetism about her that made her at once beloved and feared. Kern, *An Ordered Love*, 225.

38. As Uta Ranke-Heinemann has argued, there is a long history of various contraceptive practices within the Christian church—so much so, that between 1400 and 1750 *coitus reservatus* (also called "reserved embrace") was increasingly mentioned by theologians as a permissible method of birth control. Uta Ranke-Heinemann, *Eunuchs for the Kingdom of Heaven: Women, Sexuality, and the Catholic Church* (New York: Doubleday, 1990), 174.

39. In a privately circulated paper Noyes defended himself against charges that he had taken sexual liberties with pre-pubescent young women by asserting that he always considered their social and emotional development and cared less about their age: "I have never made free with girls, as they have come to the natural development of sexual feelings, and I have not felt bound to inquire their age, or whether they were past puberty. . . . I know that I have been accused in many cases of sexual intercourse with them when there was only sportive familiarity in the way of external contact. I admit that I cannot swear that I have never had sexual intercourse with persons of less than the legal age, because on the principles before stated, I have not referred to age as the rule to go by; but I swear that I have never had sexual intercourse with anyone who did not give what I considered evident tokens of a mature state of passional and physical development." "By J.H.N." in "Francis Wayland-Smith Journal," n.d.

Some members of this class of young women remembered their sexual experiences through a romantic and benign prism. Jessie Kinsley, for example, later wrote: "Always there were, too, the changing and steadfast lovers. Some heart-ache, much happiness. What seems now to have been strange experiences was then but natural. One formed no habits that dulled the edge of love—except, perhaps, as one was obliged to maintain too rigidly the Principles of Ascending Fellowship." Jessie Kinsley, "Autobiography," n.p. Her sexual initiation came when she was sixteen and she saw it as a necessary and essential part of colony life.

40. John L. Skinner to Alanson Skinner, March 30, 1852.

41. George W. Noyes to Harriet Skinner, September 13, 1869.

42. Ibid.

43. "Consanguineous Stirpiculture," *The Circular* 6, no. 26 (September 13, 1869).

44. F. U. L. to Mr. Nash, n.d., Nash Papers, Special Collections, Stanford University.

45. George W. Noyes to Tirzah Miller, September 18, 1869.

46. Anita Newcomb McGee, "Memorandum," August 1891.

47. See Theodore R. Noyes, *Report on the Health of the Children in the Oneida Community* (Oneida: n.p., 1878); Ely Wan de Walker, "A Gynecological Study of the Oneida Community," *American Journal of Obstetrics and the Diseases of Women and Children* 17 (August 1884); Hilda Herrick Noyes and George Wallingford Noyes, "The Oneida Community Experiment in Stirpiculture," *Eugenics, Genetics, and the Family* (Baltimore: Williams and Wilkins, 1923).

48. Tirzah Miller to George W. Noyes, March 28, 1869.

49. George W. Noyes to Tirzah Miller, March 31,1869

50. Tirzah Miller to George W. Noyes, February 26,1869.

51. This musical allusion is to Donizetti's 1840 opera, *La Figlia del Regimento*, which is set in the Tyrolean Alps where a peasant, Tonio, falls in love with Marie, a young girl ("the daughter of the regiment") who had been found on a battlefield by a French regiment and "brought up by a whole regiment of fathers, the spoiled darling of the grenadiers," according to *Kobbé's Complete Opera Book* (New York: Putnam,1954), 402. During the course of the opera it is revealed that Marie is the illegitimate daughter of an English marquise. Duty compels the young women to obey her newfound mother's desire that she marry a duke. Marie acquiesces, but sings of her devotion to her other family (the regiment). In the end she marries her true love, Tonio, who had joined the army to woo her. Ironically, this scenario foreshadows Tirzah's own struggles in the memoir between romance and duty and between her selfish desires and the demands of her "regiment" of men at Oneida.

52. Michel Foucault, *The History of Sexuality* (New York: Pantheon Books, 1978), 59.

53. Taylor Stoehr, *Hawthorne's Mad Scientists: Pseudoscience and Social Science in Nineteenth-Century Life and Letters* (Hamden, Conn.: Archon Books, 1978), 66–67.

54. Orson B. Fowler, *Sexual Science, Including Manhood, Womanhood, and Their Mutual Interrelations* (Philadelphia: National Publishing Company, 1879), 72–73.

55. Tirzah Miller to Charlotte Leonard, July 26, 1869.

56. George W. Noyes to John H. Noyes, February 26, 1869.

57. George W. Noyes to Tirzah Miller, July 14, 1870.

58. Foucault, *History of Sexuality*, 66. For Foucault the history of sexuality should be written from "discourses" and the diary and the memoir are powerful examples of intimate discourse.

59. Thomas Laqueur, *Making Sex: Body and Gender from the Greeks to Freud* (Cambridge, Mass.: Harvard University Press, 1990).

60. J. H. Noyes to Tirzah Miller, July 8, 1876.

61. "Journals of Charlotte Leonard," July 10, 1876.

62. The method used to choose Tirzah's mate shows the power structure at work: Her own position in the community as both confidante of Noyes and superior biological partner gave her prominence; however, she had a limited say in who would be the father. During the stirpiculture experiment a woman's "rights" were taken into some, but not total, consideration. Efforts to subvert this system were rampant in the late seventies and this "man's game," as one woman referred to it, caused resentment among the younger generation of women, like Tirzah.

63. Tirzah Miller to John H. Noyes, August 10, 1877. Much is made in this memoir about "feeling good" because to feel despair was to stand in opposition to community sentiment.

64. Tirzah Miller to John H. Noyes, April 21, 1878.

65. Tirzah Miller to Mary Prindle, November 29, 1880.

66. Tirzah Miller to James B. Herrick, October 2, 1884.

67. Tirzah Miller to Victor Noyes, April 27, 1886.

68. Edward Inslee to Tirzah Miller, February 2, 1884.

69. Tirzah Miller to Mary Prindle, January 14, 1880.

70. Tirzah Miller to John H. Noyes (undated).

Cast of Characters

(in order of appearance in the memoir)

George Washington Noyes (1822–1870), John H. Noyes's younger brother and the father of Tirzah's first child, was an early convert to Perfectionism, a respected leader within the group, and someone Tirzah loved and respected. Both in this memoir and in her letters to him Tirzah displays her affection for, and desire for greater intimacy with, her "Uncle George." She became pregnant by him in 1870, and their child was born after George's sudden death of cholera later that year.

Harriet Noyes Skinner (1817–1893), Tirzah's aunt, joined the Putney and Oneida groups and married an early convert to Perfectionism, John L. Skinner, in 1841. They had one child in 1842. She was an active editor and leading figure but had no children within the community. After the breakup she went to Canada with her brother.

Helen C. Miller (1847–1932), Tirzah's sister, worked as an editor and bookkeeper in the community. She had a child by J. H. Noyes as part of the stirpiculture experiment. At the breakup she married Homer Barron, with whom she went to Canada. They had one child while at Niagara Falls.

Augusta Hamilton (1845–1914), Tirzah's close friend and confidante, had two children in the community. She left in 1878 to marry, then rejoined, only to leave again to go to live in New York City.

Constance "Consuelo" Bradley Noyes (1849–1917), Tirzah's cousin and the child of Sarah Bradley and John H. Noyes (though Constance later denied that he was her father), worked as bookkeeper and in general service. She had two children in the community, one by James Hatch and one by Homer Barron. She left the community at the breakup. In 1884 she married a former community member and had one child.

John H. Noyes (1811–1886), sometimes refered to as "Father Noyes" by Tirzah, was the dominant force in her life and in the life of the community. He was the political, religious, and social fulcrum at Oneida and he confided in Tirzah about every aspect of community life. She was his favorite sexual partner and he thought of her as both "daughter" and a potential mother of his child. He fathered thirteen community children, but none by Tirzah.

James B. Herrick (1837–1912), the father of Tirzah's third child, was an Episcopal curate with degrees from Columbia College and the Virginia Theological Seminary. He joined Oneida in 1864 after leaving his wife and five children. During 1866 and 1867 he traveled to New York City to try to convince his wife to join. She refused, and in 1873 she divorced him. At the breakup Tirzah married Herrick (whom she called "Jamie") and in 1880 they moved to Canada with other Noyes loyalists. There Herrick suffered a psychological breakdown but recovered after a rest cure in a sanitarium.

Charlotte Noyes Miller (1819–1874), Tirzah's mother and the youngest sister of John H. Noyes, was a devoted member of both the Putney and Oneida communities. She had three children prior to joining Oneida, but none within the community. She died of malaria.

Edward Inslee (1845–1929), father of Tirzah's second child, joined the community in 1855 with his family. They had been members of a Newark, New Jersey, Perfectionist group affiliated with Oneida. A machinist and an accomplished musician, he had a tempestuous "special love" relationship with Tirzah. After leaving the community in 1875 he was in constant conflict with Oneida over his rights with regard to his and Tirzah's child. Eventually he moved to California and played with the Los Angeles Philharmonic (led by another community descendant, Harley Hamilton).

Homer Barron (1835–1924) entered the community in 1854 with his parents and worked as a trapmaker. He had a turbulent relationship with Tirzah, and at the breakup married her sister (and Noyes's niece), Helen Miller.

Frank Wayland-Smith (1841–1911) was Tirzah's confidante, a fellow musician, and a leader among the younger generation. He attended Yale and had one child in the stirpiculture experiment. At the breakup he married the child's mother and remained at Oneida, where he played a prominent role in the newly formed corporation.

Erastus Hamilton (1821–1894), chief "architect" at Oneida and a prominent leader, was an early supporter of Noyes. He converted to Perfectionism in 1843 and joined Oneida with his wife and children in 1848. He became smitten with Tirzah in the 1870s and at the breakup accompanied other loyalists to Canada. He was president of Oneida Ltd. for a short period in the 1890s.

Ann Hobart (1846–1908) entered the community with her mother in 1856. She worked as a teacher and typesetter, had a "special love" relationship with Theodore Noyes, and was seen to exert considerable influence over him and the community in the 1870s. As a result she came under considerable criticism. She left in 1878 to marry Joseph Skinner, who fathered her only child.

Harriet Worden (1840–1891), editor of *The Circular* and a strong supporter of John H. Noyes, came to the community with her father and sisters in 1849. She had three children in the community, including a child by Theodore Noyes as part of the stirpiculture plan, and was sexually involved with James B. Herrick. Tirzah was jealous of that relationship.

Myron Kinsley (1836–1907) was an early supporter of Noyes and a prominent community elder for much of its history. He was superintendent of the spoon factory at Wallingford and was considered a prime candidate to father Tirzah's third child. At the breakup he went to Canada.

Henry Hunter (1859–??) joined the community in 1873 when he was fourteen. Four years later he entered into a passionate affair with Tirzah that unnerved them both. At the breakup he left the community and the area.

Desire and Duty at Oneida

Beginning of Autobiography

T. C. MILLER

I WAS BORN SEPTEMBER 13, 1843 in Putney, Vermont. My mother was the youngest sister of John H. Noyes, the founder of the famous Oneida Community. At the time of my birth the nucleus of that Association had just started in the Noyes family. Mr. Noyes converted his two younger sisters and brother to his own peculiar views of religious and social life, and then having arranged their marriages with persons of similar views, he entered into co-operation with them, having common ownership of this world's goods and forming themselves into one large family with himself at the head.

During these first years I had only boys to play with. There were Mrs. Cragin's three sons, George, Charles and John; Mr. Noyes's only son Theodore, and Mrs. Skinner's (Mr. Noyes's sister) son Joseph. I remember romping with these boys (all of whom except Johnnie were a year or two older than myself) in the woods and down by the brook in pleasant weather and then on rainy days having great sport in the garret at the top of the old Noyes mansion. In that garret was a huge chimney around which we used to chase each other and once, becoming very dossy, I rolled down the stairs which were near by, cutting my head and variously bruising myself so that I was grandmother's pet all the afternoon, coddled up on her bed, diverted with stories and treated to prunes and raisins.

My first recollection of Mr. Noyes is when I was three years old. There was a lounge in the sitting-room all around the edge of which were pretty silk tassles of variegated colors. One day one of these tassles was cut off and someone accused me of doing it. I did not do it, and of course denied the soft impeachment; but I suppose my denial must have been called in question for my next remembrance is of being perched on Mr. Noyes's knees while he, with his arms folded, regarded me with a searching glance and told me to "look him in the eye and tell the truth." This was my first experience of fear of a human being and a kind of terror seized me; but I must have held to my first assertion for I do not recall any further punishment and the matter was soon passed by and forgotten by everyone but me. I remember Mr. Noyes afterwards as very kind and gentle to children.

A little incident that mother told occurs to me. She said that when I was about a year old I was sitting at a high chair at the dinner-table. Coming in Joseph, a year older sat by me and for some cause struck me in the face, when I turned on him such a grieved, reproachful look and gave such a sob of wounded feeling that Mr. Noyes remarked, "Charlotte, your little girl has a large heart."

[Here the narrative breaks off in the middle of the second sheet.]

1867

My Room, 1/4 to 10, P.M. W.C. [Wallingford Community], September 3, 1867

They tell me that Uncle George has just arrived from New York.[1] Thank God! When I heard this morning that he safely disembarked from Europe in New York yesterday, I thanked God for his goodness in bringing him back again. Something said to me, "Why thank God for what was merely the result of human science and skill?" Then this verse of David's came into my mind in direct contradiction: "Except God build the house, they labor in vain who build it. Except God keep the city, the watchman riseth but in vain."[2] So I said: "Except God had guided the ship, the helmsman had directed its course in vain, and the wisdom of captain and crew had been of no avail." Thus God is to be thanked for everything. May I ever learn to bless and praise him for all his goodness!

I began writing this before going to see him; it seemed to satisfy me entirely to have him here, and I quite forgot for a while the absurdity of my staying here writing, when all the rest were greeting him.

Monday, Oct. 28, 1867

Mary and I commence our editorial career this morning.[3]

1868

Oneida, March 24, 1868

Left Wallingford the morning of the 10th in company with Harriet, Cornelia, Ella, Mary V., Alfred, and Edwin B.[4] As Uncle George bade me "good-bye" he whispered, "Watch and pray." I owe to my acquaintance with Uncle George during the past three years a thousand blessings. From him I learned that it is truly the glory of a woman to love and be receptive to good men; he taught me that pride is despicable; he led me to the knowledge and love of God. These lessons I have learned, not by his teaching me in words, but by following his example and getting in rapport with his spirit. I have every reason to honor and love him.

Arrived here at midnight. For several days I felt strangely. It seemed as though there was no action in my heart. Thursday, the 19th, Theodore criticized me for not co-operating easily with him in regards to the paper, for having a spirit of diotrephiasis in regard to it, and for making Mary [Bolles] stand in terror of me.[5] Aunt H.H.S. [Harriet S. Skinner] was there. Said Theodore: "She is full of the diotrephian spirit lately. I don't see how it got into her." H.H.S.: "I do; it is natural to her. That is where she is just like me. That spirit was always natural to me."

I felt very thankful for the criticism. It softened my heart, and did me good in many ways. I do hate this spirit of hardness which comes over me sometimes. I felt a new purpose to keep in unity with Mary, and be humble in regard to her. In her the heart stands in much greater prominence than the head, while with me the opposite is true. I can learn from her, and have need of her.

Sunday we got out our first Circular at O.C. [Oneida Community]. The work on it has passed off pleasantly, and I have enjoyed being receptive to Theodore. Monday I just tried the piano. I had a purpose that I should not touch it until the first paper was printed, for I was anxious that music should be no diversion to me from duty.

Thursday, [March] 26.

Father Noyes came Tuesday night. Mary and I got up to see him. He was in fine spirits. He told us about the rapid reconstruction of the W.C. family. "I never grew so fast in my life," said he, "as since all you folks got away. Even Charles Joslyn and Mr. Whiting are getting to be exemplary saints!" Though he spoke laughingly, he made us understand that he was independent of the old relation to us. "Augusta [Towner] and Helen [Woolworth?] have done for me since you girls went away," said he. Mary felt some bad about it; but I didn't at all. I was glad we were out of the way, so that those other girls could get the same benefit from association with him that we had. I was glad he felt so independent of us, and wanted us to be independent of any sentimentalism in our feelings for him. Last night he asked me to sleep with him, and I never realized so much as I have to-day what a life-giving thing it is to have fellowship with him. I had an unusually nice time, and felt happier and younger today than any day since I came. He gave some interesting talk in his room on old-grannyism, and the spirit of the second generation. "I feel that there is a strong spirit of old-grannyism in this Community, and that Mr. Cragin is the top of it.[6] I'll tell you what I am going to do. I am going to favor the young in an insurrection against the old. The devil has tried a great many times to do that thing; but now I believe that God has taken hold of it in his own interest — to carry on his work. What this Community needs is to let the young blood rise. If folks will be old grannies, they may; I shall not spend my strength in trying to drag them out of that state. But they must not get into the center; they must keep on the circumference, and in a small corner, where they have little or no influence. If folks will be old grannies, we must expect that their children will rise and go ahead of them. We have got a strong battalion of young folks, and what we want is to let them rise. This young set are, as a whole, more continent, more wise, and more nearly right about the subject of love than the old folks. What Geo. E. and Charles Cragin need is to become independent of their father — go on and leave him behind, and be men by themselves. If Mr. Cragin wants to be an old granny, he may; I will not stop to pull him out of that state, but I will encourage his boys to go ahead of him. I think they are ahead of him now in continence about love. I feel confident that [Consuelo] is more sure of taking care of herself, of going right, and of keeping herself out of temptation, than her mother is, and I should tell her to go ahead of her. So Mary P. ought to go on, and leave her mother, and the Worden girls their father, and so on. God strikes into young life at about the age of twenty-two, and if folks don't keep up with him, he leaves them, and strikes into the next generation at that age. When folks fail to keep hold of God, and settle into old-grannyism, they must expect that their children will go ahead of them. I shall. But I don't expect that my children are going to be smarter than I am, as long as God inspires me. My son is strong in spiritual things, and strong in finance, and he has an army of young folks to sustain him. I have just 'saved my bacon.' I have got a son who is able to lead in spirituality and in business, and he has a strong company of young folks to uphold him. This second generation is a peculiar one; perhaps there will never be another one like it. They have had experience in the old state of things, and have come through into wisdom and continence about love, without having their hearts burnt out with idolatry. Folks have said we should fail when the second generation grew up, but we should fail if it were <u>not</u> for this second generation. It is the second generation that is going to be the salvation of us. If this Community is a hell, it is so just so far as old-grannyism keeps on top, and holds the young life down. I want to see that young life rise and rule. God wants the best life, and will have it. But this second generation must look out that it does not fall behind, and let the next set rise and be smarter than it is." I report this as well as I can from memory.

April 24.

Uncle George has come and gone. Strange talk with him. We never talked so freely. He thought I troubled him some—bewitched him. We had it back and forth in lively style for a while. But our talk was <u>very satisfactory</u>. We are no longer <u>lovers</u>, any way until I don't trouble him in the least. I told him just what I owed to my acquaintance with him. He did me, too.

June 16.

Father Noyes put the responsibility of the paper on me to-day, relieving Theodore. I told him I wanted to do right. "You <u>will</u>," said he, "I don't expect anything else. I shall make a good editress of you."

July 15.

A most splendid time with Mr. Noyes this afternoon. "The word of God to me now is," said he, "<u>talk less, and love more</u>! This is to be my final work, to sanctify amativeness.[7] This is the way to preach salvation from sin. What <u>is</u> salvation from sin? Why, it is being saved from our passions, and amativeness is the king passion. This is the way to do—preach it <u>practically</u>. Other folks may stop, or grow indifferent, but I am going on higher. I have had some splendid times this summer." I told him how I like to begin "my month" with him—that he really controlled my amativeness. If I was in rapport with him I had good times with other folks—otherwise I had little attraction. He was very much pleased, and told me to ponder it in my heart.

Friday, Aug. 7.

The Croly party came to-day.[8] I was one of those delegated to take charge of them. It was a very pleasant affair indeed. Mrs. Croly is a charming woman, because she is sensible, refined, and intellectual. Not a bit afraid of her. Mr. Noyes said the New York press had come up here to inoculate me, and make an editress of me. He talked and laughed with me about their coming a good deal. He said he wanted the Community to make a stunning sensation, "and I want you to lead off." "I don't know but we had better, all hands, practise before the glass until we can get on an expression of <u>high intelligence and conscious superiority</u>!" said he.

Sunday, [Aug.] 9.

It has been very delightful to have Uncle George here a week. I haven't troubled him this time either. I tried not to, any way. We had a nice little chat this afternoon of an hour or two. He says he told Father Noyes that he had the difficulty about me that he (J.H.N.) used to have about my father, i.e., get fascinated by me, so he was unable to see my faults. Queer, isn't it? Then he related some of his European adventures to me in his own bewitching, unapproachable way. He goes tomorrow. Mary [Bolles] has been at Willow Place a week, and expects to stay there now indefinitely.

Monday, [Aug.] 17.

Father Noyes is very kind to me. I get his breakfast, and wait on him at night, and am with him on editorial matters.

Thursday, Sept. 17.

Room with Ida, Aunt Harriet, and Consuelo in the Middle House.

Tuesday, [Sept.] 22.

Father Noyes said this evening: "No one knows what a blessing it is to be free from pain. I haven't been a moment without pain in my throat all summer. I never came so near dying—never got so close to the old monster. A terrible burning in my throat, and the worst of it was, I could feel it creeping toward my lungs. But I am getting over it once more."[9]

Sleeping with Mr. Noyes the other night he said there was an immense difference in women in regard to power to please sexually. "Why, is there?" said I. "Yes," he answered, "there is as much difference between women in respect to ability to make social music as there is between a grand piano and a tenpenny whistle!" Then applying his remarks personally he said: "I always expect something sublime when I sleep with you."

October 31, 1868.

Father Noyes said to me tonight of my piece "Among the Autochthons" in this week's paper: "I like your piece very much. It is pretty. It is somewhat rambling, but as you write more you will learn more regard for unity. But I enjoyed this piece very much. It is quite charming. Keep your freedom to ramble; you will grow into unity of style. Keep near to Harriet Skinner and me, and you will become a good writer. Remember, above all, that fertility is the gift of God, and he will give you inspirations."[10]

Dec. 27.

J.H.N.: "I shall wait and study the matter, and if inspiration shows it to be a good combination, I shall go ahead with you as quick as I would with anybody. It is among the possibilities that must be submitted to God."

1869

Jan. 19, 1869.

J.H.N.: "I suppose you haven't decided yet whom you will choose for the father of your child, have you?" Consuelo told me that J.H.N. told her today that he "liked Tirzah because she liked to come and have good long serious talks" with him occasionally.

Saturday, March 6, 1869.

Last night I slept with J.H.N., and he talked with me for more than an hour. He began like this: "I want you and Harriet Skinner to go into the study of literature. Dig into it, and show it up, as I am American socialisms. Theodore and I will attend to the sciences; you and Harriet attend to literature. Study the science of literature. Get at the causes of literature. Find out how this infernal German atheism got sifted into so much of our literature." He said we must read magazines, and find out all we could about the leading novel literature, with analysis and criticism in view. Criticise all the authors; contrast old English literature with the Boston. Those English authors, taking Shakespeare as an example, wrote with an honest intention to entertain people; but these Boston and German writers try to influence their readers with their atheism and hatred of revivals. Such work is dishonest, and ought to be kicked out. "I guess I can't let you have a baby for some time yet. I want to get you into this work. You must get so you can criticise Miss Peabody first. You can make a better critic than Margaret Fuller, or Miss Peabody, or Miss Q-body."[11] I told him I was in no hurry to have a child, and had had a kind of impression that I should not for two years. He said he thought that was probable. He talked a great deal more about what he wanted us to do.

Saturday, March 27.

Last night J.H.N. talked with me about having sexual intercourse performed on the stage. "We shall never have heaven till we can conquer shame, and make a beautiful exhibition on the stage."

April 6.

Slept with J.H.N. I dreaded to go, because I knew he must discover my unmagnetic condition. He did fast enough. In the night he said: "Would you like some criticism?" "Yes, I should very much." "Well, there is no disguising the fact that you don't attract me. You impress me with the feeling that your sexual nature has been abused by your entering into sexual intercourse without appetite. Spirits of men which are indigestible to you have come between you and me." "It is true, that I have slept with men without any appetite, and a great deal lately." "But why do you? I thought you promised me once you wouldn't." I told him I had not quite dared just follow my attractions in that aspect. But he said I <u>must</u>, or it would spoil it all for me. That is true even now, for I have been away so much this winter in a kind of duty-doing spirit with folks for whom I had no attraction, that I have lost all appetite for intercourse with men whom I love, and have always had splendid times with. I have felt that it was a great expense to me, and was taking all the romance out of life; but I didn't know what to do, and thought I was doing my duty. Oh! I feel so relieved! I had hardly dared to hope I need do nothing in this line but what I felt an attraction for.

April 26.

I have felt rather bad lately, fearing that if I remain so unmagnetic Mr. Noyes will not love me any more. Tonight he asked me if I would like to sleep with him. "I hope I can <u>sometime</u> again," I said. "Let's try it tonight." "No, I am unwell now." "Well, whenever you are ready, and feel like it, we will." "Father Noyes, I think it puts a ligature on my life to be separated from you in this way." "No, I guess not," he answered. "You are getting united to me in a different way." "I hope so." "Let's go off and take a long walk in the woods." "Oh, I should like that." "Well, some day when the weather is all right, and you feel like it, we will." During the conversation he said: "But how much have you been with these other chaps lately?" I told him I had only staid away twice since his talk with me, and meant to follow the course of attraction. He was much pleased with that. He said he thought I had done well with the paper during Aunt H's absence.[12]

Sunday, May 23, 1869.

Took that walk with Father Noyes. My last day on the paper. I petitioned to Father Noyes yesterday for a release. Aunt H. said to me last evening: "I think you deserve a great deal of praise for your course on the paper. You have done well, as I have always told you, and am glad you can have a release. You need not feel the least condemned for wanting to get out of it. It has been a steady strain upon you for a long time. You deserve a great deal of praise. You have been faithful over this, and you will be put over something greater."

Sunday, June 13.

Finished two delightful weeks at Willow Place.[13]

1872

O.C., Dec. 23, 1872.

I awake this morning to find myself again editress of the Circular. It is exactly two years and seven months since I left the position. I feel no confidence in myself, and I should never have sought the office; but I know that the angels are "looking kindly down" upon the paper, and will see that it is issued every week in strength and edification, as it has been for years. I desire to dedicate myself anew to the service of the truth and communism.

1873

Jan. 1st, 1873.

Let me thank God that I am where I cannot long be left to go astray into idolatry and the insincerity of false love. Though my intellect and common sense acknowledged the justice of our criticism, yet my heart felt so hard I almost feared that I had so fallen away that there was no more opportunity for me to renew unto repentance; but, I said, if I must go to the devil at last, I will, while life continues, struggle for salvation. I determined, with God's help, to become more <u>faithful</u>. My life thus far has stranded on the rock of <u>unfaithfulness</u>. I resolved, also, to give up H. [Homer Barron] entirely, unreservedly, leaving no thought of future connection with him. I give all my hopes and desires in that direction into God's hands. If there is anything good, he will save it. I need take no care of it myself. I will not mope or be sorrowful. Perhaps God will in due time soften my heart with the sorrow which worketh repentance. I want no other.

March 16, 1873.

Left music for writing. Father Noyes said that I might consider that I had made a good career in music, and now call it ended, and put the energy I had expended in music into writing. It is like the death of a cherished friend.

March 18.

J.H.N. spent about two hours in my room this afternoon talking about the paper, and the way that music may be made an aid to it. Musical education is a good foundation for making a good writer. Music and literature are counterparts. Boston is the headquarters of music and literature in the U.S., Germany in Europe. Music should teach rhythm, unity, fine modulation, and graceful cadence in writing.

March 20.

J.H.N. talked to me this morning about voluntary and involuntary actions. He said involuntary thinking about those we love is the same as nocturnal emission.

March 23.

My literary criticism. J.H.N. gave quite a discourse. Mr. Herrick, Alfred, William, Geo. Miller, Mr. Cragin, Geo. E., Mr. Woolworth, H.H.S., Miss Dunn, Mrs. Bushnell, H.M.W. were there. Less severe than I expected.

Mr. Herrick said he thought I might study the matter of subjects for the club. Was tempted to feel proud of me; glad that we had women who could occupy such a position. Thought one or two of my papers the best Circulars he had ever seen.

March 25.

J.H.N.: "Don't you think I shall be able to keep hold of you, and carry you through all this?"

T.: "I hope so."

N.: "You won't get so as to think of me as a grim, crabbed old hunks, will you?"

T.: "No, no!"

April 9.

Circilar [*sic*] full of stirpiculture—breeding in and in. J.H.N. said this morning that I was just the one to lead off on that subject. I had deviated from the ways of the world, and must defend my position.

April 12.

Dentist's at 1/2 past 12. The first thing which met my eye on entering the room was "L.W. Apr. 5, '73." written on the wall.[14] It hurt like an arrow through my heart. Just a week ago! What was he thinking of? He loves me still I think.

Thursday, April 24, 1873.

I sometimes wish I could be obscure in the sense that Mary B. [Bolles] and A.A. [Alice Ackley] are, and less under the scrutiny of Mr. Noyes's almost omniscient eye; but when, after trying to hide myself, he reaches out for me, and hunts me up, my heart goes out toward him with that passionate devotion, inspired not only by his being the one man on earth in whom I absolutely trust, but also by the fact that he is the only father I have known since childhood. I have been a little "off" now for several days, brooding over some of those doubts and fears which seem to come upon us so much more heavily at thirty than at twenty. This morning he called me to his room to see what the matter was, and began probing my very soul. I longed to tell him all, yet shrunk from giving him pain. At last I said: "Does Theodore feel just as he used to? He does not seem as he did at Wallingford or at Willow Place. I have not had a word to say to him, and yet I can't help feeling as though he were also troubled by some of these temptations which are depressing me." As soon as I mentioned Theodore's name, Mr. Noyes leaned forward in his chair, his arms folded, his eyes flashing, and his brows quivering with an almost alarming expression. After a moment he broke in on me with the greatest emphasis: "I have long had this same doubt about Theodore. You go straight down to the office, and charge him all what you have said."

This was a very unexpected turn of affairs, and one I would rather have avoided, but I must obey.

I found Theodore alone in the inside office, and reported to him what had passed between his father and myself, ending with his father's last remark. An expression of the most intense relief crossed Theodore's face, and he drew a long breath and straightened back his shoulders like one eager for an affray in which he would not have taken the initiative. He said he was glad he could now unburden himself, and tell just what he was, and throw off the cloak he had been wearing. I was shocked and confounded by his revelations—his unbelief in existing institutions having carried him so much farther than I had gone. After talking with him awhile, I went back to tell his father what he had said, as I knew he was waiting impatiently to hear the result of the interview. He had a great deal to say in reply, and as neither wished to meet the other face to face, I passed back and forth between them steadily from noon till 7 o'clock in the evening. Neither wished to have notes taken of his remarks, so that I had to remember as well as I could what each said. One remark of Theodore's gave considerable pain, although I did not really believe what he predicted. He said the Community would inevitably go to pieces before many years, and that when that catastrophe occurred he meant to be on hand to see that justice was done. He did not look upon the prospect as one of unmitigated evil, but on the contrary seemed to have little regret about it.

Friday, [April] 25.

Back and forth between father and Theodore all day. It is a painful ordeal to them, and I sympathize with them both, but more with Mr. Noyes, because he has more fully won my confidence, and because his suffering seems deeper. The effect on me of Theodore's apostasy has on the whole been to strengthen my own faith. His father attributes his change principally to his connection with the Bailey family.

Saturday, [April] 26.

Back and forth again between Theodore and his father pretty much all day. Talked twice with Theodore three hours in the stretch, besides several short talks.

Sunday, [April] 27.

Long talks with Mr. Noyes. Theodore submitted to a criticism committee.

Monday, [April] 28.

Mr. Herrick and Mother's wedding. Mr. Herrick, who has been here five years on probation, joined the Community by marrying Mother as its representative.[15]

Tuesday, [April] 29.

Awoke with black spots and bright circles before my eyes. The long strain of these talks with Mr. Noyes and Theodore, scarcely eating my meals or sleeping on account of the excitement, seems to have given me a slight break-down. Mr. Noyes was very kind, and told me not to trouble myself about the Circular (of which I am editor); he would look after it—but to drop everything and rest myself.

[Here the memoir jumps back two weeks. No explanation is given in the typescript for these repeated dates.]

April 13, 1873.

At a criticism committee to-day of which I took notes. J.H.N. talked about our taking an hour at least every day for spiritual practice—reflection, prayer, and communion with God. O.T.T. related an experience, but I had some difficulty in reconciling it with the "L.W." at the dentist's office.[16]

Music is to be abandoned this year.

April 14.

Wrote below the "L.W." in phonography: "Man ought always to pray, and not to faint."[17]

April 16.

Walk with J.H.N. on the hill east of our house. Nice time when we got home. I think I have been unbelieving about my social experience. I am going to take a new start.

April 17.

Edward's disaffection.

April 22.

Asked Father Noyes to contradict a story I heard circulating that [Edward Inslee—blank here in typescript] had been one of those who wanted to leave the Community. He went right down and saw him, and said he was satisfied he had never been tempted to leave—had only had involuntary thoughts about it, and he would contradict the story.

April 27.

While talking with J.H.N. this afternoon he said: "I love to talk with you. Somehow I feel real good every time I have a soak talking with you."

April 28.

Mr. Herrick's and Mother's wedding. J.H.N. had no objections whatever to "O.T.T." and I practising "Wedding March" together with the others.

April 29.

Here I am at Joppa.[18] Awoke with my eyes feeling badly yesterday morning—spots and bright circles. Told J.H.N. this morning, and he told me not to trouble myself about the paper, he would take care of it. There was a party coming here, and mother sent me. James Hatch, Mr. Thacker, Mr. Reynolds, Emily Otis, Mrs. Newhouse and I make up the party.

Couldn't help smiling as I ran by him this morning.

May 2.

Gone to the Villa [a building at Oneida Community] to live for a little while. J.H.N. says I must not think of being reconciled to having my eyes out of order. I mustn't let Theodore knock me off the track.

May 4.

Stunning proposition. Edward has been under more temptation. J.H.N. told me this evening that he sent Mrs. Ackley to him to propose to him to have a baby by me. He was pleased, he said, and overwhelmed, and said he didn't deserve it. J.H.N. said he liked the combination very much. What will my darling, my [Homer—blank in typescript filled in by hand], my dearest say? Brother George says he will comfort him. I see no reason why it should make any difference with me.

May 5.

Edward came to see me, and we had a very pleasant talk. He was very affectionate, and said if he had his choice he should have liked me. He said he would love me and be faithful to me forever.

May 6.

Edward proposed to sleep with me tonight, so that we could get acquainted a little before — —; but I was taken this afternoon.

May 7.

Left for N.Y. Does he know? Found my waist.[19] I am sure he has had it at the Dye House, and has washed it.

May 11.

H. [Homer] arrived this morning from N.Y., and sister Helen told him. Took it in a very good spirit; said he should trust God for grace to behave well. Said that he had retained his respect for me through all our trying experience, and that I was a good girl. He behaved nobly at the ceremony tonight.

> "Our Father, on these two who kneel,
> Our blessing with thy blessing seal;
> And grant in coming joyous days
> A noble child may lisp thy praise."

May 12.

Found on his table: "Sunday, May 11, 1873. The last are first, the first are last—the very last!"

Is it possible that there should be a sensation in the womb the very next day?

May 14.

How sad he looks! Edwin B. told me today that he said that a great blow always numbed him at first, and then he suffered dreadfully afterward. So it had been about this. He had felt very bad since the first day.

May 15.

Curious phenomenon. Stood in the distributing-room. Looked up at the window. There were "O.T.T." and two other men. Old hat pushed tightly over his brows, hands on hips. Gazed a moment. The image remained like a sun-spot on the retina for ten minutes afterward, growing fainter and fainter, but the exact outline of my friend.

May 16.

Father Noyes said to me this evening: "When are you and I going to have some more of our good long talks?" Then he told me that he had taken me into special spiritual drill which so prepared me, that when the need came, he hurled me against Theodore. I had sustained some damages—there had been a kind of "smash-up"—but I must learn to make quick repairs, as he might hurl me against Theodore again.

May 18.

Curious coincidence today, which shows there is still a sympathetic connection between us. I awoke with my mind full of the idea of writing something against "baby-talk." I went right about it, and after getting it done I went to read it to H.H.S., and she said that at the Committee this morning H. criticised Miss Pomeroy for her propensity for baby-talk.[20]

May 24.

Looked at me in meeting. First time in a long while.

May 25.

Looked at me when he went out of dining-room.

June 15.

Father Noyes came out against Theodore in meeting.

June 16.

Felt distressed about "O.T.T." [Homer Barron] last night, and again tonight, because he says nothing in meeting lately, and now if ever is certainly the time to make himself felt. I felt a mighty force within me, and took a resolve. I went straight down-stairs from the meeting, and said to him abruptly, "Why don't you take hold and help, Homer?" We sat down in the Reception Room, and talked till ten minutes of eleven. At first he was hopeless, discouraged, and somewhat hard—inclined to think his lot a harder one than ever man was called to bear. I never talked with anyone more earnestly. I told him I thought it time that we put aside our troubles, and helped Mr. Noyes. If we have an atom of faith in God, there is no need that we worry ourselves about the future of the Community. Rather than that it should become merely a great successful institution, I would rather that it were broken up tonight. I appealed to the better nature in him, which I had known so well. He softened completely, and declared that he would never give up his faith in God and loyalty to the Community. There were inevitably some allusions to our personal relations. How was it possible that I could inspire such idolatry?

June 18.

Best time E. and I ever had.

June 22.

Came out good and strong in meeting. He is a good boy.

July 13.

"Taken" this morning at 2 o'clock. I am glad of the humiliation. I needed it, and my conscience reproaches me with idolatry toward I. [Inslee?] still, and with having let him see it. Would to God we were back where we were a month ago! I rather be in uncertainty of his love, and have justification, than to know he adores me, and feel that I have in any way defiled my conscience.

July 18.

I have been in a struggle for several days between my sense of duty and my natural inclination. My first feeling on hearing about Frank and Helen was, that I didn't see why H. and I couldn't as well as they; but I was able to say and feel sincerely before I went to bed last night, that <u>God is good</u> to me, and I <u>have everything to be thankful</u> for, if I never have what my heart longs for. It is my duty to be <u>thankful</u> anyway. Made up my mind that I must make a holocaust of what I have received lately, before beginning another month with Edward. I had not quite the courage to do it last night, and though ready in other respects I postponed till tonight. Just before we went to bed I ran down-stairs and put the notes in the stove. Felt a better conscience. Determined to do my duty fairly, and expect God's blessing either way.

July 30.

My death-warrant.

Aug. 5.

Perryville Falls.[21] Superb! Accident with the horse. My first thought was not for my life, but "Oh, Edward! Edward! I must save myself, for you asked me to be careful!" No injury done to anything. Felt thankful for God's care. (Manly, E.A. Miller, James, and I.)

Aug. 9.

A peaceful week. No temptation. That love is dead. I shall never love him like that again.

Aug. 10.

Felt a gush of love in my heart for him today. I am glad it is not gone. It will only be better.

Sept. 6.

Georgy was telling me a story this evening, and he said, "Papa said get up, too." "Who is your papa?" I asked surprised. "Why, Mr. Homer," he answered, and went on with his story. Pretty soon he said something about "papa" again. "What do you mean, Georgy? Who is your papa?" "Ruth's papa is my papa," he answered, as though I ought to know. I said to H., "Are you sometimes kind to Georgy?" "I hope I am." And I told him what G. had said.

Sept. 7.

What a beautiful, radiant smile! I never saw such a smile. It seemed as though he were all aglow with the smiling radiance of love from head to foot.

Oct. 19.

Talk with Homer. Says it will kill him.

Oct. 23.

Wrote to Homer, telling him I dare not have him feel toward me as he seems to. He must give me up to God.

Nov. 6.

The dear baby begins to assert itself. For an hour before rising it kicked me quite vigorously.

Nov. 10.

E. left for N.Y. My love and respect for him grow continually.

1874

Jan. 25, 1874.

My life has been so full of incident since the beginning of this year that I must hasten to make some record of passing events. About three weeks ago Father Noyes had some talk with me in which he said that he had sworn in his heart that he would have the use of me, and he was not going to have his plans about me frustrated any longer by stirpiculture or special lovers. For several days we seemed to be in rapport, and I hoped that I was going to get back into my old relation toward him, only a better one; but there came a change. I knew I did not please him; but I did not heroically acknowledge to myself the cause which my conscience suggested. A week ago last Friday morning I was sent for to attend a meeting which was holding in J.H.N.'s room. The subject was the non-necessity of pregnant women having husbands to take special care of them, and Edward's and my case was especially treated of. My pride took offense at the manner of this criticism. I thought to myself that I had lately held myself ready for less communication with Edward, and would gladly have changed my course on receiving a hint from J.H.N. in private. All my old life assumed a porcupiny attitude. Mother implored and entreated, but I grew harder and harder, I wanted to yield, and yet something wouldn't let me. I thought I knew how king Pharaoh felt. I continued in this condition until Sunday morning, when I became alarmed concerning my salvation, and the fate of my unborn child. I accordingly wrote a note to J.H.N. beseeching him to help me, carried it to him myself, and made a complete surrender. He was divinely charitable to me. "God knows" he said, "that I rather suffer myself than see you suffer so." I told him that I had been full of evil-thinking toward him, and yet it seemed as though I couldn't help it. He said he knew I couldn't help it, and he forgave me for it. Edward came to my room the evening before, and though we made no frank confession of our feelings, it was evident that we were in the same state. Soon after my surrender I saw him again, and told him what I had done, and what a change had come over my spirit. This immediately affected him; but he had written Mr. Noyes a letter in the morning which he wished to give to him. After reading it I asked him to modify some parts of it, and told him that he would best express my heart by being soft and docile in his attitude. In the afternoon J.H.N. told me that he had received this letter from Edward, and did not like it—thought it was written in a hard, unyielding spirit. I went up to E.'s room in the evening, and told him what J.H.N. said. He was feeling bad about it himself, and had been ever since dinner, and wished he had not given it to him. Then I told him I thought he had been more affected by his Newark visit than he supposed. He admitted it, and said he wished he had followed an instinct he had a while ago to go to J.H.N. and tell him all about it. He promised he would in the morning.—After talking with J.H.N. the next morning (Monday) E. came to my room, and threw himself on the bed in a passion of weeping, and said it was he who had caused me all the trouble I had had, and so on. We had been talking for an hour, and he was just about to leave feeling some better. We were standing face to face, and the baby had just kicked him twice, when the door opened and J.H.N. came in with my mother. J.H.N. was very much in earnest, and after making some remarks showing how serious would have been the consequences of that Newark visit, he told Edward that he must not come to my room or see me any more, until that was thoroughly repented of. "All right," said E., looking as white as a sheet. In the afternoon J.H.N. and I had a very animated, magnetic talk—"fiery" he called it. "How do you know but I shall have a baby by you myself?" said he. I told him I should like that. He said he believed it to be his duty, and he had considerable curiosity to see what kind of a child we should produce. He said to combine with me would be intensifying the Noyes blood more than anything else he could do. He was just waking up to a full sense of his duty, which is to pursue stirpiculture in the consanguineous line. God willing, he intends to have a child by Helen, Constance, and me. Ended by lying down. Tuesday Edward wrote a good sharp letter to Julia Inslee.[22] J.H.N. told me in the evening that I had better write to her, too, without letting Edward see it. He told me to send a regular bombshell among those relatives who were trying to get Edward away. I began that night, and finished in the morning. J.H.N. liked what I wrote, and I sent it in the afternoon. Found afterward that my letter went before Edward's did. Thursday afternoon I went into the Hall to practise a little, and had not been there more than five minutes when in came Frank, and seated himself on the stage. I asked him what was going on. "Why, George E. had appointed a meeting of the Quintette; hadn't I been notified." I knew nothing of it, and asked if he were sure all were coming, for I thought if E. was coming he must have consulted J.H.N. "Oh, yes," he said; so I waited to see how things would turn out. Theodore came. We heard a noise over head and Theodore and F. shouted to Edward to come down. Silence. Finally he came into the ante-room, where we could not see him, nor he us, and called to Geo. E. to come there a moment. Geo. E. went. Said Frank: "Is there burnt woolen in the air?" and he and Theodore put on mock solemn faces. Soon G. returned, saying: "He says he is not at liberty to associate with the pianist at present." "How natural that sounds!" said F. "I have been in that situation toward this very pianist for the greater part of my natural life." Of course we all laughed. G. said he was going to see J.H.N., and soon returned saying that he thought we might as well postpone for the present. We dispersed. I went into J.H.N.'s room, and he said he thought it would be rather embarrassing to us to meet in that way just now. After that my heart began

to ache terribly, and I felt sure E. must be suffering, so I asked mother to go and see him in the evening. She found him in great distress of mind; said he never had suffered so much in his life as since the affair of the music in the afternoon. Friday noon I met J.H.N. in the hall just as he was on the way to my room, and I on the way to his. We turned and went into his room. He said he had just had a hard battle with Edward; that he came in bringing a letter written in a demanding spirit; thought he had done what J.H.N. required of him about his relatives, and now he did not see why he could not return to communication with me. J.H.N. told him he <u>never</u> should have me in that spirit, and showed him that it was special love in us that he was contending against more than anything else. He said E. was ashamed of his letter, and took it with him when he went. Then we had another magnetic talk. He asked when this baby was due, and then how soon I would be ready at the earliest to try with him. I told him in a year anyway from the time this one was born. He wanted to know if I could in a year from now, and we decided we could. He said he did not know but he should have more than one child by me. Edward sent in a good, loyal, docile letter in the evening. This pleased J.H.N. very much, and he seemed ready to give us some liberty right away, but I suspect I upset it. He said that he must manage some way so that I should not be drawn away from him again. I said I desired that very much, and had thought of asking him to help me thro' my confinement. "Oh, I certainly will," he answered, "I intend to." Then he said, suppose I have an hour of reception every day, and one day receive E., the next Homer, and the next Frank. "Can't I sleep with Edward any?" I asked. "No, I don't want to have you, unless you do with the others." Then he sat and thought for a moment, and finally said he had a plan, and that was to have Frank step in for a while as my husband—do anything I wanted, and sleep with me, and so on. I was quite taken aback by this, and told him I hoped he wouldn't urge F. any, for he and I had got so over our old feelings that he might not like the proposal. But he sent for him, and I went around to my room. Soon they came in together, and Mr. N. introduced F. to me. We shook hands. J.H.N. said: "I want to dedicate this room, Tirzah, and the baby, to Community love, and I am going to fight fire with fire." So he left us. The situation was an intensely embarrassing one. It was nearly seven, and we managed to keep up conversation till meeting-time. F. said J.H.N. told him that we might practice our music together. After meeting J.H.N. told me that my question about E. struck him rather unpleasantly. My heart was almost bursting before that from various emotions, and I went crying to bed in great heaviness and sorrow of spirit. Saturday morning F. came in, and we had an explanation about the embarrassment the night before. He told me to consider his case after all these years of waiting to present himself to me in a half-paralytic condition. Well, I told him, here was I 6 1/2 months along; and how much better was that? We had a good talk and laugh (only I was rather hysterical, and cried too), and felt better. My heart ached still, and I went to J.H.N.'s room about noon. He said that he had been thinking that my character about love needed improvement; I had become a man-killer, just as Theodore had an oracle, and it was bad for me. He thought I liked to be worshipped. I told him that was true of my natural character. "Well," he said, "I will make a league with you. I will make myself one with you. I will take all your sins on me, as though they were mine. I will have the same charity for them that I would if they were mine; at the same time I will be as sincere with them as though they were mine, and get rid of them the best way I can. I will make a better woman of you, and bring you nearer to God. I do not quarrel with your power, but I want you to have a conversion in that part of your life, so that you will use it for God, and then you will have a chance to exert it more than ever." He said he had formed an alliance with me, and did not know but he should have more than one child by me; at any rate I had better make up my mind to have as many children as I can, and emerge from it into being a mother of the Community. My heart felt soft and broken, and I wept continually, I hardly knew why. His kindness overwhelmed me. I told him that I felt very sorrowful the night before, but that I said to myself I would hold myself at his disposal. He said it was good to have our hearts soft sometimes so that we felt like crying, but he did not believe I would need to feel so much of the time, if I kept near him, and he would cry with me. Sunday Edward sent a beautiful letter to J.H.N. I had writing to do all day, and got very tired. J.H.N. was very kind, and said he would not have me do such a day's work again. He said he wanted to have Edward and Homer know of the arrangement about F., because he meant to plague them by it, if they could be plagued. I had just seated myself in meeting when he came to me and said: "If you are tired, you need not feel obliged to attend meeting," and so sent me to bed.

Monday, [Jan.] 26.

Told Ellen Nash today of the arrangement about Frank, and asked her to tell Edward. She did so, and he wrote a very brotherly note to Frank. When I went into J.H.N.'s room this noon he showed me a note he had had this morning from Harriet Worden, telling of good experience she had last night sleeping with Edward. It went through my heart like a knife, and it was two hours before I could breathe naturally, there was such pain at the center of my life. Yet I told no one and she and all supposed that I felt perfectly well about it. <u>I did, really.</u> It did not seem as though I was jealous, because I had no bad feelings toward her, but had a pleasant talk with her about it. It was like death. Terrible! What does it mean? I think I am the one that is being pinched, after all. He seems to have no particular trouble now. I am glad he doesn't. I presume my condition makes me weaker. But besides that, this arrangement about Frank has been one of intense embarrassment, so that my heart has ached ever since that began. It did not before.

Tuesday, [Jan.] 27.

Went to bed in great distress of mind last night, and with a suffocating ache at my heart. The baby was uncomfortable, and my trouble seemed greater than I could bear. Yet I knew that God was dealing with me, and I dared not rebel. I tossed about till after 12 o'clock. I longed for some superior strength to comfort, but dared go to no one. I slept but very little, awaking every half hour to a consciousness of the pain at my heart. I felt so sorrowful in the morning that after crying an hour in my room I went and talked with H.H.S. I told her how I felt about F., and also that Mr. Herrick had been very kind to me, and I should like to be free to talk with him. She seemed to appreciate the situation, and said she would talk with J.H.N. about it. I finally concluded to write to him and state my case with frankness, and then take criticism from him, if that was what I needed. I did so, and carried the note to him. As soon as he had read it he said: "That's right! I like that. That's all right, and I will go this minute and speak to Frank and Mr. H." Off he started, and then came back and said: "But wouldn't you like to have Frank free to come to your room when he wants to, and wouldn't you like to keep up your practice of music?" "Oh, yes, I should very much." The pain at my heart disappeared immediately. Not a trace of it remained. In the afternoon J.H.N. told me he was glad I had wisdom to make the choice I did; it suited him better than the other arrangement. He said Mr. H. was very willing to accept the position, and asked if he had any word for him. He told me that he might sleep with me every night, if I wanted him to, and that if he got into special love, he would get him out. In the evening I went into the library, and had a very pleasant affectionate chat with F. There was quite a gush of good feeling. He said he looked upon the freedom Mr. N. had given us as providential, because it would be safer for him to begin socially with someone like me. Well, I told him that what I had done today would make no difference about that. I went up and told J.H.N. all about it, and he was very much pleased, and said that it would make no difference, and that I might go along as I was a mind to with him now. "You see there are some bright spots," he said, and then told me an exquisite little romance he has had lately with Lillian Towner. I then went to my room with Georgy, and soon Mr. H. came in. We met affectionately, and chatted very pleasantly for an hour. He said he was very glad to accept the position offered him; it was the most attractive industry that had been given him in a long time. Just before leaving he said: "I wonder if Mr. Noyes said the same thing to you that he did to me?" "Yes, I guess he did!" I answered. He burst out laughing, jumped up as though he had been shot, and plunged out the door. "What did you do to Mr. Herrick, Mamma?" asked Georgy in amazement. After meeting mother had a long talk with Edward, showed him my note to J.H.N., and found that he was feeling rather badly, though he felt better before he went away.

Wednesday, [Jan.] 28.

Homer told mother this morning that he and Edward had a long talk last night before going to bed about me, and Homer is feeling so well now that he was able to comfort him a great deal. E. said that he thought this baby would be a rather expensive one, considering the suffering he and H. had both had over it, but H. told him he was getting so much good out of the experience that he should consider it cheap. He said he had been in a sweat for a year or so over his experience about me, but it had done him a great deal of good, and he believed it would Edward. He had had a great deal of peace himself for the last two months. E. came over from the shop in the forenoon to talk with mother. Consulted her about a note he had written to J.H.N. asking for liberty to speak to me. She advised him not to send it.

Thursday, [Jan.] 29.

Mr. H. asked me to sleep with him last night. I, of course, felt some reluctance about having him take his first impression of me in this situation, and said so; but he seemed to think that would make no difference. I did not feel magnetic, but I went for an hour and a half, and we got along pretty well. The latter part of the time he kept bursting out laughing every few moments, and I finally asked what made him laugh at me. He said the idea of my apologizing for myself struck him so absurdly that he couldn't help it. "Here you are making a fellow half crazy, and then apologizing for not being good company. Ha! Ha!"

When I spoke to Mr. Noyes about it this morning, he got the impression that I was complaining of Mr. H. I did not mean to do that, and I was at first puzzled by his taking me so; but I had to make up my mind that there was something wrong in my spirit that should draw his fire so, for he criticized me considerably. I was dreadfully tempted to feel discouraged, but toward the last of the talk these words repeated themselves over and over in my mind: "It is hard for thee to kick against the pricks."[23] I understood it then. I never shall be worth anything in a stable way to Mr. Noyes, until I am thoroughly cured of all desire for the special worship of men. I went to my room, and asked God without any reservation to purify my heart from that feeling, and never let me have any more of it. It may be sweet for a little while; but it is sure to make me miserable, and also those who love me. Take it away, O God, take it away. Give me true submission to thy will. It seems to be God's will to keep me in a humble, broken state, lest I become unduly lifted up. Let me sympathize with his ways.

Just after writing the above F. came into my room, and talked for an hour. It is some satisfaction to know that he had the same feelings toward me that I did toward him, during that long time that we loved each other so hopelessly. He said it was a constant stimulus to him, and he believed his mind was far better now that it would have been otherwise. Every new attainment he thought: "She will like this," and so urged himself forward to acquirements he would not otherwise have made. "The one thing in the world desirable." But notwithstanding this talk I did not forget my prayer. I do not want any more adoration. Told J.H.N. of the good experience I got out of his criticism, and he kissed me, and said we would call it a lover's quarrel.

Friday, [Jan.] 30.

Nice times now practising with Frank. I was just going to bed after meeting when J.H.N. came in and kissed me and said good-night.

Sunday, Feb. 1st.

An eventful day. At noon J.H.N. brought me a note he had just received from Edward, asking to see me a while. He showed me his answer, which was in substance that if he felt himself free from temptation to idolatry, he might take the responsibility of seeing me, but he should advise that the call be a short one, and that we did not talk of late experience. J.H.N. asked me what I thought of it. I hardly knew what to say. Of course I <u>wanted</u> to see him, but I didn't believe J.H.N. really thought it best. He finally left it with H.H.S. and me. I told her I would rather wait till J.H.N. invited us, and that I would rather not speak to him at all till after the baby is born than fail to do what J.H.N. wishes us to do. She wrote this to him. He wrote again to J.H.N. asking to be released from the promise not to look at me. J.H.N. answered that he would release him from that, and he also might speak to me, as he would to any other woman. The more J.H.N. thought about it, the more he felt as though Edward had a hard spirit, and was trying to make him acknowledge himself mistaken in his treatment of his case; so he wrote him another earnest letter, and came and told me I must defend myself now. I had an instinct to put myself in communication with Ellen Nash, as I knew Edward would quite likely be confidential with her. I showed her as clearly as I could how the case stood—how he seemed to be resisting J.H.N. in an independent spirit, and was relying on his own strength to keep him right, and that I was sure, unless there was a change in him, we should not be associated at all, even after the child is born. I told J.H.N. what I had done, and he said I might communicate with him through her, so she went back and forth between us until nearly 11 o'clock, and left him finally in a softer state, and desiring to have God do with him as he would.

Monday, [Feb.] 2.

J.H.N. showed me a good letter he had from Edward this morning, which pleased him very much. E. spoke in meeting, and said he had had a new ambition to be filled with the grace of God.

Tuesday, [Feb.] 3.

Very good visit with Frank last night. Communicated with Edward some through Ellen. He had a real conversion while at the shop in the forenoon, and was enabled to see what all this discipline is for. He also acknowledged that he has been dependent upon my society for happiness, and so on. He made a splendid confession in the evening. After meeting, as I was sitting by Constance in the Hall, he stopped by me a moment, and said: "I see it all now." This is the first word and look which has passed between us for more than two weeks. Now is the time for patience.

Wednesday, [Feb.] 4.

J.H.N. proposed to have us four pregnant women sit in the center of the Hall. I thank God for this change in Edward. He is very soft-hearted now. I pray for patience about seeing him.

Monday, [Feb.] 9.

The bars once let down between Edward and me we were tempted into several talks; but I felt distressed about it, and told him last evening that I did not think we were doing right, and it makes me unhappy; and that I rather he wouldn't say anything more to me until J.H.N. gave us leave. Quite early this forenoon I went into J.H.N.'s rooms, and the first thing he said was: "Well, does Edward let you alone?" So it all had to come to the light and be judged.

Thursday, [Feb.] 12.

I think I love E. better than he does me, after all. I had written to J.H.N. asking him to deal as mercifully as possible with E., and acknowledging that I believed him better than I, &c., when J.H.N. told me that E. that morning threw the blame on me, at Mrs. Ackley's suggestion. J.H.N. did not accept that, after hearing E.'s own testimony. I could not help feeling some bad about this; but it shows that there is a great deal of false love mixed in with our feelings toward each other, and this fact ought to help cure me.

Sunday, [Feb.] 22.

E. has had strange ups and downs of experience. J.H.N. gave him a number of criticisms, and about a week ago he seemed to submit himself to J.H.N.; but for three or four days he has looked very dark, and I knew last night by my own sensations and the baby's that he must be suffering. This forenoon J.H.N. brought me a letter E. had written him, asking for renewal of a certain amount of intimacy with me, &c. J.H.N. asked me what I wanted to do about it. I told him I did not wish for any change in my personal relations to him at present, but wished he would associate with others, and not make such a hermit of himself. J.H.N. put what I said into his answer, and advised him to offer himself for criticism. E. said he would do so, but wrote a reply which tried J.H.N. very much, and he had a committee get together immediately and criticise him. This seemed to produce a wonderful effect.

Thursday, [Feb.] 26.

A committee for Ann, which turned into a criticism of Homer of the most searching and earnest kind. J.H.N. said he was glad to see me thunder and lightning so.

Saturday, [Feb.] 28.

I have felt dreadfully accused and condemned ever since criticising Homer. I was amazed afterward at what I had done, for I had not thought of criticising him, and even wished when the committee began that he were there to criticise Ann. Yet I dare not take it back. No fickleness or pique prompted me to say what I did, for his personal treatment of me has been all that a woman could desire; but I do long to have him saved from this terrible principality of false love, which makes him deceitful and untrustworthy. Worn out and bruised in spirit J.H.N. went to Joppa tonight, leaving a Talk which saddened us all, and stirred us to earnestness. It is a fact that this second generation has thus far had its attention more on its social relations than on salvation. The Community will die if this continues.

March 1st.

I believe E. is established in the right way. He has remained of the same mind for a week.

Thursday, [March] 5.

Distressed to find a note in my room this morning from E. Did not read it, but asked M.L.P. to give it to him, and tell him I had not read it, and did not think he ought to write me without asking J.H.N.

Friday, [March] 13.

E. again in a quarrel with J.H.N. A committee to criticise him behind his back.

Saturday, [March] 14.

J.H.N. told me today that though yesterday had been one of the hardest days he ever knew, each encounter with E. resulted in bringing him nearer to me. He felt very near me, and that our hearts were knitting together. E.'s criticism read in meeting.

Monday, [March] 16.

Thank God! Thank God!! A letter of humble submission from E. to the family. J.H.N. said to me after meeting that the struggle had finally come to a good termination. He said he had been in travail of spirit about E. for the last two or three days, and it ought to effect something, and he believed it had. I have been tempted to feel sorry for E.; but during this last struggle I saw clearly that J.H.N. was the one who needed sympathy, and I did pity him most. E. has been possessed by a principality which has transformed him. For the first time in several weeks the baby let me go to sleep in tranquility very soon after retiring last night. There has been a mysterious connection between E.'s state and the way the baby has acted. When he has been quarreling with J.H.N. it has hurt me cruelly sometimes. It has not been any less lively today; but the movement has been pleasant.

Wednesday, [March] 18.

Yesterday afternoon I tramped through the drifts over to the clearing in the woods by the railroad with Aunt H.H.S., Theodore, Cornelia, Abby B., Helen, G.R.K., Martin, G.N.M., Carrie Bolles, and Frank. Frank very kindly escorted me. We had a nice "sugaring-off" with some hot liquid maple sugar which G.R.K. and Martin brought in a kettle and deposited on a bed of coals produced by a brush fire.[24] I enjoyed myself very much, and did not feel much fatigued; but I awoke a little before twelve, and was so troubled with anxiety that I arose, and sat up until nearly three. I have lain down nearly all day today.

Sunday, [March] 22.

Moved into the "lying-in" room.[25]

Wednesday, [March] 25.

O E! If you think I don't love you, how little you know me! You cannot have had a pang that has not struck an answering cord in my heart, and yet I know this discipline is right, and that we need to be separated.

Friday, [March] 27.

Have felt depressed for a week or more, and troubled with misgivings about the baby. Called for criticism. I know that I need to trust God more. Prayed all day that I might, and felt that my prayer was answered.

Mar. 29.

I feel no jealousy about M.W. [Mary Worden], but an unaccountable disgust came over me at the idea of his lying in her embrace, kissing her, and so on. I never had this feeling about anyone before. I am grieved, too, that he does not look higher. It is none of my business, I know, and perhaps my feelings are altogether wrong; but though I have nothing in the world against her, her life seems so coarse to me, that the idea of very close contact is repugnant. I never thought I could kiss her. Men probably think differently, though I remember that used to be J.H.N.'s opinion about her.

Mar. 28.

Auscultation with Theodore. 140 pulsations a minute. Probably a girl.

April 2.

Pictures taken.

April 3rd, Friday, 1 o'clock A.M.

I am almost inclined to think that I have begun to "be sick." For two hours the pains have come about once in five minutes. I had some pains yesterday, and the previous night, but as I had preliminary pains so long beforehand the other time, I thought I need not—(A pain!)—be alarmed; but these tonight are getting serious. If I am really in for it I shall consider it a strange providence and an answer to prayer. I have had the most intense heart-ache for the last few days, and have been overwhelmed with temptation. As my time grew nigh I longed for Edward. It seemed as though I could not stand it to enter into my confinement without some communication with him. Added to this I was tempted to think that my criticism of him, and the trying experience we have had (A pain!) might have so estranged him that he would lose all love for baby and me. I almost made up my mind to write to J.H.N., and tell him frankly how I felt; but the more I reflected and prayed about it, I saw that the best way was to leave the matter in God's hands, and be perfectly reconciled, whatever the result. (A pain!) If I am now sick I shall conclude that God thought it best that I should go through it without seeing him; for J.H.N. is at Joppa, and no one else has authority about the matter. It is all <u>right</u>, I know, and God is good to me.

Saturday, [April] 4.

Called mother at 2 o'clock yesterday morning, and she tho't I was "in for it." She staid with me till five, when the pains all went away, and have not returned. I slept well last night, and have felt well today.

Illustrations

Tirzah Miller
Courtesy of Oneida Community Mansion House

John Humphrey Noyes
Courtesy of Syracuse University Library

Theodore Noyes, George N. Miller, Frank Wayland Smith
Courtesy of Oneida Community Mansion House

Home Industry—The Chain Room
Courtesy of Syracuse University Library

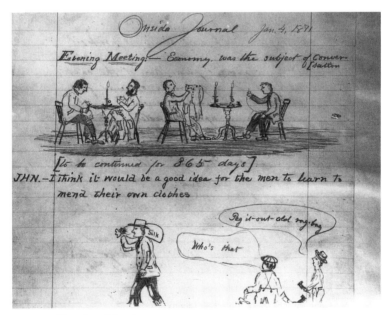

Evening Meeting
Courtesy of Syracuse University Library

Weighing the Babies
Courtesy of Syracuse University Library

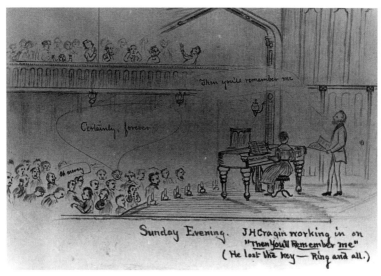

Sunday Evening
Courtesy of Syracuse University Library

Helen C. Miller
*Courtesy of Oneida Community
Mansion House*

Frank Wayland Smith
*Courtesy of Oneida
Community Mansion House*

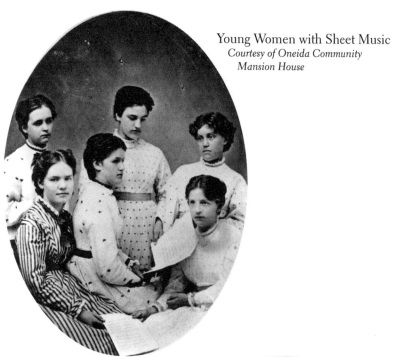

Young Women with Sheet Music
*Courtesy of Oneida Community
Mansion House*

Harriett Skinner
*Courtesy of Oneida
Community Mansion House*

Tirzah Miller, Lily Hobart, Helen Noyes
Courtesy of Oneida Community Mansion House

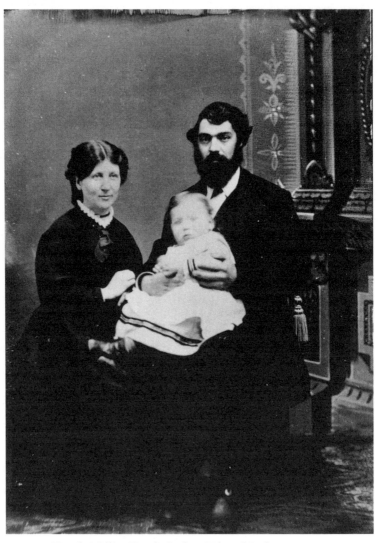

Tirzah Miller, Haydn Inslee, Edward Inslee
Courtesy of Oneida Community Mansion House

(facing page) Picnic Group
Courtesy of Oneida Community Mansion House

Harriet Worden
*Courtesy of Oneida Community
Mansion House*

George Allen
*Courtesy of Oneida Community
Mansion House*

Community Children at Gazebo
Courtesy of Syracuse University Library

James Herrick
*Courtesy of Oneida
Community Mansion House*

Ann Hobart
*Courtesy of Oneida Community
Mansion House*

Myron Kinsley
*Courtesy of Oneida Community
Mansion House*

Augusta Hamilton
*Courtesy of Oneida Community
Mansion House*

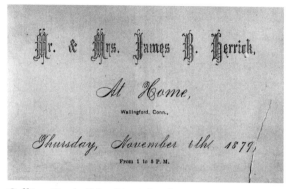

Calling Card of the Herricks after Marriage
Courtesy of Syracuse University Library

Tuesday, [April] 7.

I am now passing through the greatest trial of my faith I was ever called to endure. I wrote to J.H.N. Sunday telling him of my wish to communicate with Edward before the child is born. I had got over the heart-ache about it, and felt resigned to God. He answered he would not hesitate an instant on my account, but E. had behaved so that he should have to consider the matter. Yesterday he gave me "Mauprat," a novel by George Sand, saying that the hero reminded him of E., and he wished I would read the book before requiring him to give his final answer.[26] I sat up late last night to read, and finished the book this morning in time to go and see him before he took the 10 o'clock train for Joppa. He was surprised to have me read it so quickly, and seemed to feel quite reluctant to give his decision. He said he dreaded another encounter with E., and hoped he should not be called to endure one; he tho't if I were wise I should hesitate very much before putting myself in his power again. I told him it seemed to me that E. was very much changed, and that his will was broken. He replied that he did not come near him at all. He told me to take till Friday to digest the book, and then he would return and see me again. On his way to the train he caught me by the hand, and took me into a room alone, and told me not to worry about the matter, and not to let E. know that I was asking for him, as he thought that would be very disastrous. My God! It seemed as though my heart would break for a while. It is even worse than I feared. I had not supposed that J.H.N. intended to keep us separated all the way through; but I think he did. I can't but acknowledge that E.'s course is not calculated to make him think well of him. O Edward, if you loved me half as well as I do you (to say nothing of your duty to God and the Community) you would make some effort to win J.H.N.'s love and confidence. How can you at this serious moment dissipate your time with such a woman as Mary W., who is totally incapable of elevating you? I told J.H.N. that I would abide by his decision, and feel good about it, and I will, though the trials of this winter have caused me the acutest suffering I have ever known. Though E. tortures me so, I love him still perhaps far too much. I pray God to make my heart right about him.

A week ago Sunday E. spoke to Mr. Smith about taking my picture, and agreed upon a time with him. I told Mr. S. it was wrong for E. to do so, and set another time, so that there might be no understanding between us.

Wednesday, [April] 8.

Had an earnest talk with mother last evening about Edward, and entreated her to talk with him. She did so for an hour and a half after meeting, and succeeded in arousing him to quite a sense of the situation. He said he would make an effort to get near Mr. Noyes, and would testify every day on the right side, whether he was under temptation or not. He did speak well in meeting tonight. A good cry after meeting. I never wept so much in my life as I have during the last three months. Every day or two the tears will flow.

Thursday, [April] 9.

Begin to feel at rest again about not seeing Edward. I desire to have my will in subjection to God's will, anyway.

Saturday, [April] 11.

J.H.N. asked me if I still wished to see E. I told him I did, though I no longer felt any anxiety about it. We had a talk of more than an hour about the matter, which ended in his writing me the following letter:

> Dear Tirzah: — The hold I have upon your heart has been pretty well tested in the struggles of the past winter. On the whole you have been faithful to me; and I have confidence that you will be faithful. I feel free therefore to say to you, in view of your impending trial, that you may follow the instincts of your heart in regard to Edward, and invite him to as much intercourse as you think you can afford. Yours faithfully, J.H.N.

Felt very glad and thankful, but in no hurry to move. I long to have Edward secure J.H.N. against anxiety. Wrote to him after meeting to that effect.

Sunday, [April] 12.

Received a good letter from Edward at 11 o'clock last night, and another this morning. Took them to J.H.N., and he seemed quite well satisfied, but wanted to have me say something to him about not being with me when I am sick. Wrote to him in J.H.N.'s room. J.H.N. liked the letter, and told me to say at the end of it that he might write his answer or come and tell me. It was not long before he came to my door, and in an instant we were in each other's arms. But I cannot describe it. It was very sweet to meet him again.

[April] 17.

George Henry arrived from W.C. a few evenings since, and sent word that he wanted to see me. I had tried to dodge him, rather disliking to meet him in my present situation. His mother brought him to my room after meeting, and he staid an hour. He said he knew he couldn't get to sleep if he didn't see me before he went to bed. It is a marvel to me that he has loved me so much. (E. is carrying out his original program splendidly. We had as magnetic a time last night as ever.)

Monday, [April] 20.

(E. and I "just a minute" last night.) Awoke at 3 o'clock with an unmistakable pain. Continued without cessation, growing harder and harder. I kept about all the forenoon; was in J.H.N.'s room at 12 o'clock, N. seeing how hard my pains were advised me to go to my room, and said he would go and sit down there with me. The pains rapidly grew harder, and at 1/2 past 12 it was thought best for me to undress. Eliza kindly helped me. Swift work soon followed. At 1/2 past 1 Frank came in. In a few moments I called to Mrs. Sears that the water had broken. She thought at first that I was mistaken; but on examination sent hastily for Geo. E. Edward came in, and clasping me in his arms for a moment kissed me passionately, and then I sent him away. At 10 minutes past 2 the child appeared—a boy weighing just 8 lbs. in a nude condition— 8 - 11 1/2 oz. dressed.

Sept. 20.

My mother is perhaps dying. Dr. Carpenter said she could not live, but we cannot give up hope.[27] Friday (the 18th) J.H.N. seeking to do his duty by her, called us Miller children together, and talked earnestly with us against the family spirit, which he thought was more concentrated in me, because I have two children, and particularly because I am connected with Edward. He thought E. and I had better dissolve.

Sept. 29.

Mr. Noyes wrote to E. this morning that he thought best for him now to be weaned from the baby. He has taken him every evening.

My dear, good mother died at 6 o'clock this evening. She has suffered greatly, but has never made a complaint. She has shown wonderful faith, patience, and care for others. The last thing she said to me was day before yesterday when I had rubbed her all over: "You did it nicely, you did it nicely." The last time she saw Georgy she told him he must ask God to cure her. About half an hour before she died E. came to my room under considerable excitement, with white face and burning eyes, feeling very hard toward Mr. Noyes. We had quite a struggle, and he went away somewhat mollified. He said if I released him from responsibility about the child he should leave the Community, but I <u>said I never should.</u>

Oct. 5.

Mr. Noyes wanted to have me wean little Haydn. I consented, though it is one of the greatest sacrifices of my life. I have enjoyed nursing the sweet little fellow very much indeed. I commenced teaching him to drink a few days ago, and today did not nurse him from six in the morning till six in the evening.[28]

Oct. 6.

Went to Joppa with J.H.N., Mary P., Mr. Herrick, Miss Pomeroy, and Flora. Left the baby at home. In the evening had a talk with Homer, and found he had considerable criticism of me.

Oct. 7.

Went to Mr. Noyes in the morning, and told him about my talk with H., and suggested to him that I have a committee, and let Homer say all he had in his mind. He liked the idea, and H., Ann, Maria, S.B.C., met at 1 o'clock in Mr. N's room with him present. I am certainly under an everlasting debt of gratitude to Ann.

Oct. 8.

I was much disappointed in Homer's criticism of me. I thought that, once having been so intimate with me, and now professing to be entirely free from all special relations with anyone, he ought to be able to give a discriminating criticism of my social character; but what he said certainly seemed to me very much biased by personal feeling and resentment for my sincerity last winter. I made one reply during the committee, and then concluded to hold still. After thinking the matter over I concluded to go to Mr. Noyes, and frankly and dispassionately tell him my side of each story which H. told against me. He said immediately that he was very much disappointed in H's remarks, and he accepted what I said as more correct than H's statement.

Oct. 13.

Left for Joppa with J.H.N.'s party to stay three days. Nursed the baby for the last time this morning.

Oct. 16.

Returned, having had a very good time; but the instant I entered the house a terrible pain entered my heart.

Oct. 23.

Edward left for W.C. this evening. Came to see baby and me. (Sweetest.) God is good—better than I asked or thought.

Nov. 4.

Is Edward a scoundrel? He returned unexpectedly from W.C. Went back this evening.

Dec. 22.

What a fearful experience has been mine for the last three months! I feel now considerable peace of heart, and trust in God's purpose to make suffering work patience, hope, and all the excellent qualities of the spirit. During the time when I received the greatest emotional shocks I looked as though ten years had been put on my face.

After Edward went to W.C. on Oct. 23 he wrote me three letters which were very affectionate. I did not consider that we had had any liberty to correspond, and so did not answer. But when I decided to put Haydn into the Drawing-Room I thought it would be proper for me to write to him about it; and besides I wanted to tell him that it was not in accordance with Mr. Noyes's ideas for him to write me such love letters. So the 2nd of November I went and asked Mr. N. if I might write to E. about Haydn's going into the Drawing-Room [room where infants were cared for]. "Wouldn't it be as well," he asked, "for someone else to write?" He spoke very mildly; but I was perverse, and answered, "No, I don't see why I can't write." He expostulated with me for a few moments, and then I said I thought he dealt more severely with me than with others. We had quite an argument about it. "It seems to me," he said, "that you take the liberty to judge, and to think for yourself." "I know it; I told you I did, and I can't help it, though it makes me feel bad not to think as you do." We argued still further, and left it so. When I had nearly finished dinner Ann came to me and said: Mr. N. wanted to see me in his room. I went up. He said he should like to have Ann tell me something which she had divulged to him on his reporting to her my talk with him. She then related an incident which occurred between Frank [illegible words]. The night before E. went to W.C. he consulted F. about his legal rights and duties concerning me and the baby, and somehow

gave F. the impression that he felt quite stiff and resolute about the matter.[29] I have been unable, all along, to see E's character as Mr. N. did, or
to believe him dishonest; but as I knew that at the same time that he had
this talk with F. he professed great affection for and loyalty to Mr. Noyes
to me, I could not deny that the course he had taken was a disloyal one.
From a few remarks made by Mr. N. I began to suspect that he had not
expected E. would come and see me also that last afternoon when he
asked to see the baby, although Edward told me that he asked if he might
see me and the baby, and Mr. N. answered, "Certainly, I have not the
least objection." I therefore asked Ann to step out a moment. When she
had gone, I said: "Did Edward only ask you if he might see the <u>baby</u>,
or <u>me and the baby</u>?" N:—"He only asked to see the baby." Myself:—
"Do you mean it? Are you <u>sure</u>?" N:—"I am <u>perfectly sure</u>. There could
be no mistake about it." "Then," I said slowly, and with a strange horror at my heart, "he must have told me a falsehood," and I went on to tell
him of all that took place between us, knowing now that it was without
his sanction, and that the story would probably give a shock to the whole
Community. I, however, told Mr. N. that I considered myself more to
blame than E. for the sexual part of the transaction, for I had doubts
about Mr. N's having given us permission, while E. appeared like a man
who was perfectly sure he was doing right. I was surprised when E. asked
me, not having thought of such a thing, and expressed doubts three
times, but was reassured by him. It therefore seemed to me that I was
much the most to blame for that; but Mr. N. said it was not so—that a
man in making such a proposition to a woman incurred all the blame,
and it was no matter what took place after that. After some more talk I
became so much convicted of the injustice I had done Mr. N. that I
threw myself at his feet, and asked his forgiveness.—It gave me great
distress to think of E. as in any way untruthful, as I had never had any
reason to think so; but Mr. N. would not listen to the proposition that he
had not heard him, so there was nothing to do but to choose between
them; and really the insincerity of E's treatment of Mr. N. was the same
thing as falsehood in <u>spirit</u> if not in letter.

Two days after this (on Nov. 4) I had been up with the baby between
five and six, and had locked the door. Suddenly I heard someone try the
knob softly. As quick as a flash I thought, "It is Edward," though I had
reason to suppose him to be three hundred miles away. I did not open
immediately, but waited a few moments to still the beating of my heart,
for I thought he must have left the Community. There he stood smiling
and holding out his hand. With a great effort I controlled myself. I drew

away my hand, and told him that Mr. N. said he did not ask to see <u>me</u> that day. "<u>I certainly did, Tirzah</u>. <u>You know I cared a great deal more to see you than I did to see the baby</u>." The accent of truth was in his voice, and I shall never doubt that he <u>did</u> ask to see me, for Mr. N. is certainly very deaf; but then, E's course toward Mr. N. is utterly inconsistent with loyalty and Community honesty. I only said a few more words to him, and then went upstairs and waked Mr. N., and told him. E. returned to W.C. in the evening.

Dec. 28.

Another heart-wringing today. A telegram from E.H.N. to Mr. N. telling him to send Edward back to W.C. We do not know what it means, but it looks as though he had gone away from the Community. He promised me never to do anything of this kind without telling me, and I shall not believe that he has done so until facts prove it.

Tuesday, Dec. 29.

I felt every time I awoke in the night that I should see Edward here in the morning. My instinct proved true. I almost feared that he had come to settle up and go away, from his coming so in the face of Mr. N's wishes; but he did not. Frank and Theodore talked with him, and he said he had finished his work, and so came home, but acknowledged that he had not acted in the wisest way; said he had no intention whatever of leaving the O.C. Frank, Theodore, & and I had a talk about him with Mr. N. in his room, and he was an angel of mercy, and easily entreated. He was at first indignant and for taking severe measures; but we all advised a different policy, and he most generously put the case in our hands, and said that he would agree to any course we fixed upon, though he thought he ought to practically take back the move he made in coming here. So he was advised to return tonight to W.C. and remain until invited back, or until he had thoroughly finished the work there. Then Theodore said his plan would be to have him come here and go right into the orchestra in a subordinate position, and to treat him generally with all the confidence we safely could. I had the baby in Mr. N's room in the evening, and we had quite a chat about Edward, Mr. Noyes seeming very good-natured; said he began to see the providential uses of his behavior. One was to compel the second generation to come forward, and learn how to deal with a case among their own set; another, that he had been forced to expound principles which might not for a long time have been so thoroughly worked out among us. By and by I said, "I don't think Edward has seen a glimpse of the baby." "Why," he answered most sympathetically, "I would let him see him by all means. Get somebody to take him to him." This was most unexpected, and made me very grateful and happy. The baby was with his papa for an hour. E. left at eight o'clock. Theodore and Ann said that Edward at first expressed himself as somewhat exasperated at me. Said he considered the relation between us ended forever, and he should never speak to me again unless I took back some things I had said. They said he afterward took this back, however. I expected he would hate me; but I love him still as much as I ever did.

1875

Jan. 9, 1875.

My experience is far from being settled into the even flow characterized by those who have attained undisturbed peace. My mind is much exercised about the future of the Community. Ideas connected with that subject are the last of which I am conscious at night; they obtrude themselves immediately in the morning, and in the night I am thinking, continually thinking. A great revolution is taking place; there is no denying that, and a greater one, perhaps, than the first generation is yet aware of. When Mr. Noyes dies how are we to exist? The course Theodore has pursued for the last few years makes it utterly impossible for us to receive him as leader, unless he undergoes a vast change. It is unlikely that we shall ever allow anyone the absolute control which has been exerted by Mr. Noyes—certainly not unless his mantle falls on a successor who shall equal him in spiritual power. An aristocracy of the Noyes blood has grown up in the Community. The original four were certainly men and women who deserved to take the places of highest honor; there was no question of their superiority. But look at the second generation of Noyeses! Where is there one among them who has inherited anything like the original faith? Certainly Theodore, Joseph, Constance, and I have not. George Miller has perhaps a greater measure of the spirit which possessed the founders than any of us; but he has few of the qualities of a leader. All the world is pushing against the monopoly of the aristocracy. Now an aristocracy of blood in this Community is inconceivably more unjust and senseless than the aristocracy of the nobility. It is contrary to the genius of communism; it is practically antagonistic to many of our doctrines. One of our dominant ideas is that the natural should be subjected to the spiritual—that the Community has a right at any time to step in and set aside the natural when it interferes with the spiritual. We are taught to consider the children as belonging to all the Community with equal claims on our love. Why should not this doctrine be applied to the Noyes children? Is not Mr. Noyes <u>as</u> likely and even more likely to transmit his spirit to those who have adopted his faith than to those who are of his seed? The only kind of aristocracy possible among us is a spiritual aristocracy; the aristocracy of Christ, when he said: "they that do the will of my Father in heaven, the same are my brother, and mother, and sister." To that we may bow down; but anything short of that it is useless to talk of submitting to. Members of the Noyes family—as for instance, Constance—have been set up as examples, when it was only because of the power back of her that she held any place in our respect in that position. Her intellectual inferiority, her arrogance, and her inconsistent and imbalanced social and spiritual career are facts but too apparent. I am conscious that I myself have in the past held a position which I by no means merited.

On the other hand it should be remembered that when the members of one generation become greatly renewed, their children are in a great measure eclipsed and paralyzed by the brilliant reputation of their fathers. They may be persons of excellent parts themselves, who, were it not for the glory of their predecessors, would rise into positions of eminence. It is certainly true of myself that when I was younger the remarkable goodness of my parents and the transcending virtues of the Noyes stock were often held up to my view in such a light as to cause not only discouragement, on my part, but actual polarity.[30]

Jan. 13.

I have been disposed to place great confidence in Ann; but I feel compelled tonight to return to original instincts. A long talk with her. She seems sore to me in her attitude about her position like the prima donna who will not do things without a certain amount of begging. It may be that I do her injustice.

Jan. 26.

Edward is here again. J.H.N. wrote me that if I am likely to be unhappy here, he hopes I will feel free to go to W.C. Edward is still far from reconciled to J.H.N. I must keep clear of becoming in any way involved with him.

[Jan.] 27.

The great lesson I seem called on to learn now-adays is humility. I just found it out tonight. I think I have been in a hard, evil-thinking, envious state of late. Yes, it is humility that I need, perhaps more than anything else in the world. It has been a lack of humility which has led me into most of the errors of my life.

Feb. 9.

Here I am at W.C. Took a sudden resolution yesterday afternoon, and Ann, W.A.H., and I started at 8.15.

Feb. 24.

Returned to O.C.

Apr. 7, 187[5].

N.: "Don't let him know that you are calling for it, or he will set up such a tremendous growl as never was heard."

April 14.

"Love's Embrace." Most exquisite.[31]

Newport, Rhode Island, Aug. 5.

Yesterday afternoon [apparently at Wallingford] I received a letter from Edward saying that he <u>must see</u> me to talk over our affairs, and that he should consequently make his appearance in my room to-morrow night at eleven o'clock. I showed the letter immediately to Ann and Theodore, and they carried the matter to Mr. Noyes. He instantaneously planned that I should choose any man I liked, and take my departure for regions unknown. He said at first that I might have Homer; but it was finally concluded that that would perhaps not be best, and so among others suggested I choose Charlie Cragin. The evening was spent in hasty preparation. Mr. Noyes told us not to let any one know where we were going, and told James Hatch not to even let folks know the station from which we started. Mr. Noyes concluded also to leave for O.C. himself this morning with Mr. Herrick. Charlie and I arose at 1/2 past five, and James drove us to the Yalesville station by a circuitous route. We went from there to New Haven, where we remained until 4 o'clock, when we took the train for Newport, R.I. (Here follows an account of the trip to Providence, Boston, Springfield, Northampton, Brattleboro, and Putney.)[32]

Putney, Aug. 10.

Only a month today since I left O.C. What a checquered life mine has been since! It is so dull in this village—my native village—that I cannot support the idea of staying over night, so we are going back to Brattleboro at 9 o'clock. We reached here at about 12 noon, and now it is 6; but the time seems longer than all the rest together almost. Got a letter at 7 o'clock. Oh! Joy! Mr. Noyes wants us to come to O.C., and thank God! Edward has consented to try living with Theodore at W.C. for a while. Charlie found a telegram also for "Cragin" (his name is "Adams" you know) from Mr. Noyes, telling him to bring me on to O.C., and "All is well." It came here this morning, but we could not have gone but a few hours sooner if we had found it then.

Aug. 12.

Reached Oneida at 1/2 past 1 this morning. I am put to room opposite Mr. N's room. Mr. N. is very kind to me; called me in to sit down with him this forenoon, and then told me this afternoon: "I had a real attraction for you this forenoon. I did not feel it at all while at W.C., and it is a sure sign to me that you have changed." I am to help him on the "Socialist," he says, and not go back to my old place here at all.[33]

Aug. 22.

Wrote to Mr. N., asking how I could get into more fellowship with him, and telling him that I wanted to open my life to him as to a surgeon's knife.

Aug. 23.

Mr. N. came into my room this morning before I had got up, and said he had something to propose which would cut, but he thought it necessary, and that was to break myself off from all communication with Haydn—have nothing whatever to do with him. He said he was "a pretty baby, a very pretty baby," but that he was a link between me and Edward. I told him I should obey him heartily, and I have had good experience today in doing it. It seemed to be the thing I needed to keep my heart free from distractions, so that my faith should be bright continually.

Aug. 24.

Mr. Noyes asked me to get up a ride for him. So this afternoon Mr. Herrick, Carrie Bolles, and I went with him to the top of the east hill. We took our dinner, and had a charming time. Mr. Noyes expressed a great deal of enjoyment. I lent Mr. H. my handkerchief. When we came away he left it on the top of the hill. He discovered that he had done so after we had ridden a short distance, and Mr. N. had him drive back to find it. I was very glad to get it again, because it was mother's.

Aug. 25.

Mr. Noyes came into my room, and said he had a suggestion to make, which I need not entertain for a moment if it did not suit me, and that was to change Haydn's name. He said the name "Haydn" was a symbol to him of Edward's idolatry toward music, and had always been distasteful to him on that account. He said: "I think he is a fine child— a very fine child—and will make a fine man; and I know from what you have said that you do not wish him to follow his father." I told him I liked the idea, and would carry it out. Just before this I went to him and told him I wished Mrs. Ackley might be forbidden to grandmother Haydn any longer. He seized on the idea immediately, and executed it instantly.

All the time Mr. Noyes was talking about Haydn's name the name "Paul" kept going through my mind, not because I had ever thought before I should like it, nor even now. After that I talked with George Miller about it, and he thought "Hayes" or "Russell" would be better.

Aug. 26.

I made out a list of names beginning with "Hayes" and putting "Paul" at about the middle, and handed it to Mr. Noyes. I called his attention to "Hayes" and "Russell," but said nothing about "Paul." After studying over the list a few minutes he said he liked "Paul" the best; so he wrote a letter to the family about it, and now my dear little boy is no longer "Haydn" but "Paul." I thought there were excellent spiritual reasons why this change should be made. It will be a great help in separating both him and me from the associations of spirit connected with his father. Then the boy will probably grow up to a very different man with the name of the great apostle from what he would with that of the composer Haydn.[34]

Aug. 27.

Constance's criticism. Mr. Noyes made an overwhelming defense of me. What a friend he is! How strange that I could desert him a moment for such a man as Edward! He said of me this afternoon to Emily Otis: "Every one of you young folks ought to help her, rather than pull her down with accusations. Ever since she has been with me I know she has been absolutely honest. She has not swerved for a moment."

Aug. 30.

Mr. Noyes was somewhat anxious yesterday morning lest Edward should make another raid, and undertake to get the little boy. He told Mr. Towner to keep watch of him.

It seems to me we have plenty of evidence that those who, after hearing Mr. Noyes's sayings, <u>do</u> them, are like the wise man who built on a rock; while those who do them not are building on a sandy foundation which washes away every time a storm comes. "Strait is the gate and narrow is the way which leadeth unto life, and few there be that find it."[35] How small every act of self-denial in this world ought to seem, while we are striving to enter in that narrow gate which <u>few</u> find!

Sept. 1.

Rather an agitated night. Mr. N. asked me after meeting to hunt up a remark Edward had made, and then showed me a paragraph in a letter he received from him last evening, in which he still insists that I am just as responsible for his visit there as he was. The more I thought about it after going to bed, the more I felt as though the time had come for me to deny that, I have taken care not to do so before, because he has been so positive that I did not know as I remembered all that I might have said. I remember perfectly what he refers to in his letter asking me to meet him, where he says that I asked him why he did not "<u>insist</u> on speaking" to me on certain occasions mentioned. We were talking of things which happened two years ago, when he felt himself to be un- justly accused by Ann and Frank, and came to speak to me about it, but I refused to say anything to him. Talking this over I said that under sim- ilar circumstances he should <u>insist</u> on seeing me, for I would certainly hear him another time. But it seems to me that this agreement did not at all cover the meeting which he finally proposed, and says I promised him. If it did, our understanding of it was very different.

We received a telegram during the day to meet one from W.C. Of course I anticipated something about E. Ann arrived in the evening, and brought the dreadful, <u>dreadful</u> news that Edward left the Community last night, and he desired her to get papers of release of me concerning the support of the child and all obligation to myself. Mr. Towner left for N.Y. on the next train for that purpose. Mr. Noyes dictated, and I wrote: "Edward Inslee: I will sign any papers which Mr. Towner will make releasing you from all obligations to myself and the child." I thought this would kill me, and I almost drew back; then I did it as I would put my head on the executioner's block, or as Queen Elizabeth signed the death-warrant of her favorite Leicester.

Sept. 4.

Ann left during the day, and during meeting I gave way for the first time to the heart-rending anguish which has been all I could bear up under for several days. I did not think that the legal document would be read in meeting, or I would not have gone in. I could bear no more, and got out as quickly as I could, and sent for Mr. Herrick. I had an uncontrollable fit of screaming.

Sept. 7.

Mr. Noyes came to me this morning and said that he thought during the night that the reason I found it difficult to be cheerful was the fact that there is so much marriage spirit in this family, and if I could not stand it I must go back to Wallingford. I told him that everything reminded me here of Edward, and that I dreamed I asked him last night to take me back to W. Then I went up [to the garret] to make beds. I had been there but a few moments when Mr. Herrick came up and said that Mr. Noyes was looking all around the dining-room after me. So I ran down and said: "Did you wish to see me?" He turned and answered: "I will go with you just as soon as you want to go." "Thank you!" I answered, my heart giving the first bound of joy for many a day. Then I went to his room after breakfast and said: "Will you go tomorrow morning?" "Yes, just as soon as you say." Then he asked Mr. Herrick to go too, and it was all arranged in a few minutes. Talked with Ella in the evening, and Mr. Noyes had me have an affair with G.K. and A.H.B.[36]

Sept. 8.

Arrived at W.C. at 11 o'clock, taking folks by surprise.

Sept. 13.

Thirty-three today. I pray God to help me to become a true soldier, and to do as Christ did when he said: "They that do the will of my Father in heaven, the same are my mother and brother and sister." Found this morning that Aunt Harriet had been writing to Mr. N. some impressions she and Ann had had about me, about Homer, and so on. Talked with Ann, and felt much better after it. Convinced her, I think, that I rather not say a word to Homer than to cause her the least anxiety. Good God! How can a woman in the situation I am in give her heart much to any man!

Sept. 14.

How <u>could</u> he leave me and our beloved boy, who calls for him every day? But if he ever gets as desperate as I was to save his soul, he will forgive me for what I did. I was only looking ahead beyond the now to our eternal happiness; but if he cannot see it, the sooner my heart is weaned, the better.

Sept. 15.

Cozicot. — [37] Mr. N., H.H.S., Ann, Theodore, W.A.H., Abram, G. Easton, Marion, Irene, and I came down here this afternoon. Mr. Noyes's purpose is to have a contest with William.

Sept. 18.

Mr. Noyes did not have his talk with William this morning.

Oct. 10.

Aunt Harriet leaves for O.C. in the morning.[38] She told me this evening that my being here had been a help to her, and that she was thankful I felt so <u>strong</u>. Knowing how very, <u>very</u> weak I feel, this was a great surprise to me, and seemed almost like mockery. But I believe I am learning somewhat of the truth of Paul's saying: "When I am weak, then am I strong."[39] I am so weak and tempted that I have to pray to God almost continually to give me moral strength to be faithful. I should not dare tell the temptations which harass me.

Homer and I kissed each other a week ago Saturday. "Mine will last a hundred and fifty thousand years, if you want to know."

Oct. 26.

Mr. Noyes, W.A.H. and I moved into the new house today.

I have been through some agonizing temptations during the last three weeks, but have felt more at rest for two or three days. I think I have inherited the Hayes hypo in full force.[40] It has been difficult for me to believe that there is anything in me which is likely to be of use to the Community, and it has seemed a great waste of labor for Mr. Noyes to exert himself so much to save me.

Oct. 30.

If Edward and I meet in the Great Hereafter, he will know that I loved him, and that I only left him because my conscience would not let me choose the world and have any peace.

Nov. 3.

Went into Mr. Noyes's room this noon, and he handed me a letter he had been writing Aunt Harriet, which he said he wished me to read. I learned from it that Mr. Towner had said to him that he thought Paul needed a father, and Mr. N. suggested that he act in that capacity, to which Mr. T. acceded; and Aunt Harriet was asked to see that all necessary arrangements were made. I was not even alluded to, and I did not see as there was a chance for me to say anything, as it seemed to be all decided without any reference to me. I felt pretty bad about it, and perhaps a little inclined to be resentful that I should be thus ignored, after all the suffering I have been put through, and am now in, about that child. I concluded my best way was to write to Mr. N. just how I felt. I had of course thought more than anyone else about the necessity of having someone act as father to him sometime, but the idea of replacing his own father with someone else is still so painful that I had hoped to postpone it longer. I told him I thought that between me and whoever took that position there should be mutual respect, esteem, and freedom of speech, but that though I highly respected Mr. Towner, the relations between us had been very formal.—At first Mr. Noyes was quite stirred up that I should say he had not consulted me. He said that was his very purpose in showing me the letter, and that I should have said what I thought right on the spot, and not waited an hour or two. "You are too quick," he said; "I had no idea of acting arbitrarily without reference to you." Well, I saw that I might have taken his showing the letter to me as an act of consultation, (though I did not so take it at the time) and acknowledged that I had been through stupidity unjust to him, so we made it up. Then I said: "I guess I will send the letter now." (I had taken it from the envelope.) "No," he said, "I guess not." "But what will you say to Mr. Towner?" I asked. "I shall tell him to consult you." Mr. Towner came to me awhile afterward to consult me, as though I had heard nothing about it. He quite won my heart with his sympathetic interest in the dear boy. He says he feels it a good deal, having both his parents taken away so suddenly, and asks after his father and me quite frequently. It was so touching to think of, that I wept all the while we were talking, and could not help it to save my life. He said he would do by him as by a child of his own, and already loved him. I told Mr. Noyes of our talk, which pleased him, and then I asked if he had any objection to his writing to me about Paul, and he said he had none whatever. Then he began laughing to himself, and said: "I can't help laughing to think how you and I both fired up. I was as mad as I could be for a few minutes. It never occurred to me that you could have any objection to the arrangement, and I had no idea that you would flare up; but, as I see it now, I think you had some reason." Wasn't that clever? I thought I had reason, but I had no hope that he would see it as I did. I was glad the affair happened, because I see that he means to treat me as a woman, not a child, and wishes me to say what I think of any such move on the spot. I minded this little oversight much more from the fact that in all his dealings with me during the last few months he has heretofore treated me with great consideration.—He finally sent the letter, adding the following P.S.: "Tirzah has been consulted, and thereby hangs a tale."

Nov. 8.

Had a nice long chat with J.H.N. this afternoon. I went in to show him that a letter which I had received from brother G. indicated that he and Aunt Harriet had been quite misled by the P.S. referred to above. G. wrote that they had some "surmises" about me, &c. I told Mr. N. that I could guess what they thought, and that was that I was going to try for a baby with Mr. Towner. We had quite a time laughing and talking about it, and about the plans he and I once had of consanguineous stirpiculture, he saying that he is so nearly in hades now, that it would be like posthumous work for him to make any more attempts.[41] By-and-by I said: "Theodore said awhile ago that I must make up my mind to have three more children. What do you think of that?" "Well, I guess Theodore is right about it," and he asked why T. didn't take hold himself. I said I didn't know as T. believed in consanguineous stirpiculture for himself. Then he asked me to "lock the door." When we got up he said: "There! I didn't!" Then he added significantly: "I suppose Theodore would think Homer Barron a better one to mate with you, wouldn't he?" I was very much surprised, and answered: "I don't know; but he has behaved real well, hasn't he?" "Yes," he answered heartily, "he has behaved first-rate." This and one other thing he said made me feel very happy. He said he had been wanting to say to me that when he is silent and solemn, I mustn't think he had anything against me; but his throat felt so badly that he had to shut himself off from folks in order to feel comfortable. "I often wish," he said, "that I could have a nice sociable time with you; but I can't."

Nov. 9.

Mr. Hamilton has been here nearly a week. I have enjoyed his visit much. There seems to be a perfect reconciliation between us.

W.A.H. and I started with the double carriage for Cozicot this morning, so that the party there could return, while we take our chances walking back tomorrow. Homer is here, and I had some difficulty in keeping from telling him what Mr. N. said, also what Ann said when I reported it to her. She seemed very much pleased, and said she wanted the privilege of telling him, if it should come off. — Just a year today since Edward and I walked to Joppa.

Nov. 10.

Reached home a little after 7. Ann reports that she has talked over the matter of my having a child now, with Theodore; but she could not get him to express any opinion whatever about the combination of Homer and myself. He says he must go over all the men in the Community, and select the best scientific combination. He thinks, she says, that I am one of the strongest women in the Community, and can therefore afford to combine with someone who it is desirable to have propagate, who is not so strong. When I was talking with Mr. Noyes about the matter the other day, he asked if I had any desire to have more children. I told him that my past experience had not been such as to make me very enthusiastic about having more; but that there was one reason why I should like to have one more, and that is the condition of my head and eyes. Since this last great strain on me of giving up Edward, I have had almost constant pain in the nerve of my eyes. A fit of crying almost incapacitates me for anything. I have thought that the rest of my head, and the recuperative effects of pregnancy, might make me more useful to the Community, if my sphere is to continue to be head-work. Dr. Bacon examined my eyes about two weeks ago, and said they were not diseased, and that the vision was clear, but that they showed great over-use, and that I had been subjected to great nervous strains, and that I ought not to use them for some time.

Nov. 19.

F.W.S. has been here for a few days. He leaves tomorrow.

When I carried J.H.N. his pitcher of ice-water this evening, he said very affectionately: "Why, poor dear, what a deal of pains you take for me, don't you? Well, I am very much obliged to you." And he kissed me.

There has been a little outbreak between Theodore and William lately. Mr. Noyes is doing his best to harmonize them.

Nov. 25.

Theodore, who has been at work for some time on a scientific combination for me, gave a list of eight men to Ann today, which she handed to me this evening. The list was written in the order of preference. It was as follows: G.D. Allen, J.B. Herrick, J.H. Barron, F.W. Smith, H.G. Allen, W.A. Hinds, Alfred Barron, F.A. Marks. Ann wished very much it might be Homer, and Theodore said he considered him about as scientific as the two whose names he put first; but he thought we were not quite so sharply contrasted temperamentally. Of course I showed the list to Mr. Noyes. He first thought W.A.H. a good one; but I said I could not do that for several reasons, and particularly because he is in some trouble with the Community. Then he said I might do just as Theodore and I decided. But after a while he went up-stairs and talked with Theodore about it. I was in Ann's room with her, and Homer was in his room opposite. Of course Theodore had to talk very loud, so that we couldn't help hearing, and were all the time in distress of what H. might hear, as we had told him nothing about it. Then he told me afterward that he didn't want to have sentiment get control of the matter at all. "I may choose the same one that you would; but I sha'n't do it for the same reason that you would, or Ann would." So we concluded to let the matter drop for a few days.

Nov. 26.

Homer came to me, and asked me what I was going to do. "Read with Mother Noyes," I answered. "No, I don't mean that," he replied significantly. "What have you heard? What do you know?" I asked quickly. So we went into the reception room, and I told him all about it. "Oh!" he said: "I would accept <u>any</u> conditions. I would stay two years in Africa." &c. But I discouraged him in regard to it.

Nov. 30.

First entertainment. Assisted. J.H.N. and W.A.H. in more trouble.[42]

Dec. 1.

Told Ann I had made up my mind that I would be thoroughly scientific about the matter of having a child, and would take G.D.A. if Theodore said so. Told her I hardly thought Homer and I were ready yet. At any rate, I should not want to proceed on a reluctant consent from Mr. Noyes.

Dec. 2.

Told Mr. Noyes this evening that I had made up my mind to be thoroughly scientific. He smiled, and said he was glad to hear that. I said

I supposed it would be George Allen, as Theodore considered him the most scientific. "Does he, now?" he asked. "I don't know; but he did then, you know." "Yes, but does he now?" "Do you think Mr. Herrick more scientific?" "No," he answered, "I don't; and I don't care a snap which one you have, only I want to have it come entirely from Theodore, and not from your choice or Ann's." I told him that I did not feel my heart was set at all on having a child by anyone in particular, and I was ready to do as Theodore said. "That's it; leave it all with Theodore, and it will all go right." How queer he is! It would almost seem that he wants me to have Homer, after all. What <u>does</u> he mean?

Dec. 4.

Ann told me today that Theodore keeps turning our case over and over in his mind, and don't [*sic*] know exactly what to do; that the only reason why Homer is not just as scientific for me as G.D.A. is because we were once "special." He says that from the way his father acts he is inclined to infer that he wants to have Theodore suggest Homer without any suggestion from him.

Told Mr. Noyes that I had felt tempted to write to Myron, and he said: "By George! Write to him!" Afterward he read the letter, said it was first-rate, and told me to tell him that if it would do any good for me to talk with him I might go right on to O.C. for that purpose.

Dec. 7.

Theodore told me yesterday afternoon that he was going to present the stirpiculture matter to his father this morning. This afternoon Ann came to me and said: "It is decided." "Who is it?" "They are going to send for George Allen." "Yes. How soon is he coming?" "Theodore is going to write tomorrow." Then she burst into a laugh, and added—"—but not for you!" "Who <u>is</u> it then?" I asked more eagerly. "<u>Homer!</u>" Then she said that Theodore told his father that he considered me the best scientific combination for H., and if he could feel at liberty to ignore the fact of our past combination, he should recommend him for me. Mr. Noyes answered that that was what he wanted all the time, but he didn't want to have it come about by my choice. I asked if she had told Homer, and she said she had just been down to the shop on purpose to tell him, and he was "dreadfully tickled," and exclaimed: "I love you dearly." I told her that I had mingled feelings about the matter, and she said she could understand that it would be so. Although I love Homer, I cannot but remember Edward, and all the love and trouble I had with him. God help us!

Dec. 8.

We <u>did</u>, last night. Why should he care for it so much?

Dec. 10.

A disconsolate letter from Myron Friday. He thinks nothing can help; but Mr. N. had me write again.—If it "is so," it is so <u>now</u>. Night before last after meeting I had some talk with William, and he said it seemed impossible that he could leave the Community. Even if he could leave other things, he could not get away from Mr. Noyes, and he guessed the Community would have to make up its mind that he is a permanent institution. I repeated this to Mr. N. I had been asleep about an hour when he (Mr. N.) came into my room, saying that he had discovered at last the root of the trouble with W. Then he went on to give me a long talk about it. He thinks <u>Myron</u> is the dynamic member of the duality, and he drew a very discriminating and sharp contrast between the two men, praising William quite highly. W. thanked me this evening for my mediumship in helping to bring about the reconciliation. I told him if I had been any help it was through prayer.

Dec. 11.

Help needed at the "Socialist" office at O.C. to set type. No one wanted to go to stay. Mr. Noyes finally proposed that each of us girls and women take turns going for a month. Ann goes first, tomorrow.

Dec. 16.

Negotiated with Mr. Noyes and Theodore about the "introduction" or initiation of Virginia.[43]

Dec. 18.

Nothing like things of this kind to take the romance out of life. It doesn't go first-rate. You know there never was much sexual attraction between us, and now, with my heart bleeding still for E., it is anything but what it would have been 4 years ago. In some respects I see it might have been pleasanter to combine with someone whom I had never loved. I wonder if he does love me, or does he love the memory of that summer? I am a totally different woman from what I was then.

Dec. 19.

Letter from Ann about having Alfred Barron stay at O.C. Consulted Mr. Noyes about it, and he concludes he must go on there soon himself. I of course wish he would take me with him, though I do not at all expect him to.

Dec. 20.

Spoke to Virginia again last night for Doctor Noyes. Long talk with him this evening about it. He really did it last night, and very wisely and discreetly, too. He is a good man, I am convinced.

Wonder what my duty is about telling Ann Eliza about H. and me. Her extraordinary duplicity 4 years ago has made me slow to trust her since then; still it is evident that she has changed. She wrote a letter to Mr. Noyes today which he liked, and he got me to call a meeting to praise her. He attended. I want to take the course about this matter that will be the best in the long run, for if H. and I do have a child, the relation between us and her will last our life-time.

Dec. 21.

Mr. Noyes set me at work copying his "Gilpin Commentary," and said he should stay until that was over, but he thought we should finish it by Monday.[44] Mary Prindle is coming here. Her mind has been much troubled with the many strains we have passed through, and Ann wrote to Mr. N. about her condition. He told me to write to have her come on immediately.

Dec. 22.

Poured out my overcharged heart to C.A.C. a little this evening. Sometimes the anguish is greater than I can bear. He is always friendly and sympathetic, and yet the relation between us is so platonic that I know he will never misinterpret anything I do or say. Besides he always reassures me how utterly hopeless it is to ever expect that Edward will come back again.

Dec. 23.

Poetized a little this morning:

> An angel came to me one day
> With sad reproachful eye,
> And took my choicest pearl away,
> Nor stopped to heed my cry.

Dec. 27.

Good talk and a good time with H. last night. The reason why he has not got along better has been because he thought I was perfectly indifferent to the matter, and didn't like him very well.

Dec. 28—

Mr. Noyes made up his mind yesterday morning to start for O.C. today. At noon I received a letter from Ann, saying she wished very much I could come with him, so he thought I had better. This morning Mr. Noyes, Mr. Herrick, and I left W.C. Reached O.C. at 8:15. Ann and I had a good hug.

1877

Jan. 5, 1877.

Helen and Ann left for W.C. this morning. Helen is enceinte by J.H.N.[45] He is extremely pleased, and she is quite queer.—I still continue. Breast[s] began to be very sore on the 2d—grow worse and worse. Keep feeling as though I should be—ever so many times a day.

Jan. 9.

"Came round" today.[46] Went a week over. Wrote a note to H. this morning, giving him some hope, I am afraid. Wrote again this afternoon, and destroyed it all, and besides told him I felt as though I ought to give up the idea of having a child by him anyway, because others who are in special relations may be stumbled, although I know there is no exclusive love between us. I am afraid I have made him feel bad.

Jan. 11.

Mr. Herrick and I have taken Temple to father and mother.[47]

Jan. 12.

Began playing with Henry Hunter. Mr. Herrick talked with me about him this evening; he thinks he likes me, and wants me to have my eyes open to his defects.

Jan. 15.

Letter from Ann. She and Theodore really want me to go on, and I find from talking with Maria again that she and Minerva think no one will have any of the feeling I feared. Ann said if I concluded to proceed, to telegraph, and he should come. I sent the following telegram this afternoon: "I wish he would, I am waiting."

Jan. 16.

Telegram from H. that he would be here tonight. Trains are delayed, however, by the snow.

Jan. 17.

H. arrived this morning at about 4 o'clock. Went to see him at 7. Myron left yesterday. I talked with him Sunday, and Monday and Tuesday many [words missing here]

Jan. 25.

We got along a little better at first than we did at W.C.; but now it is about the same. The great difficulty I see is the pain which remains in my heart about Edward, and H. is so sensitive he feels my moods in spite of me. We had a frank talk about it the other night, the first we have had. He had not seemed to realize that my attachment to E. was so deep.

Feb. 2.

I have encountered so much opposition lately to the idea of my having a child by H., among those specially interested in him, that I have felt almost crushed by it; and then when I spoke to Maria about taking the matter of John and Minerva to Mr. Noyes, she said she did not wish to, because John would be so provoked at her, and then said: "And it won't do for you to do it on account of your affair with Edward." I thought if that was the way folks felt, I could be of no use to Mr. Noyes, &c. &c.[48] I felt so badly that I talked with Mr. N. about it today, and he was quite indignant, and said: "I have my opinion of your character, and you ought to take that, rather than that of all the rest of the Community put together." Homer came in to see me a little while before meeting, and I told him about it, and he went on to tell me of other things folks had said to him against me; and before I had any idea of what I was going to do I got to screaming pretty badly. Fidelia rushed in, and between them they quieted me after a while.

Feb. 3.

Dreadfully weak all day, and head-ache. H. Hunter came into my room after meeting to see if he could magnetize the head-ache away. He did so. Quite an affectionate time. Kissed.

Feb. 10.

H.M. Worden has shown so much interest in Henry, and has lately begun singing with him twice a day, that I began to think that he would prefer to read with her, (we have been reading the Bible every day). So I went to Mr. Hamilton this forenoon, and suggested that Harriet take the reading with him also, and that I drop all responsibility about him. Mr. Hamilton did not sympathize at all with this idea, and said he had been reflecting about Harriet's relation to Henry this morning, and had said something to her about it, and thought they had better stop singing together. I had to tell Henry this in the afternoon, and told him also I had no idea of stopping, but had proposed to have him read with her also. He seemed almost offended at that, and said he would not have read with her any way. Then he went on to tell me all that had passed between them. He had not liked her, but knew that she was trying to get him to do so; said she had written him a great many letters, and showed me one he had in his pocket; she had told him private experience, had asked him to kiss, &c. &c. I sat and blushed to hear so young a man talk in such a way about a woman who has had so much experience. He said it would be a great relief to get away from her.

Feb. 12.

Considered it my duty to tell Mr. Hamilton all that Henry had told me, though I asked him to save her feelings as much as possible. He was much stirred up at her insincerity about it, as she had substantially disclaimed to him the idea of there being anything between them.

Sat in my room with Henry till after 12 o'clock last night. He came to read after meeting, and then stayed and talked. I wish I could give a verbatim report of our conversation. It would do for a scene in a novel. He began by giving a great sigh, turned pale, clenched his fist, and said he felt desperate. I saw that he was repressing some very strong emotion, his lips trembled so, and his countenance looked so strange, but I could not guess what. He said he had for years—ever since he began to feel anything—pursued the policy of suppressing all emotion, chaining down his feelings with an iron hand, and he meant to do so. He has grown more reserved in his treatment of me lately, so that I had concluded that those who said he cared something for me were greatly mistaken. Well, we talked on, getting nearer and nearer a certain point. He said finally that he did like someone, and had for a long time—that he told Jane Kingsley who it was a number of months ago, but made her promise not to tell. Then he asked me to guess. I couldn't guess. While he was talking about Jane I was more and more convinced that it was not I. But after a little, he said it was I, but that I seemed so far away he thought it no use. Then he threw aside his almost supernatural self-control, and kissed and embraced me ardently. We had a delightful time. I have not felt so much affected by any one since Edward left. He said: "I don't feel one bit more toward you this minute than I have for a long time."

Feb. 13.

Henry was very ardent last evening. He is fast making a powerfully magnetic man; but this romance is nipped in the bud, and perhaps wisely, for I feel that I could love him intensely. Mr. H. told me this forenoon that he found himself feeling anxious about it, and he thought I had better drop it. He had no criticism, but thought H. ought to get into the revival spirit, and he feared love would stand in the way. I have not seen him yet. Mr. Hamilton's views regarding the matter had changed so suddenly that I felt sure that someone had suggested to him the ideas he expressed, though I could not guess who. I told Homer about it this evening, and after a while he told me that he went to Mr. Hamilton and told him his temptations about me to feel jealous of Henry, &c. I was very much surprised, and told him it seemed unreasonable to me. We had considerable talk, and he seemed convinced that his feeling so was a mistake really for his own interest, because, just as sure as this world, my attraction toward Henry would have helped my relation to Homer.

Feb. 14.

Told Henry about the probability that we should not read. It affected him a good deal, and he thought he could not stand it.

Feb. 15.

Henry neither eats nor sleeps; neither do I. I hardly understand why the affair should affect my nerves so.

Feb. 16.

Henry came to me today, and said he could endure it no longer, he must go to Mr. Hamilton. He looked and acted very fierce, and said he felt ready to fight the whole Community. I showed him the folly of that way of feeling, and begged him to go to Mr. H. in a docile, obedient spirit, ready to take any course he wished. He reported the talk to me after meeting, and he had a more subdued spirit than I ever saw in him

before. He said Mr. H. criticised him a good deal, and he wept in spite
of himself; but he felt nearer to Mr. H. than before, and said he left him
with the liberty to read with me. We both agreed that the feeling between
us is safer.

Feb. 17.

Henry came to read, and I told him I had made up my mind to leave
it with Homer, so I went to see him. He said we might, as he saw it would
make no difference. He said he knew he didn't feel right about me, and
didn't justify himself at all in being jealous, but he couldn't help it; and
"God knows I would if I could," he said. Henry and I concluded to give
it up.

Feb. 20.

A talk with Henry in his room this morning, and a good experience
with Mr. Hamilton afterward. Told Aunt Harriet, and she was so much
pleased that she told Mr. Noyes, and he said it was splendid. You know
how the great dread of my life has been to sleep with Mr. H. I have had
such times with Homer lately, and worse than ever last night, that it did
seem to me this morning as though I couldn't stand it any longer. While
at my work I prayed that I might have "a good spirit" to get along with it
as long as necessary, and the result was a gush of love in my heart for Mr.
H. I met him when I came back to the house, (I was making the store
beds), and I went with him to his room, and told him. He was much
pleased, and then we went to bed, and had excellent experience. The
fact is, Homer would be much more attractive to me if he felt less as he
used to, and was entirely free from any anxiety about my feelings toward
others. He has not got along so far as I expected.

"Centennial Views" this evening.[49] Sat by Henry. Delightful Back-
gammon afterward; but concluded that we would not talk any more for
a week.

Feb. 23.

Homer returned to W.C. this evening. He was very sober.

Feb. 25.

It is wonderful to me the amount of emotion which Henry has
aroused in me. I would never have believed it possible. Began to feel
last evening as though we were expressing more to each other than was
right under the circumstances. Told Henry so today in the South Sitting-

Room during a mock game of back-gammon. A curious talk, both extremely agitated. Spoke to Mr. Hamilton in the evening about reading with Henry again, and he said he was doing so well that he was afraid it would be a distraction to him, and that I must not forget that I am a very powerful social magnet; and that I didn't know how terribly the idea of giving me up wrenched Henry. I felt mortified some at my position; it seemed like that of a child teasing for something.

Feb. 26.

Constance is considerable of a temptation to me. Since her late conversion she has been pushed and has pushed herself forward very fast. There is something so managing and domineering in her natural tendencies that I hesitate to take her as a spiritual leader. It seemed to me, considering the defects of her natural character, and the long career of independence and disloyalty she has passed through, that she ought to plough under this conversion, and let it improve her character, rather than seek to dictate and lead and tear down. Said some of these things to her today. She complained to Aunt H.

Feb. 27.

Aunt Harriet talked with me this morning, and on the whole sympathized with my view, and thought Constance needed me as much as I did her. The thing that first threw me out with C. was her saying that she thought Mrs. Bushnell stood nearer to God than Aunt Harriet. I told her I could not agree with her. After Aunt Harriet talked with her again she took that back, and took what I said of her also in a good spirit.

Feb. 28.

Talked with Henry till 11 o'clock. When he went away Aunt H. came in, and she had felt distressed all the while he was there. We had quite a talk, and I couldn't feel quite as she did.

March 1st.

Wrote to Mr. Noyes about Henry, but he would not give any definite answer as to whether we might go on.

Mar. 3.

A long talk with Aunt Harriet this forenoon. Told some temptations I have had about her manner of criticising me, &c. I tried to have a good spirit in what I said, and she said she felt good about it, and thought I did have.

Mar. 4.

What a strange, strange attraction this is! I never would have believed I could be affected in this way.

Mar. 5.

Aunt Harriet, on thinking over the matter more, wrote to Mr. Noyes this morning about the affair between her and me, and between me and Constance, without telling me. Mr. Noyes spoke to me about it immediately, criticising me sharply at first, and thought I ought not to judge Constance; but after reading the letter C. wrote Aunt H. after the affair he came and said that he saw that my criticism of her did her good, and he saw that everything was working right; that we were all knocking each other into place, and the result would be to bring us nearer together. I had one of my hard cries—cried for two hours and a half, and did not get to breakfast till 12 o'clock.

Saw Henry in the evening, and he grows more and more urgent. When he knows his power he will be very much such a man as Edward.

Mar. 6.

Letter from Ann inquiring if this was the last of the trial between Homer and me. Commenced to answer her that I supposed of course it was, knowing how Mr. Noyes felt about it a month ago; and then I thought I would first go and speak to him to be sure, and was amazed to find that his views had changed most astonishingly. He said he didn't think Homer had a fair chance. At first he chuckled to see that he didn't have things quite as he wished, but before he went away he was as jealous for him as he was himself; said he tho't my associating with Henry would be a snare to me, and he wished me to drop it; said he thought his feeling toward me was likely to be very similar to Edward's. Told Aunt Harriet about it, and that I would tell Henry myself. Spoke to him after meeting, but we did not get a chance to begin our talk till about 1/2 past 9. We went into the tower room, and talked till 2 o'clock in the morning. Dreadful, I knew it would sound to everybody, but there were reasons for it which made it seem almost necessary at the time. Still, I do not justify it. I told him how Mr. Noyes felt, and he wished to know if there was no hope in the future. I said, No. Then he talked in quite a desperate way about it, and about going away, &c. I told him a good many times that he <u>must</u> go, but I was very weak in spirit, so that I let him hold me there when I knew he ought to go. Every time I rose to go he would stand against the door. He was so thoroughly respectful to me, that of course if I had insisted in any way to show that I should take offense, he would have done just as I said.

Mar. 8.

Mr. Hamilton came to me this afternoon, and asked me to promise him that I would say nothing more to Henry; said Henry reported his talk with me to Clarence, and Clarence had come to him about it, and said that Henry told him when he went away that he didn't want to live any longer. Of course I gave him the promise, but I told him I thought he should hear what I had to say.

Last evening I was in the children's South Room, and Henry came to say that he felt better than when he left me in the morning, and thought he could get along very comfortably if we could be ordinary friends. Just then Mr. Towner brought Paul to bid me good-night. The little fellow put his arms around my neck, and hugged me, and though his lip quivered, he obeyed, and went away without crying. "He did well," said Henry admiringly. "If I could only do it as easily as that!" I thought this one of the prettiest compliments I ever had. Aunt Harriet saw us speaking together, and not knowing where I was this evening, she went to Mr. Noyes, and poured on him the full pressure of her alarm and anxiety. He sent for Henry during meeting, and gave him a very sharp talking to—told him he should send him out of the Community if he didn't stop his intimacy with me, &c. After meeting he sent for me, and gave me a thorough criticism.

Mar. 9.

Told Aunt H. some things about Henry's and my long talk; for one thing, how he stood against the door when I proposed to go. I told her I did not tell it to blame him or excuse myself, but merely to show that he was a man of strong feelings, and not a boy to be dealt with easily. I said that for one instant I had such a sense of his great strength, that a terror went thro' me of what he was able to do with me; but that I immediately reproached myself for the thought, because he had treated me with such genuine respect that I knew I had actually no fear of him. Aunt H. wrote to Mr. N. the bare facts that he held the door, and that I had that instant of terror, without any of these modifying remarks, and Mr. Noyes went down to the office, and gave Henry a fearful denunciation. It seemed to me all day as though I should die of self-condemnation, because of having got so young a man into such a dreadful scrape. Mr. Noyes thought he ought to be judged, because he is a medium of a bad principality. I couldn't feel good at all to have him blamed, when I am so much older. It seemed to me that I ought to take it alone.[50]

Mar. 10.

Wrote to Mr. Noyes, and asked him to put me in the lowest place in the Community, so long as I am so liable to come under influences alien to him. Called a committee [for a criticism session], too. I never felt so thoroughly crushed and humbled in my life, and expected to be almost annihilated; but to my surprise all except H.W.B. were very kind and charitable. Mr. Noyes wrote to the committee that his power of recall over me was greater in this than in any previous case, and that when he made up his mind to haul me in I came. Felt very thankful for this; but still it seems as though I ought hardly to stay in the Community, and certainly deserve no place of confidence. Although there are many things in this judgment which are very hard to bear, I can see that God is dealing with me, and planned it all to humiliate my old life.

Mar. 11.

Henry had a committee this afternoon, and Mr. Hamilton told them about his holding the door, &c. Oh! dear! I know he will think it very unjust told in that bare way, and yet if he had heard what I said I don't think he would have found any fault with it, and I had no idea Aunt H. and Mr. Noyes would feel so about that any way.

Mar. 16.

A letter from Ann. She writes as though offended or ashamed of me. Good! I feel as though I had got my release. I have had too much reference to her good opinion, and I am glad I have lost it. — Talked with Mr. Hamilton Monday, and told him it seemed unjust to me to have it in any way represented that I was afraid of Henry that night, or that he forced me, &c.; but he and Aunt Harriet both thought I was inclined to justify him, and refused to do anything about modifying the statements.

Mar. 18.

Wrote to Mr. Noyes about the part of the affair with Henry that troubled — my being "afraid of his violence," &c. — and he had quite a talk with me. Said it was a small matter for me to worry about, and he wished I would put it out of my mind; said he would see that Henry was not abused. Went into his room this evening after the dance, and he said he had been thinking about me a good deal during the day. He said I must get my affections into such a state of obedience to God that I should let my heart out to some-one, and then take it back again instantly at the word of command, just as the dancers obey the call of the manager. I told him I had been tempted to think I must crush out of me all love; but he said if I could get this obedience to God, I could love more intensely than now.

Mar. 24.

Constance told me of some talk she had with Henry a few days ago. She said he was very soft, but it was very hard for him to give me up. He said he had found out that he <u>could love</u>, &c.

Mar. 25.

Asked Constance to tell Henry about my probable condition, and she asked him afterward if that wouldn't make it easier for him to give me up. He said: "No, that would make no difference."

I have taken considerable criticism from Constance lately. She has been a true friend to me. Mrs. Bushnell I have learned to love very much. She is a thoroughly good woman.

Mar. 26.

Got Mr. Noyes to write to Homer for me. I have known well enough that he was greatly tried and offended at me, so much so that I doubt very much whether he will not be more displeased than pleased on hearing that I have started. Thought perhaps he would take the news better from Mr. Noyes. After writing one letter he said if that didn't suit he would write another. I said I wished he would, so he did, and I sent both, as they were both good. Talked with Maria this evening, and found from her that he has written dreadful things about me to her. Well, I have too much respect for him to believe that he will retain this resentment all through the nine months, and if he does I shall not trouble myself about it. I have made what reparation I could for my bad treatment of him, and the child will cost me a great deal more suffering and hard work than it will him. But I feel reconciled to God about it all, and know that he arranges my circumstances.

Mar. 27.

Ann arrived. Met her a little cooly at first, as I did not know exactly how she felt.

Mar. 28.

"Taken" at about 11 o'clock this morning. Talk with Ann this afternoon. Perfectly reconciled. She says Homer is talking very badly about me. Wrote to him this afternoon to relieve his mind as soon as possible about the idea of having a child by me. Don't feel at all resentful toward him; but I am very glad that God had destroyed his idolatry toward me. I think it is a blessing. These two weeks of going over my time have been an excellent experience to me. When I first thought it might be so I had a great struggle in my heart about giving up Edward. I saw that though I had consented to try to have a child I had not estimated the bearing an event of that kind would actually have on my future, and on my relations to Edward. I found I had to give him up and become reconciled to God in a way that I had not done.

Mar. 31.

H.M. Worden showed me this morning a note she got from Homer several days ago in which he made quite a coarse remark about Henry and me. A short time afterward Mr. Noyes showed me a note he received from Homer today, an answer to the announcement that I <u>was</u> and was not enceinte. After reading it I said: "Well, what am I to do now?" "What do you <u>want</u> to do?" he asked. "I don't know," I answered, my eyes filling with tears. "I guess there isn't anything to feel bad about, is there?" said he. "<u>You</u> don't know," I replied. "Well, I <u>ought</u> to know." So I told him some how Homer has talked and written. He was very indignant, and said Homer had no business to say one word about Henry and me, after he knew that he had criticised us — that was the end of it, and whatever he said he should have said to him. "You are better than he is," said he. I was surprised at this. He said I must keep so near him that I should not care what anyone else thought of me. He sat right down and wrote to Homer, reproving him. I told him also that I had had to endure a great many evil-thinking remarks made about me by various ones, which had tempted me to feel that I was hated and despised, and had no place in the Community, but that I had tried to remember all the time that God was dealing with me, and I did not get any more blows than were necessary to make me hate my old life . . "Forsake them all, and <u>I</u> will be your friend," he said. "Now I will tell you just what I think of that matter of Henry Hunter. I am glad it all happened just as it did, and considering everything you did well about it. It is plain enough that Homer needed it." Wrote a note to Mr. Noyes in the evening. He said it was right up to the mark, and that he could see plainly enough that, though God judged me, he was using me to bring <u>men</u> to judgment. "You are a great trap. It is pretty hard on you; but in one sense you ought to be glad if you are all used up in bringing the false love of men to judgment, for that is what you are doing, and I can see great benefit coming out of it all."

April 2.

Brother George appeared from W.C. unexpectedly this evening. Theodore sent him to harmonize the two families.

April 3.

George is revolutionizing a great deal. Called a meeting this morning, and proposed to have the Bible classes dropped. He thinks there is a tendency toward a morbid state of things here which is bad.

April 4.

Mr. Noyes had George send for Theodore.

April 5.

Another meeting called by George with the young folks to prepare them to receive Theodore in a good spirit. Theodore arrived in the evening.

April 10.

The days since Theodore's arrival have been crammed full of events. I have been back and forth between Mr. Noyes and Theodore a good many times in reference to the plan of concentration which Theodore suggested. There has been distress on the part of some; but things are going quite well now. Constance has had a great deal of difficulty in adjusting herself to Theodore. His father settled it this evening by saying that the difficulty between them was the fact of their relationship.

I had a talk with Theodore several days ago about his stirpicultural plans for me. He said I was one of those women (Ann was so too, he said) who was liable to be magnetized by a certain class of men. He said it was nothing derogatory to me, but was a fact which I had better calculate for. He had a desire to consolidate about himself a number of those which are likely to stand nearest him, and so far as stirpiculture would help this object, he should use it. He thought I needed a head, and perhaps Frank, by being responsible to him, could become my controller. There was much more said about his plans of organizations, &c.

April 11.

Constance decided this morning to go to W.C. and live with Theodore a while. Mr. Noyes came into my room this forenoon, and said: "You don't think of going to Wallingford too, do you? Heavens and earth! I can't have you go." I told him that I rather thought not, and I certainly would not go if he had the least wish to have me stay with him. He said I had better not leave him. I told him something about Theodore's plans concerning Frank and me. Mr. Noyes seemed to be amused at the idea of F's exerting moral control over me, but said he liked the idea of a conjunction between us with reference to the paper. But he said he himself was my natural head. "I have courted you a good while," said he, "and we had better go along together. I want you to stick by me as long as I live." I told him he had practically been a head to me, and that no one was able to do anything with me in reference to Edward till I went to him; and that I was learning that the way for me to keep out of trouble was to go to him with everything—that if I had told him in the first place about Henry Hunter, there would have been no difficulty, and that I meant to tell him things even if I plagued him. He said that was right.

Mr. Noyes criticised George Miller some yesterday for not consulting him more, and I told him I thought George was learning the same lesson.

April 12.

A great deal of writing to do these days. Write out reports of evening meetings with Mrs. Campbell, and then today Mr. Noyes talked to me, and I made a report of that. A glorious talk, and he said that he felt ready to burst. Everything seems to be going favorably now with regard to Theodore.

April 13.

Deliberately made up my mind to speak to Henry Hunter today, and did so. It is five weeks yesterday since we said a word to each other. I met him, and said: "How long are we going to keep this up?, I am tired of it. Did anyone tell you not to speak to me?" He looked astonished at first, but glad. Said he took it that he must not speak to me from what Mr.

Noyes said to him—told him to let me entirely alone, &c. "It is perfect foolishness to do this way, I think," said I. "Yes, it only makes it a great deal worse." But he said he had tried to obey Mr. Noyes just as well as he knew how. He said I could not be any more tired of it than he was; yet he had some hope that things would be different before a great while.

April 16.

Theodore, George, and Constance left for W.C. Constance told me before going that she had had a conversation about Theodore which reconciled her to me. She was really quite fanatical. She was sick one night last week, and attributed it to contact with me, which brought Theodore's spirit upon her.

Talked with Mr. Noyes about Henry, telling him I wished I might be free to treat him as I did other young men. At first he said I might; then he said this time of year was so enchanting and romantic that it might be dangerous, and he guessed we had better go on about as we were till Theodore comes again, when he might look after us. Told Henry in the evening, and he looked much pleased. I asked him if he had a good supply of patience, and he said, Yes, he had.

April 17.

Henry came to the window this evening at the Piano house, where I was practising, his gun on his shoulder, and his girdle about his waist. I talked with him a few moments, and then told him I thought we had better not speak to each other.

April 20.

Paul three years old today. I can't help wondering if his father will remember it. I can scarcely keep him from my thoughts today.

April 22.

Met Henry in the Court this evening with two fragrant bunches of trailing arbutus in his hand, one of which he asked me to take, and said the other would go into the sitting-room. I had missed him all day, and he said he had walked down to Joppa and back, and that he should have put the flowers in my room, if he had not met me.

April 23.

Letter from Ann, saying that Theodore recommended me to try with Frank.

April 26.

Got drawn quite unintentionally into a plain talk with Aunt Harriet. I have had a great deal of trouble about her the last two months, but I did not expect to say anything to her about it. When we got through I tho't I should have to take the matter to Mr. Noyes, in order to be able to get along with my relation to her; but after a few hours I felt that I loved her, and wished that we might settle our difficulties ourselves. It seemed to me we might if she would treat me with more confidence. I looked for her, but could not find her. After meeting Frank and I played, and when we had finished Deming handed me a note from Aunt H, desiring reconciliation, and we had a pleasant talk afterward.

May 1.

I said yesterday to Mr. Noyes: "I am working in the Printing-Office." (He had been gone to Joppa.) "Yes," he said, "I noticed it, and wondered if it was a very good plan to be there with your 'snare,'" meaning Henry. This disturbed me a great deal, and we had quite a discussion. Renewed it this afternoon and evening, finally ending in his having me send word to Henry by Mr. H. to give up <u>forever</u> any idea of loving me or my loving him—entirely and completely, and never think of it again.

Talked also with Mr. Noyes yesterday about the matter of trying, and tho' he said he had no objection to my trying with Frank, he said he would rather I would take Mr. Herrick. So I said I would. I spoke to Mr. H. last evening, telling him he might feel perfectly free to decline. He said he should be glad and pleased.

Joppa, May 3.

Mr. Noyes, Mr. Hamilton, Mr. Kelly, Cornelia, Charlotte, and I came down yesterday.

May 5.

The rest of the party returned on the cars, and Mr. Kelly and I walked home this afternoon. Funny time laughing at Joppa.

May 7.

Mr. Noyes asked me to give up music, and become a writer. I was almost paralyzed at first. Then I told him he could ask me nothing that would hurt me so much, and we had some pretty plain talk—perfectly respectful and good-natured, for I told him I should obey him at any rate, though it was like turning the world upside down.

May 9.

Mr. Noyes thinks he has got at the real root of the difficulty with me now, and he is mightily pleased. He said it was distressing to have me do well for a day or two, and then all down again. "And besides," said he, "I don't believe you are that kind of a woman. I believe you are a person who can form a purpose, and follow it persistently." I told him that I had never given my best efforts to writing, that music had been the passion of my life, and that I had never turned the fire and force of my ambition into any other channel. How he did talk! He said to William Hinds (who arrived yesterday): "Here we are to have our poetess, authoress, editress, and what not. Edward Inslee has been over her for the last two or three years, making her think she hadn't any literary talent. But he was only a kind of stopper, to keep her from being too precocious." And so on, ever so much more. "You can make a <u>splendid writer</u> just as easy as not, if you are a mind to," said he to me. "You are too big a woman to be thumping the piano; leave that to the small fools."

May 10.

Actually got under an afflatus, which I could not get rid of until I had worn it out.[51]

May 11.

Frank and I made a compact tonight to devote the remainder of our lives to helping Mr. Noyes about the paper.

May 12.

Mr. Noyes liked my article. He said it treated of a great problem, and perhaps he could help me to say something more about it. I told him I had a great deal more to say myself, and I should be glad to have him make suggestions.

May 13.

Mr. Towner invited me to take a boat-ride with him and Paul. The little fellow, on the way to the river, astonished me with an exhibition of his memory. We took a little different course from what we used to last summer, and he said, pointing to the usual path: "That's the way, mamma. We went that way when my papa took me and Georgy to ride in the boat." He has not been since he was two years and four months old.

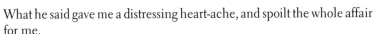

What he said gave me a distressing heart-ache, and spoilt the whole affair for me.

May 17.

Theodore and Ann came day before yesterday. Mr. Noyes made his proclamation this evening. Frank told me before meeting that Theodore wondered that I had not spoken to him, so I went to assure him after meeting that I had nothing in the world against him. Got into a most fearful muss. Ann came in, and we did not get through till half-past eleven. It seems that on the first day of the discussion between me and Mr. Noyes three weeks ago, he wrote a letter to Theodore about it, but on the next day, when he understood my difficulties better, he wrote another to explain. Meanwhile Theodore answered, and was afraid that I felt offended at what he wrote. I had such a sense at first of what a plague and burden I must be to Mr. Noyes, that I told them I saw no way but that I must go away from the Community. They scolded me a good deal about that, and I just sat there in amazement to see what low motives Theodore imputed to me about it. He seemed to think me incapable of any but a very low and mean motive for wishing to go away. Edward did not enter my mind, when I spoke of it. Theodore forbade me to tell Mr. Noyes anything about the affair.

May 24.

Paul has had times lately of talking about his father as a "naughty, bad man," saying that somebody told him so. This was agonizing to me, and I spoke to Mr. Noyes about it to see if it were necessary that anything should be said to him at all about his father. At first he said he would stop it, but this evening he concluded that it would be better for him to grow up now with the idea that his father is a bad man. We had a long talk. "I can assure you most lovingly," said he, "that God can reconcile you to this matter, and take away all the pain, and no one else can."

May 25.

It has been so hard, so hard, for me to believe that Edward is the wicked man that Mr. Noyes thinks him; but he said today I must make up my mind—must choose between him and E. I said I had done that, but I asked him if he would be satisfied if I should suspend judgment, and banish the subject from my mind too. He said that would not be enough. I thought and prayed about it all the afternoon, and finally wrote to him: "I am going to accept your judgment of E., cost me what it will." He said that was right; that God had always treated him like that —put him into a tight place where the only way out was to trust in God. "I can feel the great and mighty power of God reaching out after you, determined to save you," he said.

Then I went up and had a talk with Mr. Towner, as Mr. Noyes had talked to him about Paul. After a little he said: "I learned something about Edward when I was last in Newark, which I have hesitated some about telling you. I have only told his father. It has nothing to do with his reputation." Then he stopped. My heart gave one of those horrible contractions which sap the lifeblood, but I said calmly: "I have been expecting to hear that he would get married; it is probably something of that kind." "Yes," he answered, "Miss Mary Leonard told me it was generally expected in Newark that he would marry a Miss Ricker at almost any time now." I made some inquiries about her. All he knew was that she is a girl of good reputation—a pianist. Although I have dreaded to hear this, it is really a relief to me. Now I shall set myself about the task of forgetting him with all my might, asking God to help me.

May 28.

Mr. Noyes asserted this morning that Edward was a wicked man before I was acquainted with him, and that I was in no way responsible for his condition. He set Mr. Towner this morning at proving that assertion historically, and proposed having the matter up in meeting. I made some objections to being up for discussion again, saying that I had been talked about so much the last two or three years, I was morbidly sensitive about being mentioned in public. Mr. Noyes criticised me some about that, so I went ahead and put it thro' myself. I also made a few remarks showing that I am convinced that, judged by the true standard of righteousness, Edward is a wicked, unprincipled man, and was so before I knew him. Horrible as this seems, I really felt more light-hearted after thus committing myself than I have since all this tragedy occurred. I asked them all to help me forget him.

June 7.

Another three hours' talk with Mr. Noyes, brought about by his announcing to me that he had some suspicions (or rather, someone had told him) of my talk with Theodore and Ann, and so he had written to Theodore to find out about it. He began by saying that I must not think it strange if he kept things from me occasionally, so long as I did from him. He did not like it at first because I had not told him about that talk, but seemed to feel different when I told him Theodore forbade me to tell him. On the whole the talk resulted well. Told him that Homer and I did not speak, and he sent Mr. Herrick to talk with him.

June 9.

Homer asked to see me, and we talked an hour. He is trying his best to feel well toward me, but I can see it is very hard for him. It is as I thought. He says he did not suppose I felt badly about Edward at all. Astonishing!

June 13.

Quite a pleasant picnic ride father Noyes got up, inviting Homer and me. We did not have much to say to each other then, but had quite a pleasant talk in the evening after meeting.

June 16.

There has been considerable steady magnetism between Frank and me for a long time, though we can't "stay" together. He said the other day that he thought we should have a honeymoon when we are sixty. "It has been seventeen years already," said he, "and we haven't lost an atom of attraction yet, and I don't believe we ever shall." My health is superb now-a-days. He complimented me in regard to it today, and said: "You look just as fresh as a rose," which is pretty well for a woman of thirty-three, who had been dragged through the misery that I have the last two or three years. — Theodore and Ann arrived today.

June 23.

A frank talk with Ann yesterday, and succeeded in clearing up a number of mysteries between Theodore and her and me, and she said she would talk with Theodore. She did so, and I did too today, and things are much more satisfactory. The fact is, Aunt Harriet, who is in miserable health, has fallen into one of her morbid fits of evil-thinking of Theodore and Ann, and when it first came on a few weeks ago, it let in a good deal of light on my experience with her. I could see that her imaginations about them were unjust, and I began to feel justified in concluding that things in her treatment of me which tried me so were of the same character. I told him so, and he accepted it as a fair explanation. Aunt Harriet is in a perfectly morbid state of mind, and tho' I love her, and feel very sorry for her, she has caused me a great deal of harrowing experience.

June 24.

Portia told me today that I looked the best this summer that I ever had since she first saw me nine years ago, and Constance said to me two or three days ago: "I was thinking only yesterday that if I were a man I should be sure to fall in love with you, you are so bewitching." "Why, do you think I am attractive?" said I perfectly astonished. "Yes, very, and I don't blame Henry at all for loving you. I don't see how he can help it. You seem just as bewitching as you did five years ago!" I put these things down, because my own ideas of my attractiveness are so very different. I should be insincere if I did not admit that I know I have been one of the most attractive women in the Oneida Community; yet I have thrown away with indifference so much love that has been offered me, and lavished so much on my one attraction to Edward, that I now feel quite poor in lovers, though my first love—Frank—told me yesterday that he felt more of this magnetic, electrical attraction toward me than toward any one. Although I do not feel that consciousness of power which I once possessed, yet I feel still that there are many persons whom I might attract if I cared to do so. But things of that kind do not possess the zest they once did, and it would indeed be a bore to me to be again "popular."

July 10.

A year this evening since I saw Edward.—I asked Ann if I might stop trying with Mr. Herrick, as I have no faith in it. She sympathized; but he has just had two hard criticisms, and felt so badly when I "came round" the other day, that I had not the heart to propose it this time, so said I would go on one month longer.

July 15.

Homer Barron is a mystery. He treats me quite pleasantly unless we get into some personal talk, and then a strange look comes into his eyes, as though he had all he could do to control his temper, and I have a sense of something revengeful in him, as though he would like to make me suffer all that I have made him suffer. He should remember that he made many women suffer before he loved me, and if he could believe it I think he would see that I have met my retribution in the suffering I have had about Edward. Sometimes I think I will bow and bow before his displeasure, and let him have it that he was the only injured party, and then again I feel as though I would treat him with contempt, and flame out at him in scorn and denial of his accusations. I trust I shall have a Christian spirit.

Temple talked with me quite a while today. He is only a boy of 14, and is struggling already never to succumb to passion. But he told me that he told Henry that it would be very easy to like me, if anyone was a mind to, and he didn't wonder at all that anyone should.

July 17.

A talk with Homer this morning which was so distressing that I talked with Ann about it, and then she talked with us together. I don't know what the result will be.

Charlie Burt said to me this evening: "I saw you walking on the lawn the other day, and your hair was drawn back in such a way as to look as though it were done up. I thought if you had long hair, you would be a dangerous woman to have here in the Community.[52] Some of us fellows would go crazy over you." Then he asked: "Have you given up music?" "Yes." "Our only artist at the piano!" he exclaimed.

July 19.

Theodore is having trouble with Ella, and he asked me yesterday to take charge of her and be responsible for her spiritual state.[53] We had a hard time with her today—a committee this forenoon, and this afternoon she had the hysterics in my room, and softened and yielded in spirit the most that I ever saw her. At the committee Ann told some appalling things which Edward told her just before he left the Community of the deception which Ella practised in regard to him, and which he allowed. She made Mr. Noyes and the Community believe that she loved and suffered about Edward, when it was really Edwin Burnham, and then afterward acknowledged to Edward that she put it on him because he was already under criticism about me, and laughed and joked with him about it. Shocking as this is in her, it shocked me to have to believe him capable of associating with one whom he knew to be deceiving in so flagrant a way. He would be in the Community now, if he had not associated with her. Although I have no reason to think that he loved her, intimacy with her engendered evil-thinking in him, and willfulness and independence.

July 20.

I knew that I was very tired when I went to bed last night, but was not prepared for the result which took place today—chills and fever. I have wondered sometimes if I should not come down with the fever and ague. I went to W.C. last summer in just the nick of time to take it, and was also in an extremely reduced condition physically, mentally, and spiritually.

July 22.

Another chill today. The doctors decide I have really got the ague, and this evening began to administer quinine. Homer has kindly rubbed my back several times.

July 23.

Offered myself for criticism. I enjoyed Theodore's remarks very much. He was very sincere, and also very kind. He criticised me for general indiscretion. I only wish I had had what he said told me ten or fifteen years ago; but I shall do my best now to learn the lesson.

July 24.

How strange to feel so much out of harmony with what must be really true! Here I sit in my black cassimere,[54] with my thick woolen shawl wrapped about me, while I see from the window many signs that the heat of summer is at its height. There is a dreamy, shimmering haze in the atmosphere, the insects buzz with that peculiar tone of midsummer, and the large, dark-blue wasps come droning in at the window. While I shiver in my woolens, it is almost with a sensation of horror that I observe the girls come along in their muslins and with fluttering fans.

July 25.

A strange, sweet dream about E. this morning. I had not been thinking about him specially, but I wished the other day, when I was lying with my eyes closed, that I could see his face, as I did that of others among the shifting images which pass before the closed sight. I dreamed that he had returned to the Community, and that there was a deep, bubbling joy in my heart about him. Mr. Noyes was kind and sympathetic, and left me free. I thought that, although I had been trying with someone else, Mr. N. had me try once with E., which was all that had passed between us until the time of my dream. I ran upstairs to his room (where it used to be, in the garret), and not finding him, went down. After a while I went up again, and found him reading in the Testament, and studying phonography. He was very loving, though not passionate or vehement, and a quiet, peaceful expression radiated from his beautiful eyes. I put my hand on my heart, and said: "I know in here that the child will be yours," and put up my arm to clasp his neck. He at the same instant turned, and bent on me his dark, tender eyes, full of soul-love, and I awoke. The impression left on me was one of <u>goodness</u>. He seemed as he did when in a good spirit, and I know God is able to release him from the terrible control he is under; but I must build nothing on a dream. Let it pass!

August 10.

Convalescent again. Quite a fit of sickness for me. Taken on the first of August. Ann Eliza was my nurse, and Homer, Mrs. Dunn, and others were very kind to me. Well now, only rather weak. "Came round" also, when it was time for me, so I suppose I shall not have to try with Mr. Herrick any more. There is certainly an "incompatibility" between us, which has seemed to me more and more apparent.

Aug. 11.

Wrote to Mr. Noyes saying, if he sympathized, I should prefer to give up trying with Mr. Herrick, to which he said: "All right." I wrote also an account of the state of things between Homer and me. But he said he guessed I had better leave well enough alone.

Stayed with Frank, and we had a very cozy, affectionate time, and a plain talk about the matter of having a child together. He said he had never found a woman before who so completely satisfied him as I do, and that if he could only stay with me a little while every day, that would be all he should want, &c. About having the baby, he feels just as Edward and I did—that he would prefer to go on and have all his children by one woman, and having begun with Cornelia, he would continue with her; but he sees that is impossible in community, and so if he is to have another child he would rather have it by me than any one else. I told him I understood perfectly how he felt about having all his children by Cornelia, for it seemed to me as though I could not have one by any one but Edward, and that was really one of his greatest causes of discontent with the Community.

Aug. 12.

Told Mr. Herrick what I wrote to Mr. Noyes, and I was surprised to find how badly he felt about it. He asked if there would not be a chance for him again sometime; said that it would be a tremendous giving up for him, and that he would rather have a child by me than by any other woman in the Community. He also said he didn't think he had quite a fair chance last month, as he was feeling badly about his criticism, and I was not well. He said he knew it was asking a great favor of me, but he did wish he might try once more, and I felt so sorry for him that I said I would. When I saw how badly he felt, I couldn't think of myself, but when I got away from him I found it put a great weight in my heart, which had felt very light just before.

Aug. 13.

Talked with Homer. He does not want a child by me now. Ann says he is afraid to trust himself, and thinks he shall have trouble. The talk made my heart ache.

Aug. 14.

Frank and I had a very satisfactory talk today on the relation which exists between us. He says he can work and harmonize with me more easily and fully than with any one. This is mutual, and we both agreed that it would be better to preserve our musical, literary, and magnetic relation than to have a child, if so doing would be likely to destroy this superior relation. He says he really loves me more now than he did years ago, and we think we are adapted to form a life-long intimacy which will be a mutual help.

Eliza told me this evening that Homer told her this morning that he could not get to sleep last night, and that if he were she he should go to his room and throw himself on the bed, and make the pillows wet. Poor boy! poor boy! But he is so proud he won't believe I love him, or let me love him at all since I do not feel just as I used to. I said to him last evening that I had not changed so much as he had. "No," he said, "it would not be at all the same to change from one degree above zero to one degree below, as it would be to change from a hundred degrees above to one below." He also said: "Your combination with Edward was not half so painful to me as having to give this up last winter."

Aug. 16.

It is curious what an amount of attention, or attraction, I can feel is directed toward me. Men tell me they love me, whom I had not been conscious of attracting. I suppose my having been out of circulation for so long is one cause of it.

Aug. 19.

Helen's baby (a nice girl) born at 19 minutes to 8 this evening. I was with her from 1 o'clock P.M. till half-past 12 at night. Homer was also one of the assistants, and a very excellent one he is. He thinks I didn't love him last winter, but while Helen was in her travail I couldn't help thinking that I have not been, and am not now, really <u>willing</u> to go through the agonies of childbirth for anyone but Homer; (I mean by this that my feelings about E. are held in suspense); though of course I shall do what I am told, hard as it may be. It seems wrong to me to try with a man whom I feel such a reluctance to stay with as I do with Mr. Herrick. He said he wanted to have a visit with me this month; but I dread the idea very much.

Aug. 21.

Frank and I got into the "intensities" a good deal last night. He says he has come to the conclusion that I understand him better than any other woman.

Aug. 23.

A pleasant party of aristocrats from Syracuse—Rev. D. Ely and wife, with Mr. and Mrs. McLean of N.Y. with mother and aunt.[55] Mrs. McLean is daughter of General Sumner. I wonder if Edward ever thinks of the cruel position he has left me in in regard to our child. Paul is such a large, handsome, healthy boy, that people always want to show him off as a specimen of scientific propagation; <u>but he has no father.</u> These people today expressed a great deal of admiration for him, and Mrs. McLean asked me if I loved his father. I told her I did, more than I ever loved any one else. "How <u>can</u> you endure to have him associate with any other woman!" she exclaimed. Fortunately she did not ask whether he were here. Oh Edward! <u>Edward!</u> Was the sacrifice right or wrong? I can hardly tell; but I know I believed I was doing God's will.

Sept. 11.

I feel convicted of unthankfulness. I am continually reaching out for, and grieving because I cannot have, certain unattainable things, instead of being thankful for the blessings which I actually possess if I would only recognize the fact. God must look on me as ungrateful. I have felt perfectly indifferent to the matter of having a child by Mr. Herrick, and have been quite prone to see his defects; but there is certainly a great deal of good in him, and I don't know as I deserve a child by him. I certainly don't by any one, unless I am thankful and reconciled to God for his dealings with me.

Sept. 13.

Thirty-four today. The weather has been perfect. A large picnic stopped for two hours in the afternoon, and we had a lively time waiting on them. Took Paul to walk in the meadow where the ducks are, and while we were loitering under a tree we heard distant voices calling to us. Looked up and saw Florence, Mabel, and Ida, with Henry Hunter, engaged in a butternut-crack. Joined them, though of course I said not a word to H. By the way, I went to Theodore three or four evenings ago, and asked him if he and Ann would not consider the matter of allowing us liberty to speak to each other again. He said if he really had the management of the case, he should deal with it quite differently from what had been done. I told him that I must say for Henry that he had been extremely obedient; but that the present restriction was and had been dreadfully humiliating to me.

We are having a great pressure of work at the Fruit-House.[56] Enjoy it tho'.

About to begin the month with Mr. Herrick again. It does not seem right for two persons to try when one feels as I do. I dread it fearfully, and more and more every day.

Thirty-four! My weight is 110 lbs., and I do not look as old as I am. My hair is a little gray, though not noticeably so except on close scrutiny; my complexion is still tolerably fair; a few crows' feet have laid their marks about my eyes, and my moustache is becoming quite heavy. How about my heart? I hardly know. I sometimes think I am growing more and more materialistic; then again I revolt against that idea.

Sept. 16.

Mr. Herrick came without notifying me last night, and after the trial was over he said: "Poor little martyr! I know the best part of this to you is for me to go away." I made up my mind I would make a clean breast of the difficulties between us, and show him wherein it seemed to me he had not treated me fairly and justly. I began with late affairs, and ended with that affair last spring, when he wrote to Theodore and got me into such a muss between him and his father. I told him I had no doubt that his motives were good, and that he had no intention of making me trouble; but I thought he acted of impulse without getting a clear idea of what he was about, and it had made me dread to get into any relation to him where he would feel as though he had a responsibility about me, as I should never be able to calculate what he would be likely to do. He said he was glad to find there was a foundation in fact for the aversion I

seemed to have toward him; he had been afraid my feeling was merely one of fancy—that I disliked him, and could not tell why; he had felt
all the month that I had a growing aversion for him, and that I could not
"endure the idea" of trying again. I told him I had not in the beginning
an aversion toward him, though I never had felt any spontaneous attraction for him. Well, we left it that we would "try" no more, until there
was a better state of feeling between us. He said that at the time he asked
me to let him try one more month he never felt more attracted to any
woman in his life than to me. The reason why (though I did not tell him)
was because I felt so glad to be free from the engagement with him, that
I treated him quite genially and naturally; but that all changed of course
as soon as I gave him the promise to go on again. Tossed about till half-
past 12, then went up to Frank's room, and we had a good talk which
quite strengthened us in our resolve to make the most of ourselves during
the next thirty years. Got to sleep about 3 o'clock.

Lorenzo asked to talk with me last evening after meeting. He said
he wished very much to have a certain embarrassment between us removed, so that he could feel at ease in my society; he had felt strange ever
since two years ago, when I declined an invitation he sent me.[57] I told
him that I did not suppose at the time that he would care any because I
refused him, but I would now tell him the principal reason why I did, and
he could see that it was not strange that I did. I then told him how jealous
Edward was, and how he confessed to me the next day that he went into
the entry outside the office-bedroom, and heard and saw all he could. I
was very much surprised that he should feel so about Lorenzo with so
little cause. He seemed ashamed of having given way to this temptation,
and confessed in quite a broken way; but I did not feel as though I could
ever go with Lorenzo again, while there was any danger of his feeling so.

Sept. 20.

Mr. Herrick and I had quite a plain talk in Helen's presence. We
were both somewhat angry; but we finally made up in quite a friendly way.

Sept. 26.

Ann told me this morning, in reference to what I asked Theodore
about (H.H.), that she and Theo. did not know whether they were to deal
with me or not—i.e., whether I belonged to their parish or not. So I wrote
and asked Mr. Noyes, and he sent back quite a long answer to Theodore
(he brought it to me), which made me feel both well and ill; well, be-

cause he spoke charitably of me, and as though he expected I would become an assistant mother in the family; and ill, because I realized how
differently he thinks of me from what Ann and Theodore do, and how
little he understands their system of government, which, so far, admits of
no directing power except their own. Authority is, in fact, very much
contracted. Even in the direction of ordinary affairs the class to which I
belong has been entirely passed over, and offices have been given to
Annie K., Charlotte M., &c. Well, Mr. Noyes said if what he had written
did not suit he would try again, or he would not write at all; and that I
could take time to think it over before showing them what he had
written.

Oct. 1.

A long talk with Theodore and Ann last evening. More satisfactory
than I expected. They both said they felt good toward me; and I feel a
new purpose to be loyal and a help to them.

Oct. 2.

Mr. Noyes returned from Joppa yesterday, and met me very affectionately this morning. Then this afternoon I went into his room, and
after talking some he said: "It will really be quite a satisfaction to me to
go back to Joppa (he goes tomorrow) knowing that you are feeling good;
I was afraid before that you didn't like me, and were mad at me. I feel
better about you than I ever did before, and I did then, only I thought I
must be terribly sincere, seeing I was going to pass you over. But I think
a great deal of you." "Why, do you?" I asked. "Yes, I do," he answered. "I
think a great deal of your good opinion. I always feel bad, when you feel
bad." And we both wiped tears from our eyes. We had a very affectionate
talk, and I feel more as though I could sacrifice my life to this good old
man than ever before.

Oct. 3.

Asked the Doctor and Ann if I might begin practising. They left me
free to do as I thought best.

Oct. 19.

Nearly two weeks "over my time." Can it be possible I am to have
another child?

H.H. had a hard criticism yesterday, and the fact was evolved that he
is in a quarrel with Mr. Noyes about me.

Nov. 8. — Joppa. —

Came down here last Saturday. I wanted to get away from O.C. for a while, I was so afflicted with nausea, &c. Oh, Edward, <u>Edward</u>! Is this the end? Do you ever think of the mother of your boy? I thank God that I believe in Providence. Were it not so I should find it very difficult to be reconciled to my present circumstances—with child by a man whom I have no love for, and the one of all others whom Edward disliked. But I know there is a God who orders our circumstances, and I believe good will come of the present unpleasant arrangement of things.

Nov. 10.

Returned from Joppa. Talked with Mr. Noyes, and he criticised me some for my feelings toward Mr. Herrick. Thought it a part of the insanity which made me love Edward. Said he was hardly ever so much pleased about anything in his life as when he heard I had started. "It will be the finest child you have had yet, and the one that will give you the most comfort." Talked with Mr. H. afterward, and felt some better.

Nov. 11.

Dizzy and dreadfully sick all day.

Nov. 20.

Nausea still continues, though not quite so unendurable.

Nov. 23.

I ought to mention that in the talk I had with Mr. Noyes about Mr. Herrick, he said he <u>prayed</u> that he might be successful in impregnating me. He looked upon it as salvation.

Mr. Herrick asks me once in a while if I want anything. I generally say, No, but the other day I said I did want some nuts. After a few days he brought in a most munificent supply of English walnuts, filberts, pecan nuts, almonds, and Brazil nuts. I was very much surprised, as I had not thought he was that kind of man.

Dec. 28.

Wrote to Mr. Noyes last evening that I did not like to have him talk as though I didn't belong to him (he having said to me the other morning that I seemed to write more now than I did when he had charge of me), as I had not taken up writing at Theodore's suggestion, and that I had not transferred my allegiance to Theodore, only as they are one. After saying several more things, I said I had had as much as I could do to mow away temptations I had had about Theodore and Ann, which I should like to talk freely with him about sometime, though I could wait, if he thought the right time had not come. He answered quite unexpectedly that he should be glad to talk with me, and I would find he had more to say than I had. Then he asked me to hunt up some facts about Ann.

Dec. 29.

Mr. Noyes met me on the walk this morning, and said: "I have one thing to say to you: I <u>don't like</u> Ann Hobart. I consider <u>her the devil of the Oneida Community</u>." I felt myself turn pale, but I answered that I had long had great doubts of her. Then he took me to his room, and astonished me with the documents which had accumulated already on the subject.

1878

January 2, 1878.

Charles Cragin died at Wallingford this morning. Edward has been at Wallingford. Yesterday morning Mr. Noyes came to my room (the little bedroom around the corner from the Upper Sitting-Room), and said he wanted me to room nearer to him, and he thought also it would be a good ordinance of disobedience to Ann for me to move. I accordingly moved into the second room on the east side of the main avenue from the Hall. Edward, it is said, called at W. ostensibly to see his boy. Frank saw him in New York in November; said he inquired about me and the boy, &c. F. told him I was going to have another child. He asked if it was by Mr. N. F. said, No, but did not tell him who. F. said from his present condition there is no hope whatever of his ever coming back to the Community. Though he has some romantic notions about me, he had no remorse for his treatment of Mr. N. and the Community, and is drifting farther and farther away. The Lord have mercy on his soul!

Jan. 15.

The last two weeks have been crammed full of events, and we have lived at railroad speed. Ann has lost all reputation, and all chance of ever again rising into power; Theodore is deposed, and never can hold the reins again except as he takes his father's judgment of Ann, and can never come in with her. I knew this day must come, but did not expect it so soon.

Jan. 20.

Theodore had a long talk with Helen today, and finding that she felt as most of us do about Ann he said he saw he should have to class her with Tirzah and George. He said George and I were diotrephians, scrambling to get the place held by Ann, and that his father felt about us just as he did. Helen reported the talk to Mr. Noyes, and afterward he came to me twice to tell me that he didn't feel at all about me as Theodore did. On the contrary, he never liked me better in his life. He said the only thing he had against me this long time was that he thought I was somewhat unreliable about Edward, but he didn't feel so even about that now, and it was only in reference to that point that Theodore had any foundation at all for what he said. He said he thought a great deal of the Millers, and Theodore would do the same sometime.

Feb. 28.

I seldom note down anything here; but this winter has been full of events. For six weeks I was extremely busy reporting, copying, getting evidence, and in other ways assisting Mr. Noyes about the judgment of Ann. That judgment is not yet ended, but Ann has begun to confess some, so that what is now done is left pretty much to her own conscience.

Henry Hunter has left worshipping at this shrine, and transferred his allegiance to Alice A. Ann set him last fall at helping her take care of her baby. I thought I divined her motive at the time. She imagined it would be something of a trial to me to lose an admirer. She was mistaken; I was only glad to have him have a friend. My feelings toward him were never of a kind to make me jealous, and I am truly sorry to have him come to grief, and sincerely glad that I am not the one involved.

Dreamed about E. last night. The scene was the Hall, and we seemed to be about to hear a lecture or something of that kind. I went in and took a seat by Carrie B. Looking up after a few moments I saw that I had sat down directly behind E. He soon became aware that Carrie was there, but did not see me. By and by I leaned forward, and whispered: "Edward!" He turned instantly, his eyes meeting mine and melting into that humid expression of unutterable tenderness which I remember so well; then he caught me passionately in his arms, murmuring: "Oh, my precious, precious darling!" and carried me out of the room. The rest of the night my dream was spent in going with him from one place to another trying to find a room where we could talk without interruption. I thought his knees and elbows were patched, and that he said he was not doing so well as he had been.

Mar. 4.

I suffer a good deal in my mind now-a-days. I wish I could show Mr. Noyes all that is in my heart about Edward. I don't see how I am ever to feel differently from what I do. For three years before Mr. Noyes became convinced of the fact I believed Ann to be a dishonest woman; and I feel just as sure that Edward is <u>not</u> dishonest.

Mar. 10.

We are having a series of musical criticisms for the purpose of getting the musicians into such a state that we can have a regular campaign summer in the line of concerts and entertainment for visitors. We began with a criticism of T.R.N.

How strange it sometimes seems to me to be having a child under such circumstances as the present, when I contrast my feelings with what I know they might be under different conditions. Mr. H. and I rarely speak to each other, and nothing in the way of endearment or caressing ever passes between us. He asked me several times to stay with him during the first two or three months; but I told him I would rather not, and now for some time he has said nothing about it. I feel good toward him, and when away from him I think I will treat him with more cordiality the next time I see him; but when he comes about a strange paralysis of feeling comes over me, and I am sometimes at a loss what to say. A strange embarrassment makes me seem colder than ever. I desire to have a good spirit, and I expect things will be better after the child is born.

Mar. 11.

Helen asked me today whether I expected to have Mr. Herrick help me to take care of the baby; said he told her he did not mean to get his heart set on it, as he thought I did not like him, and would probably prefer to have some one else help me. I told her to say to him that no idea of the kind had ever entered my mind, and if he would like to take care of the child, I should certainly prefer to have him rather than any one else; and besides, I expected that when we had a mutual interest like that, it would improve our general relations to each other.

Mr. Woolworth arrived. Queer developments about Ann. She has been writing to Joseph, and is now in Albany with Myron. She would find it difficult to live without the excitement of making a sensation.

Mar. 12.

My musical criticism today. They were kind and sympathetic mostly. The only trouble I have about it is that some spoke of my playing old pieces. I think nobody but a superior genius would have been able to do much different under the conditions which have controlled my musical career. Self-taught, with little chance to hear good music; stopped frequently, and for months and even years, it has been all I could do to retain even what I had.

Mar. 18.

Ann actually left the Community Saturday, and is married to Joseph. Theodore acts perfectly unmanned by the turn events have taken, and finally prevailed on his father to allow him to telegraph and also write to her. I can't help remembering how Theodore and Ann drove Edward out of the Community, and then showed no sympathy whatever for me. I thought when he talked with me last spring he was cruel and hard. He seemed to think I ought to have no more feeling than a machine, and give up Edward without a pang, and consider it good riddance in fact. I could feel a great deal better toward him if his present suffering would make him remember how hard and unfeeling he has been toward others, when going through as great, if not greater, suffering; but it does not seem to have any such effect yet.

Mar. 20.

Mr. Noyes found out that I was feeling bad, (the present affair brought up all my agony about Edward afresh), and he talked with me today about him in the most encouraging way that he has at all since he left. He said that if he could save Theodore and Joseph, he should not be discouraged about Edward, and he would assure me that if any opportunity offered he would do everything in his power to save him. It has seemed so terrible to have him talked of as though he were a reprobate, that I felt today that if I could be assured that Mr. Noyes had hope of him and would do his best to reclaim him, I should not care if I never saw him again in this life.

Mar. 22.

Theodore talks of leaving the Community. He has three children by three different women. I don't see how he could possibly justify such an act, or ever sit in judgment on any one else again for dishonorable neglect of duty.

Mar. 29.

Theodore left the Community today. The struggle with him has been a strange one. He wanted at first to take Marion Burnham with him, and was also very demanding about property matters; but he has finally gone without Marion, and left it to his father to say what he should have. He leaves three children by different women, and claims that it is not his fault, but the fault of the system. What does it all mean? I cannot think that it was any more difficult for him to live here than it is for many of us. The outlook for the future looks very dark for the women, if men can desert their children with so little compunction. Few women could do it. I feel extremely unhappy, and yet there is a certain feeling I have about Mr. Noyes which makes it impossible for me to leave him. I have sacrificed my happiness in this life to that feeling. Sometimes in thinking over all that last experience with Edward, it seems terrible, and I wish that I might have done differently; but I could see no other way then, and if I had a chance to do it all over again, it might end the same, because there are two things I cannot do: <u>I cannot desert Mr. Noyes, and I cannot take George W. away from the Community</u>. No matter what my temptations, or how much I long to be with Edward, I always have to come back to these two fixed facts in my life. So why cannot I accept the inevitable, and be happier? Why waste my life in vain wishes that things might be different? Edward and I can only come together again in one way: he must come back.

Mr. Noyes told me this afternoon that there had been as much fellowship and as little chafing between him and me during this long war, as between him and anyone, unless it was Aunt Harriet. He said he thought I had done splendidly, and he felt proud of me.

Mar. 31.

Mr. Noyes called a meeting this morning, and gave a talk disclosing a new policy which he means to adopt toward deserters. He says he does not consider them reprobates, but on the contrary thinks them better material, so far as efforts at conversion are concerned, than people we know nothing about. Spoke of sending missionaries to them, &c. Mentioned Edward. Is there really hope that Mr. Noyes will change in his feelings toward him? It seems to me that he must do so, or else consider his own son a bad man, for certainly Theodore personally abused him to a degree that Edward never did, and he also revolted at interference of the same kind that Edward did, though Edward bore injustice and law for years, while Theodore only put up with it for a few months.

April 18.

I am in continual torture of mind concerning Edward, and it seems to me I can never have any peace unless I can in some way communicate with him. I suppose Mr. Noyes would think I am quarreling with him if he knew all that is in my mind; but I do not think it is really so. I have never felt as though I could leave Mr. Noyes, and yet I must have some things different about Edward, or I shall go crazy. If he had been treated altogether right, I believe that I should before this time have felt at rest about him.

April 20.

Paul four years old. Put pants and jacket on him for the first time, and Eliza and I took him to ride. He looked very bright, and healthy, and handsome, and I would have given a great deal if his father could have seen him. Paul said to me in the morning: "Mamma, I wish you <u>would</u> ask papa Noyes if he won't go and see my own papa, and talk to him, and bring him back. I want to see him." "So do I," I answered. I had a long talk with John Norton about Edward the other evening, and he told me all he knew about his call at Wallingford four months ago. He met our agent, Bristol, first, and told him that he used to live in the Community, and was obliged to leave under peculiar circumstances; but that it pulled very hard, as he had very dear friends here. Poor boy! poor boy!

April 23.

I have good news to begin my journal with. Aunt Harriet and I had a little falling out last evening. She said to me that Augusta had accepted Mr. Noyes's proposition to consider her going away an experiment, and not make a final settlement, &c. I answered that I was glad, and thought most of those who had gone out previously would have been glad of such an arrangement. I said some more to that effect, and she finally said that if I talked that way I would talk myself out of the Community. It seemed unfair to me for her to speak like that to me, and I spoke to Mr. Noyes about it this morning, and we three had a talk together which brought us nearer together. Aunt Harriet acknowledged that she had misunderstood me, and thought I was criticising the past. She accepted my explanation that I was glad that we could now afford to treat those who went away differently from what we had been able to do in the past. Aunt Harriet said she thought I had my mind on Edward a great deal. "Well," replied Mr. N., "I have given her leave to think of him in quite a different way from what she has done, and I can't very well blame her for that." Then we went on to a very free talk about him, and Mr. Noyes expressed an interest in him, and a hope that he would come back, and said his feelings about him had very much changed. I thought I might as well, while things were so favorable, tell Mr. N. a number of things about Ann's treatment of Edward, which have long troubled me. I accordingly went to my room, and wrote about her misrepresentations of him for three years, and her final sending him away from the Community. Mr. Noyes said he had no doubt it was all true, and that he was convinced that Ann thoroughly abused Edward, and had behaved very wickedly about him. He also said my instinct was undoubtedly true that she was actuated by enmity toward me rather than toward him; that it was her purpose to destroy me, and she knew she could keep me down by abusing the man I loved, better than in any other way. I do thank God that there has come such a change of feeling toward Edward. I believe we shall some day have him back. Mr. N. also said: "It may be (in view of my late theory about women) that I shall find you more or less responsible for his state." "You certainly will," I answered; "I told you so when he went away, and also that he was in no way responsible for my doubts and temptations about you and the Community, for I had them all before I associated with him; but you would not believe me then." "Well," he said, "I couldn't believe it then."

April 26.

A good letter from Mr. Easton showing that he has had communication with James Van, reporting to him that he had received a letter from Mr. Noyes expressing friendly feelings toward all the deserters. Mr. Noyes was very much pleased with it, and said James would tell the rest. —Frank reported that when he saw Edward in N.Y. last November, he felt in him a very soft, tender spirit toward the Community, and that he said not a harsh word about it; he had evidently suffered a good deal, and instead of being hardened, had been softened by it. My prayer is that he may come back to Mr. Noyes.

May 6.

Free concert. Great plans, and ever-expanding, about what we are going to do to entertain visitors this summer. Some of the musicians want me to get at playing as soon as possible after confinement. Frank even said he was almost sorry I was going to have a baby just at this time.

Mary Prindle, who left for W.C. last week, saw Theodore in New York, and wrote me today some things she learned about Edward, the best of which is that he is really out of fellowship with Julia on account of her opposition to the Community. The letter made me feel both happy and sad, and certainly very thankful that he is growing better rather than worse under his trials. I showed the note to Mr. Noyes, and we had a pleasant chat over it. He was very much pleased to learn that Edward had broken with Julia—"that wicked woman," as he called her—and said that now he had found her out, if he ever came back, she would not be able to tempt him away again. He said it would be a splendid thing to have him back to help us in our musical campaign, if he would take hold under him. Mr. Towner also saw Theodore, who told him that Edward said his heart was in the Community, and that he never could marry that Miss Ricker of whom we have heard so much. He also asked Theodore if he supposed the Community would let him see his boy. I have talked quite freely to Paul about his father lately, and he speaks of him very frequently, often saying that he wishes his "own papa" would come back. The other morning he said to me: "I wish my own papa <u>would</u> come back." "I think he would," I answered, "if you would go and ask him." "But I don't know the way to find him," he replied in a plaintive tone; "but if papa Noyes would go with me, then I could ask him." Mr. Towner said he asked him suddenly a few evenings since: "When my papa Inslee comes back, will you be my papa then?" It is wonderful the way things are working, and I have every reason to thank God for his goodness.

May 22.

Moved into the "lying-in" room today.

May 23.

Slept very little last night. The room was so haunted with memories of Edward that I could not get my mind off from him. It seems to me that I <u>must</u> say a few things to him before my confinement. Homer received a letter from him which he was so kind as to show me. I made an extract which certainly shows a good spirit: "May 20.—I was in hopes that you were parentally interested in T's present condition, but they say it is Herrick. I have felt a good deal of pity for you ever since I first heard how you felt about me. If I had known it before the deed was done, believe me, I would never have done it. But I presume it was all for the best, even if we cannot understand it now. I should like very much to see you. Ever yours fraternally, E.P. Inslee."

May 27.

I wrote to Mr. Noyes about three weeks ago requesting that the law which he put on me more than a year ago not to speak to H.H. might be removed, as he had long ago (as I supposed) transferred his affection to Alice, and it seemed to me to keep up a restriction of that kind was a humiliating farce.[58] Mr. Noyes complied. I reported to Alice what I had done, and there let the matter rest. I had no special wish to speak to him, and so said not a word, not even informing him of the change. The law was intensely galling to me, and I resolved I never would expose myself to the possibility of being treated so again. A few days ago he said something to Alice about its being so embarrassing not to be able to speak to me, and she told him that he could, and supposed of course I had informed him; so today he spoke to me, and said he felt just the same as he did a year ago, &c. I told him that we must be very careful indeed in our treatment of each other, and that he had better go on as he was without minding anything about me. He said he had learned a good deal by all he had gone through.

June 4.

Paul stood looking out my window today at the tulip tree which is in blossom, and said: "Mamma, when my own papa comes, won't you ask him to climb that tree, and get me one of those pretty flowers?" The other day he said to me: "I do want to see my own papa." "You must pray to God to send him back," I said. "I do. I did last night," he answered.

I interviewed Rosamond this morning to get information for Mr. Noyes about her experience with Ann in spiritualism.[59] I had no idea of coming across anything personal to myself, and was consequently greatly astonished at a revelation she made of Ann's plans and plots concerning me. She said Ann talked with her about me <u>last summer</u>, showing beyond a doubt that it was her purpose and hope to have me go away from the Community. When Rosamond first perceived her design she exclaimed: "Why, you mean to drive Tirzah away from the Community!" "I don't deny it," said Ann. She said she was <u>determined</u> to have me go, and that she never failed in anything she undertook. Rosamond told her she would fail in this. She went to Rosamond several times after that, and said: "Do you think I can do it?" Rosamond said, "No." "I <u>can</u>, and I will, and I will prove to you that I can." This accounts for many things I felt from Ann during the last four years, and if it is really true, it was a plot of a number of years standing. That was the cause of her persecution of Edward—the hope that I would go with him.

June 6.

Paul said this afternoon: "I dream about my own papa all the time."

"Why, what do you dream?" "I don't really dream anything, only <u>him</u>." "You mean you see him?" "Yes ma'am."

July 10.

Two years ago this evening I saw my dearly beloved Edward for the last time. Although I felt goaded on by an inexplicable impulse to do something desperate, I had no idea then that so long a time could possibly elapse ere I saw him, or that any serious obstacle would ever come between us. God grant that the days of separation may be shortened, for the sake of my darling boy!

On the 6th of June Mr. Pitt left for Newark. I asked Mr. Noyes if word might be sent to Edward about the judgment of Ann, and he told Mr. Pitt to see him and tell him. Before Mr. Pitt left I had a few moments' talk with him about Ann's treatment of Edward, but said not a word about myself or about Paul.

At 3 o'clock on the morning of Saturday, June 8th, I awoke with a pain. I went about my work as usual after breakfast, saying nothing, though the pains grew more frequent. At 10 o'clock I attended a committee, and took notes for nearly an hour. At about 1 o'clock I told my nurses (Belle Woolworth and Mary Velzer) of my probable condition, and also Mrs. Conant, who had promised to be with me. A few moments before 3 o'clock Dr. Cragin was called in, and at 7 minutes past 3 a little girl with dark hair made her appearance. I immediately sent word to Mr. Herrick, who did not know that I was sick. The baby weighs 7 lbs. and 9 oz.

On June 12th I received a note from Mr. Pitt, reporting to me his conversation with Edward, and suggesting that he be allowed to make a visit here. I was horrified to have him write to me, as I knew Mr. Noyes would not like it; but I sent the letter in to Mr. Noyes, and then followed a correspondence between Mr. Noyes and me which lasted several days. It was rather stormy at first, but finally ended in a very satisfactory covenant between us. In the midst of this correspondence Mr. N. received a letter from Edward, asking liberty to visit, and enclosing a letter to me, which Mr. Noyes did not let me have, but wrote me the purport of its contents. He also told me that Edward wrote a letter to me a year ago which he kept from me. When he told me about this letter which came last summer, I was at first glad that he did not let me have it then, because I was under such fearful temptation that I should doubtless have gone to Edward, and implored him to take me. Then after thinking of it a while, I was tempted to feel provoked that Mr. Noyes had dared to interfere with my rights so, and I thought that, had I received E's letter, I should never have had this baby, &c. I went through quite a struggle, but finally saw that my first feeling was the right one, and I wrote to Mr. N. thanking him for not letting me know about the letter at the time.

July 20.

I have had a new feeling come into my heart about Edward lately, which has been quite a comfort to me. I have been able to see that, in spite of everything which has seemed so cruel and unjust in the treatment of Edward, the whole experience has been very necessary to me; and a number of times, instead of complaining: "Oh Lord! How much longer must I endure?" I have found myself praying that God would continue the discipline until he made of me what he wished. I realize that it is one thing to recognize the fact that God arranges our circumstances, but quite another to feel good about it, and contented to have him do as he pleases.

Theodore is here, and we have had several chats together. He seems quite friendly, and we have talked somewhat freely of the problem of life, and of the conditions which we should have chosen to have existed. I told him the experience I have had in regard to temptation to go away from the Community; that although I was under great temptation to do it for several years, and often came to a point where it seemed as though I could not endure the life here a day longer, I always found that an inexpungable feeling which I have toward his father stood in the way; I could not escape from it, however I might try. I told him that that was what held me when Edward went. I felt in giving him up that I sacrificed all hopes of happiness in this life; but I knew that if I went with him the remorse I should feel for having set aside this sense of duty toward Mr. Noyes would embitter my whole existence, so that I considered it better to sacrifice love than conscience and honor. He said that this same feeling toward his father was just what ailed him, and he could not get away from it.

Aug. 2.

About a week ago I wrote to Mr. Noyes about some of the trials I have had with Mr. Towner as Paul's father, on account of his legality, and what seemed to me a lack of love for him. Mr. Noyes had been for some time very much tried with Mr. Towner, and advised me to withdraw Paul from him, and proposed that Mr. Herrick be his father. I proceeded to change the child's sleeping, &c. and talked with Mr. Towner. He was so much offended at my "high-handed outrage" that he made quite a disturbance, and finally went to Mr. Noyes, who advised him to offer himself for criticism. He did so, and after a day or two had a deep conversion. This produced a great change in him which was very satisfactory to Mr. Noyes. He also came to me, and wrung my hand with tears in his eyes.

My soul is sometimes very sorrowful because of the "hope deferred" so long about Edward; and yet I know that God is doing the best thing to save us both. Yet I ask myself, How can he live away from the dear boy whom he certainly loved very dearly? How can he let him grow through all the prettiness of early childhood without seeing him? When I meet Mr. Pitt carrying Doty, or Henry Allen with Grosvenor, my heart aches for my fatherless boy, who longs for a father's love.

Sept. 7.

Arthur Bloom, just before leaving, came to my room to bid me goodbye, and was so affectionate that I was rather taken aback and a little suspicious of him. "Do you intend to make your separation from the Community permanent?" said I. "Yes," said he. "I don't see any other way." "Well then," said I, "if you ever meet Edward, don't you go and prejudice him with your troubles and temptations." "Oh, no," he answered, "I never will. I never will say anything to him to influence him against the Community." About a month ago Edwin Burnham received a letter from Edward, showing that Arthur made an appointment to meet him as soon as he entered the city, and filled his mind with all his own doubts, and made him believe that the Community was likely to break up. Mr. Noyes was dreadfully tried with Edward at first, but after I told him about Arthur's promise to me, and the newspaper attack coming on just then, showing that Arthur was filling the minds of other people with the same ideas he had put into Edward's head, Mr. Noyes seemed to feel better, and in answer to a request from me that I might write to him, proposed that he and Edwin and I all write. Edwin and I both wrote, but he has postponed sending the letters until Theodore gets into a state to be more of a help to him.

Is it possible that I love Mr. Herrick? A strange, sweet magnetism has come between us. What is it? Whence is it? I never could have believed it would be so, and yet I do love him, <u>love him,</u> and find in him a great deal that is pure and noble and high-toned. I hardly know whether he really loves me, though he is very affectionate and kind. He said to me last evening: "You never looked so pretty to me as you have today. Never in all your life have you looked so pretty to me as you have today."

Oct. 27.

There have been some exquisite love passages between Mr. H. and me, and yet there has been trouble too. The case is peculiar, and we feel that the communistic problem is put right in our hands to work out: how to love each other, and yet keep clear from the marriage spirit, and from all appearance of it. We both love others, and the fact that Helen is so involved makes communism absolutely essential, else the misery of the situation will be beyond endurance. If I followed the natural dictates of pride, I would have nothing to do with it; but I cannot do that, and the conviction of truth is so strong upon me that I cannot escape.

Today Mr. Kinsley came to me, burdened with a message which he said came from Paul. Mr. Kinsley is a very old man, shaken and broken with age and infirmity, and yet his soul is so devoted, his manner so earnest, that it seemed almost as though one of the prophets of old had come to me with a message from the Almighty. He said that for three weeks I had been almost continually in his mind. He had a time of prayer and heart-searching, asking God what he should do to rise into more usefulness, and the answer came that he must go and talk with me. He resisted the impression, and put it off again and again, saying that it was not his place to do anything of this kind, and that I might be offended; but he could not get rid of the idea that Paul commanded him to go and talk with me; it was the only answer he could get to all his prayers. This morning the call came again so strongly that he promised Paul he would obey. "Paul wants you," he said; "he wants you to abandon all worldliness, and come entirely over on Mr. Noyes's side, that you may help others to do it. There is need of a great change in order to bring the young into unity with Mr. Noyes's faith, and I have a feeling that if you don't start out and answer this call from Paul, it will not be done. There is not another woman in this Community who can do so much as you can. Mr. Noyes needs you." I told him I had never had any ambition to lead. "I know it," said he, "but those are just the ones for leaders, who do not desire the place."

Nov. 27.

Mr. Noyes wrote a kind letter to Edward, and had me copy it, and send it in my hand-writing. Edward asked again if he might visit, and Mr. Noyes says he does not wish him to do so until he can come back and join the Community again. He told him that he and others earnestly hoped he would return. He advised him to stay where he is at present, and correspond with him.

Dec. 14.

A long letter from Edward to Mr. Noyes, and cold, cruel, and heartless it is. He seems to have no real sense of the position in which he places me and his child. His own self-will is of more consequence to him than our bleeding hearts. He tries to make out that he is really all right, and shows plainly that he has no desire to return unless the government can be changed; yet he says his heart is here, and wishes to be free to visit. While reading the letter my heart sank within me, and I felt very badly for a while; but I went to bed very quietly with a feeling of hope and trust in God. "The Lord gave, he took, he will restore. Blessed be the name of the Lord."

I had a strange experience yesterday. Mr. Noyes was holding a meeting in his room with a few of us who regularly contribute to the "Socialist." He was talking, and I was interested and sympathizing with what he was saying, when all at once my heart gave one of those sickening contractions which drain the very life-blood, and I said to myself in an agony of doubt: "Oh! Is he a crazy enthusiast, who is just experimenting on human beings?" This came so suddenly and so unexpectedly that it seemed it must have been injected into my mind by someone else. I looked at the others—Alfred and Frank and William—and said: "Is it possible that either one of these is thinking like this?" But they all looked innocent of any mockery in their thoughts. Several times during the remainder of the day I wondered about it. When this letter came from Edward, I understood it. Does he still have a mesmeric power over me? It would not take many such letters as the one today to break it forever.

Dec. 15.

Theodore has been very sick for some time. I see him occasionally. He was in my room chatting for a while this evening. He is very friendly, and I feel very sorry for him.

Dec. 23.

Theodore is getting better. He comes into my room quite frequently now in the evening, and talks with me for half an hour or more. He had an inspiration to start the malleable iron business in our foundry, and it has given him new life. He came in this evening, and we had a very pleasant talk. We were speaking of his being leader, and I said: "I see but one thing that really stands in the way." "What is that?" he asked. "Why, your being one with your father, and taking such an attitude toward him as you will wish us to take toward you when you are leader." He made no objection to that; said it should be so, and that he thought he was now practically one with him in most things.

1879

Mar. 21.

How the months fly by without record here! Every day is crowded so thick with events and emotions that volumes might be written. The condition of the Community has been quite distressing of late. There was the raid of the ministers upon us; but that was nothing compared to the internal dissensions.[60] Evil-thinking of the administration and general independence have become more wide-spread and outspoken. C.A. Burt made an attack on Mr. Noyes, and such women as Alice Ackley have become very much disaffected. The agony of the situation comes over me occasionally in waves, though I generally manage to keep a faith-view of things. Today the clouds of discouragement came down pretty heavily, and yet there was a gleam of sunshine in Mr. Herrick's love. For he <u>does</u> love me; he has told me so again and again, and many times his looks and actions have said so more plainly than words. He was in a peculiarly soft state today, his beautiful eyes often filling with tears as some emotion crossed him. He wrote to me this evening: "You cannot begin to tell how beautiful you are to me." I love him very dearly, and am only fearful lest I love him too much, and become too clairvoyant about him. We have had a very sweet honeymoon which has been almost uninterrupted for several months.

(The following account is written here because I have always promised myself to write a novel some day, and I feared if I did not write down some of these love-throes while I am in them, I should forget some of the most poignant sensations which give life to a novel.) Day before yesterday Mr. Hamilton talked with Mr. Herrick, telling him some complaints the business men had made of him, about the farm, &c. I saw he suffered about it, and it of course made me feel very much as though it were myself. That evening he invited Helen; but she was engaged. At first I had just a slight temptation about it, but I immediately said to myself that I had had a pleasant time with him lately, and now I would stand back and let her enjoy him, and feel good about it. (He did not know that I knew whom he asked.) Consequently I began to treat him yesterday morning according to the agreement I had made with myself—to be perfectly kind and respectful, but to withdraw my magnetism entirely from him, so that I should not affect him, nor he me. He, of course, noticed the change, and asked what the matter was, evidently suspecting that I might be in trouble about him. I answered good-naturedly that I was not as selfish as he thought me, and that I was only adopting a new policy, that was all. He laughed, and dropped the subject. That evening he spoke out suddenly in an appealing tone of voice, while the tears fell from his eyes: "O, Tirzah! I wish you wouldn't adopt your new policy just now, while I am in so much trouble. I haven't got <u>anybody</u>—" and then he broke down. "My darling, I won't," I answered with quick sympathy; "but you know I didn't <u>feel</u> any differently toward you?" "Yes, I did know it; but I want you to be as you have been, darling." Then I told him why I had done as I did, and he said it "was very sweet of me," and went out for a walk, from which he returned in quite a different mood. This morning, although he has conquered his difficulty with Otis and others by going to God, and was very soft-hearted, it seemed to me as though he had somewhat withdrawn his heart from me. We have been reading together lately between 4 and 5 "The Lady of the Aroostook."[61] At about 1/4 past three I heard him go through the hall outside my door, and within two or three minutes afterward I had one of my clairvoyant flashes which are so troublesome. I felt that he was having the proposed visit with Helen. I would have given worlds to have felt as I did yesterday morning, but his appeal to me in the evening had swept from me that self-possession, so that I could only suffer. Yet I felt good about it, too, in a certain way, and determined to have a good spirit and behave well with God's help. I went up as usual at 4 o'clock to read. He came in a few minutes late with a flushed face, and proceeded very smilingly to read. He tried several times to caress me, but that I could not bear, and did not respond. He kept stopping to look at me with an expression on his countenance of deep affection, and said some things which would have been very sweet under other circumstances. As it was, it only made my heart ache to have him do so, though I tried with all my might to feel generous. He stopped reading a while before the time, and asked me to go walk with him. "Why—" I began in an objecting tone. "Oh, yes! Let's go," he said. "<u>You</u> may go," I answered, and we started to go down-stairs to my room. He asked what I was going to do, and I said I was going to the kitchen to strain some porridge for Hilda. "Let me go too," he said. "I want to do <u>something</u> with you." So we went down together. After we returned he sat looking at me awhile, and then wrote something on a slip of paper which he handed to me saying: "I couldn't speak it," and then went quickly out of the room. I opened the paper and read: "You cannot begin to tell how beautiful you are to me." Oh, dear! Oh, dear! If he would only have done it some other day. Now it seemed to me his apparent feelings toward me must be all inspired by his real feelings toward Helen. It was terribly humiliating, and yet I hardly could resent it without saying things which would give him a wrong impression of my real purpose of heart about him and her. Still, it was hard, it was hard.

Mar. 22.

He has been most charmingly affectionate all day today, and I have been able to put away my pride, and accept and return his love with simple hearted trust. He spoke of spending the afternoon with me, and we were together several hours.

Mar. 23.

He said some unpleasant things in sport this morning, which made me cry, and then that made him feel very badly.

Mar. 24.

He was saying this afternoon that he had never in all his experience with Helen and me been on so good terms with us both as during the past week, and he thought we were both free from all trouble about the relation. I was a little surprised that he thought so, because I knew that this week I had had my first real trouble about him, and I said enough to set him eagerly at work investigating. I was very sorry I said anything about it, for it would have been so much better to have left it as it was; and now I am afraid he will think I am hopelessly jealous of him. I had noticed that Helen felt unusually well during the last week, and I was glad it was so, and glad that I had been able to conceal my own trouble as well as I had. I ought to have left it so. Why couldn't I?

Mar. 25.

We had a long talk, which, although he said many things which ought to satisfy a reasonable woman, and especially one who has espoused a social theory like ours, made my heart begin to ache in that terrible manner which cannot be adequately described. He said two or three times that it would end the trouble if he should tell me frankly how the case stood; but he thought he had not better. "I don't want to know," I said. I went to bed, but could not sleep. I arose and dressed, and went to the library, where I read till nearly half-past eleven. Then I went in and talked with him again for half an hour, but got no relief. After I went away I began to pray and confess Christ like a drowning man reaching after something by which to rescue himself. After a few moments the terrible physical pain in my heart began to pass away, and I tho't I could sleep. I went to bed, and by confessing Christ and continually bringing my attention back to it whenever it wandered, I went to sleep at about 1 o'clock, and slept until 4 1/2, when I awoke to find that the pain had returned. I tried in vain to sleep, but could not, and so got up shortly after 5.

April 1.

A week of uninterrupted bliss. It is really wonderful how much romance Mr. H. and I have. I need not have written the last few pages, for now that I understand him, nothing he does troubles me. I find I did not really believe him before, when he said that no woman drew his heart from me—that Christ had the first place there. I believe him now, and would not have it otherwise. He tried to find me several times yesterday, but could not, and in the evening expressed a great deal of yearning of heart toward me. "I have felt more love-sick today than any day since I have known you," said he, "and I wanted to cry when I couldn't find you." He said today that I was the greatest luxury he had had since he came to the Community.

Meanwhile, although my heart is comforted about Edward in Mr. Herrick's love, I still have hopes of Edward, and cannot believe that he is a wicked man. Mr. Towner (who has continued to eat with Paul, and to have him sleep in his room, and to pay him a great deal of fatherly attention) is now in a great quarrel with Mr. Noyes, and is acting in more open disobedience to him than anyone ever did. The special point is his sitting by his wife in meeting. I am distressed to have Paul associated with him, and think he might as well have his own father as to be under the present influence. I told Mr. Noyes this morning that I wished to make a final separation between them, and he entirely justified me in doing it, but advised me to act without any reference to him (Mr. N.) in the matter.

April 12.

Mr. Noyes said to me the other day: "I want you to make up your mind that you are to be the mother of this Community. I say to you secretly that this is what is before you." "I never would choose the place," I said. "Neither would I," he answered; "but we must do it, and I shall keep at you till you do—till you get so you can master all these young folks. I see that it happens over and over again, that when I have any great move on hand, like dealing with Ann, Mr. Towner, Theodore, and so on, <u>you</u> are right in the midst of it, and it means something."

April 22.

Mr. H. and I cleaned my room today, and had a charming time. Then in the afternoon we had an exquisite experience which seemed like a baptism of heavenly purity and continence. It put a new quality into our love.

April 26.

Mr. Herrick has at last divulged to me the true state of things between him and Helen, and all that seemed so strange and contradictory and inconsistent in his behavior at times is explained. He said several times two or three months ago that he loved us equally, and could not tell which he loved best. I could see how a man might find it difficult to tell between two sisters which he loved best—especially when he had known and loved one a long time before knowing the other; but how it was possible that there should be the same kind of glow, magnetism, and ardent attraction between him and her that there has been between him and me I could not understand. My instincts told me it was not so, and yet his words often persuaded me that it must be so. Thus the suffering I have had has been caused by the inability to prove the truth or falseness of my instincts, which, in such matters, I had supposed almost infallible. I was sometimes perfectly bewildered, dazed; I was at sea with no compass. All ordinary calculations failed. My reason is now satisfied. I respect his faithfulness to Helen, and his determination that I should get no advantage over her while I might not make a good use of it. He does not now say that he loves me better, nor do I wish it; but he shows me very frankly that he feels that inspiration has led him in loving me, and that I understand him and am nearer his heart than any other woman. I should be afraid of this did I not know that he loves Mr. Noyes far more than me, and that he would instantly leave me at a word from him.

May 8.

Found after meeting last night that Mr. Towner had taken Paul to sleep with him. Felt disturbed about it, and asked Mr. H. what I should do. He went to see Mr. Noyes, and when he returned said Mr. N. thought we ought not to leave the boy there, and that he had been to Mr. Towner's room and told him that Paul's mother did not wish him to sleep there. He waited about fifteen minutes, and then went to Mr. T's room, and told him he had come for Paul, and carried him to his room. Mr.

Towner came to me at breakfast this morning, and said he should like to see me in my room. He talked for some time very reproachfully, and showed considerable emotion. He called me cruel and heartless. Finally he said the matter was one of such importance that he thought we should each choose a friend to meet with us and talk it over immediately. He chose William Hinds, and I Mr. Herrick. We started out to hunt them up. When I found Mr. H. we both went up to tell Mr. Noyes before returning to my room. Mr. Noyes advised me to remain in his room, and let Mr. H. bring the interview to a close as quickly and peaceably as he could. He did so in a way that Mr. N. admired very much. Mr. Towner afterward went about looking for me, and so Mr. N. put me in his bedroom, and kept me prisoner several hours. — Mr. Noyes has set me to looking after Ormond — reading with him, and so on.

May 11.

I could write volumes about our romance; but I shall only tell occasional incidents. I gave him the first tea-violets that bloomed, and he wrote me a pretty verse in reply. Today I gave him this:

> You are so near — so near and dear —
> My life in yours so deeply dwells,
> That love has banished every fear,
> And peace I feel that no tongue tells.

He answered:

> My life in Him I deeply hide
> Who taught us both to safely love;
> In Him in peace we now abide,
> And rapture thrills us from above.

May 12.

Paul was not well last night, so we took care of him and Hilda together. A wonderful, <u>wonderful</u> episode. We experienced the unutterable. A long nap this morning, and then the "lovers' chase."

May 15.

Mr. Noyes, Mrs. Waters, Mr. Herrick, Ormond, Geo. W., Humphrey, and I went to Joppa this afternoon. The chemistry between H. and me was disturbed at first, but the trouble soon passed off.

May 16.

Mr. Noyes asked me about two weeks ago to read to Ormond, and help to civilize him. That was why he took me to Joppa with him. O. seems to be actually in love with me, and is the purest piece of nature I ever encountered. H. and I had quite a magnetic time this morning, and then this evening we went to the arbutus field with Ormond and the boys. I made up my mind at the start that I should give my attention to H., as Ormond had occupied most of my time. As we approached the ground a charming vista into the past opened to H. and me—so vague and intangible at first that we could hardly grasp it, but very sweet. He said it was sure it could have been no one else. When we returned O. showed me that he was jealous. Mr. Noyes says he has had the jolliest time here he ever had in his life, and we have laughed a great deal. Home tomorrow.

May 20.

A strange thing happened to me last night. I went into Mr. N's room after meeting, to tell him that Ormond was going to have a visit with Aunt Harriet. We had a pleasant chat, and he asked me to come and see him in the morning, and also to get him some lunch. I had been quite heavy-hearted all the evening, and went to bed soon afterward. At six o'clock in the morning I went into Mr. N's room, and he greeted me with: "Well, you have kept me hanging by the gills pretty well." "Why, it is just six," I said. "But I expected you at 5." "Did you? You didn't tell me." "Besides, I did not get that lunch." I started up in bed horrified and amazed, and exclaimed: "That was dreadfully naughty; but I forgot it." He said he thought it very strange, as he never knew me to forget anything before, and he feared at first I might be under some excitement. "No," I said, "it was just the contrary of that. I was much depressed." Well, he said he waited and waited, and thought about me, and came to the conclusion that the bad principalities over the Community would be only too glad to get between him and me, and I must be aware of the game that was going, and escape from any snare that was set for me. "So I did not feel offended at you at all," he said. "Then you don't lay it up against me?" I asked. "Not a bit," he answered; "let's forget it." Then we had a nice time. I never saw such God-like forgiveness and forgetfulness of a wrong. Before I left he said: "And I see that you are a true daughter to me. Your tastes are like mine, and you like the same things that I do."

May 22.

Was in Mr. Noyes's room just before his time to go to the Turkish bath with Jamie, and he asked me to go into the bedroom, where he said he had an exquisite time, and repeated: "You are a true daughter to me."

In the afternoon he said: "I take solid comfort with you now-a-days." I take care of Jamie's clothes. Cornelia asked me, and I consulted Mr. N. He said it would be a good thing.

A slight incident between Homer and me Tuesday evening in the steward's room, which led to an explanation yesterday afternoon. We talked in the office-bedroom for an hour. I didn't mean to cry; but something in his tone wrung the bitter tears right out of me, and I threw aside pride, and reproached him with deserting me. He thought he was the one who was deserted, but after some things I said admitted that he might have been mistaken, and we came the nearest touching hearts that we have for two years. I told him I should hold on to all that was good in our old love, whether he did or not.

June 2.

Mr. H's criticism. Not much. We were advised not to cause remark by the appearance of the marriage spirit. We do love each other wonderfully. — Mr. Noyes talked with me about William's and Mr. Towner's course, and said if they did not change, he should make a new will and put them out of the inheritance of any authority. He also said, if he could not get Theodore to do as he hoped, he had another successor in mind, and that was George Miller. He told me to tell no one what he said; "but if I did not write this will before I die, you are witness that I have said it."

Referring to the affair that happened between him and me about my forgetting his lunch he said: "I had no business to ask it of you anyway. I had no right to make you a servant to me."

June 8.

Hilda's birthday, and Jamie and I took her in the little carriage to the "Island." All the way along we recalled the many charming episodes we have had together since her birth. She has been a blessing to us every day that she has lived. If it had not been for her we should never have known each other, and we should have both missed a great happiness. We referred to a charming walk we took last winter, early in January. We tramped a long distance across the meadows through knee-deep snow; but were so absorbed in each other that we never thought of fatigue. Nearly all the way I told him the story of "Miss Rovel." "That walk was just as full of magnetism as it could be," said Jamie.

June 10.

"What a year of romance it has been!" said J. this evening. "I never had such a romance in my life, and I never had such uninterrupted happiness in loving any one." "Neither did I," I answered. The story of our romance ought to have been written, and it would fill a volume; but the reason why I did not write during the winter and early spring was because I was often perplexed, and did not know whether what <u>seemed</u> was real or not. I know now that it was all real—and even more than I then thought. "Was there not a long time when you were afraid to love me?" "Yes," he answered. "And you did not dare let me see that you loved me as much as you did?" "Yes, that is so. There were tremendous principalities determined that we should not come together."

June 11.

I practise from 11 till 1 at the cottage. Jamie comes down frequently and plays with me, or listens to me and criticises my playing. Today I asked him to criticise "The Two Angels"; but when I turned around he was weeping, and said that I did it beautifully. It is a continual wonder to me that we two, who thought ourselves so incompatible, should find ourselves really better adapted to each other than we ever were before to any one. It is true. We are constantly remarking upon the marvelous way in which we "fit" each other. "Nobody <u>ever</u> drew me out so much as you have," he said.—He took Helen and me for a boat-ride with the babies this evening, and we had a pleasant time.—I have times of sitting and loving him all by myself, and love him so that my heart burns within. Sometimes I run down to the office just to see him and touch him a moment, and we glow to each other in the perfect radiance of love. This afternoon his love seemed so beautiful to me that I felt as though it were selfish for me to have so much of it, and I wanted others to know what a lover he is.

Frank and I are to practise together again when we have drilled in private. Mr. Noyes asked Frank to play with the piano, and F. says he told him he should prefer to play with me.

June 13.

Jamie and I were together last night, and were both most unexpectedly overcome. He was somewhat anxious as to consequences, and ran for a syringe.[62] We would both consider it a terrible calamity to have an accident of that kind happen, and cannot believe that God will let it. We talked about it some today, and agreed that we will each speak at such times, so that the other can know just what is liable to take place. I am afraid I have more of his society than I deserve. He is so sweet and dear to me that I long to have him appreciated by others. My love for him has grown constantly during the last two months. "What a continual crescendo our love has been all this year!" said he the other day.

June 14.

Mr. Noyes proposed today his privateering scheme. He says W.A.H. has steadily sought to break down respect for the ascending fellowship until now the social condition of the Community is very much that of a grab-game. It is his undying faith that in a grab-game the righteous will beat the wicked, and he resolved he would set the men who are loyal to him to attracting all the love they could from the young women and girls. He gave rover's license to Jamie, Homer, Frank, Edwin, and George E.

June 16.

Jamie went to New York suddenly last evening on business about his youngest sister, Louise. An unpleasant occurrence took place between us while packing his satchel, which made us both miserable all the remainder of his stay. He went away with a sad face, and I lay awake a great deal with the heart-ache. It was really all a misunderstanding, and there was no real cause for either of us to be offended at the other. I have felt dreadfully all day till late in the afternoon, when I got a view of my own pride which helped to remove all bitterness from my heart toward him, and then the sun began to shine. O my darling! How terrible if anything should happen to you when we parted thus!

June 19.

We did not hear a word from Jamie till this morning. I have suffered a great deal since he has been gone.

June 20.

Home again, and so glad to see him.

June 23.

The political condition here grows worse and worse, so far as outward signs go. Myron, who has lately come on a visit, told me yesterday that he has got a view of the situation which makes him feel very anxious. He says there are certainly folks inside the Community who would use the law against Mr. Noyes. Mr. Noyes left here in the night with Myron for parts unknown. The notification that parties outside are resolved to arrest him, and the knowledge of the bitter feeling toward him in the Community made him consider it best to go away. It has been a rather quiet day, so far as outward manifestations go, but you could feel great surges of feeling rushing in the undercurrents. Those of us who are loyal have had meetings, and have consulted together a great deal. Mr. Noyes wrote yesterday the codicil to his will which I mentioned on the 2nd.— There is perfect harmony between Jamie and me.

June 28.

Our life (Jamie's and mine) has been during the last four days a poem of exquisite beauty. He has said so many sweet things to me that I cannot even remember them all. "How wonderful, how strange it is!" he has often said, "this magnetism between us. No matter what happens, still it flows on, and is renewed every morning." We strolled about in the garden in the evening, and he looked down at me so tenderly, and said: "Dear! dear! How strange it is! I shall certainly fall in love with you (playfully). You quicken my circulation and send the thrills right through me." This afternoon I went to the office a moment, and got caught there in the rain. I had my white dress on, which J. likes very much (he calls me his little bride in it), so I waited for the rain to stop. Jamie and Helen were working at their desks, and he kept glancing at me when he could do so without observation. After a while he went to the house and brought me my black dress, and had me change in the inner office. He took Helen up with an umbrella, and came back for me. There was a wonderful glow and ache between us. We seemed all aflame. We hurried to the house, and then he wanted me to come to his room. Ecstasy, but alas! we went just too far. He says he has wanted just such a friend as I am ever since he came to the Community, and that I understand him better than any woman—even his wife.

June 29.

Myron returned this morning with good news of Mr. Noyes's health and spirits, though he does not tell us where he is. Mr. Hamilton called a meeting of a number of us with him at 6 1/2, and we continued in session for two hours. Afterward a very pleasant time with Myron.

Jamie and I keep in constant rapport, and it does seem as though nothing in the world could come between us.

July 4.

A wonderful day of magnetism with my beloved. In the morning, in the afternoon, and at night. We seemed to be absolutely one. "I don't believe there is another couple in the house who enjoy such rapture as we," he said. He finished yesterday reading to Helen and me a charming story, "Signor Monaldini's Choice," and he told me that in the most powerful chapter of the book Camilla, the heroine, reminded him continually of me.[63]

July 14.

Oh, this living in communism is terrible, <u>terrible</u>! I do not know whether I can stand it. J. and I talked till half-past 1 last night. Today he had a frank talk with Helen, and she with Homer, and then she came to the Piano Cottage and talked with J. and me together. Afterward he and I passed through quite a tragic scene. In the evening he asked me to ride to Oneida with him and the baby. It was quite pleasant until we were within a mile or so of home, when he said, obliviously, some things which almost broke my heart, so that I wept all the evening.

July 15.

He said to me this morning: "If I had never had a baby in my life, I would rather have one by you than by any woman in all the world; and if I could have but one, I would choose to have that one by you." I know he meant it to comfort me, but it did not.

July 16.

It is marvelously strange what savage attempts are made by unseen diabolical spirits to separate us. The control has passed off, and we are in exquisite rapport again—even reaching new heights this afternoon.

I must mention a delightful stroll we took together to the mill this morning, I with my hands clasped round his arm, and both of us in a glow of magnetism. "Is this special love?" said he. "Yes," I answered, "it is special, but not exclusive. There's a difference, you know." And that is the fact about it. I do not write these things here because the attraction is an ordinary specialty, but because it is a romance which we both recognize as a gift from God, and being such is full of a divine beauty the aroma of which I would fain imprison here, that in years to come we may again inhale its sweet fragrance. I know that Jamie is a universal lover. He first loves God, then Mr. Noyes, then all women who would make themselves brides of heaven; and I have no thought of appropriating to myself either his affection, or the beautiful words which express it.— Returning from the mill we stopped in the flower garden, where I picked a lovely jessamine, and as we parted, he going toward the office, I gave it to him and said: "That is to remind you that you are in love—or that <u>I</u> am." "Yes," he answered, "I am in love."

July 18.

We had a long, strange talk in the cooling-room of the Turkish bath this morning. I hardly know what ailed him; but he seemed to wish to reassure me of his love, again and again promising never to do anything knowingly that would give me pain. "But you must not refrain from doing what you would like to do," I said, "just to save me from suffering." "There is nothing I could have in the world that would be good enough to compensate me for hurting you," he answered earnestly. "I cannot put a knife into your heart." There were many other things he said—very, very sweet.

July 19.

E.H.H. invited me last evening, and when Olive first asked me I thought I could not possibly do it, and excused myself. When I told Jamie afterward he did not like it, and thought it would have been better if I had gone. I went into the library, and while writing there tried to feel good about recalling the answer I had sent to E.H.H. After a while he stopped at the door and bade me good-night with a very pleasant smile. This was so different from the way he used to take such refusals that I immediately felt as though I could go. I stepped up behind him and slipped my hand through his arm, and said: "I will come and see you a little while, if you would like to have me." He was much surprised and pleased, and I never knew him to be more enthusiastic or affectionate than during this visit. I ran up-stairs afterward to tell Jamie that I "repented and went."

I have been preparing to go to Joppa this afternoon. While in my room this forenoon Mr. Kinsley came in, and said he had not been to see me for some time because he was afraid I might think he claimed too much attention. I said I had not thought so. He asked if he might kiss me. I answered, "Of course he might," and put my arms around him, and returned his embrace. "That's right! Come close to me," he said. "Now I'm going to feel free to love you all I've a mind to. Mayn't I?" "Yes, I hope you will," I answered. "I appreciate your love very much." "I'm an old man," he said, "and didn't know but I might obtrude; but 'once a man and twice a child,' so I can be a child again, and love." He asked me to kiss him again, and said: "There! I can let you go now." I told Jamie, and he was greatly pleased.

July 20. Joppa.

Came down with Manly, Orrin, Florence, and E. Loveland. It has seemed to me sometimes lately that I should die if I could not escape for a while from the wearing life at O.C. I have not been so thin since I was a child as I am now. My weight is only 95 lbs., and it is trouble and worry of mind that does it. I shall expect to gain down here, and already feel hungry and dull, so far as super-sensitiveness of feeling is concerned.

Jamie said he would come and see me if he could, and I hope he will.

July 21.

The three young men returned this morning, leaving Ellen W., Florence, and me alone. The weather is perfect.

July 23.

Dear Jamie came down in a carriage for me this morning, and we started for home at about 3 in the afternoon. Although it rained several times we had a delightful ride of some more than three hours. He told me when he came in the morning how much he had missed me. Gained 5 lbs.

July 24.

The committees chosen by Mr. Noyes have been accepted. I learned last evening that Mary V. said that her "party" were so "tickled that Mr. Herrick, Tirzah, and Alfred Barron were not on the Committee, that they could put up with almost any one!"

Aug. 1.

A marvelous time of magnetism these last three days. This evening after reading till 10 1/2 we lay a while in each other's arms, when he said: "Isn't this delicious? How nice it would be for you to sleep here!" So I went down and got my night-dress. Then again we lay clasped in each other's arms while waves of heavenly ecstasy rolled over us. Wonderful! <u>Wonderful</u>! But when we tried to intensify our happiness by drawing nearer together the exaltation passed away. We fell asleep afterward, however, and once when I rose on my elbow an instant he sprang up and caught me in his arms, calling me by the most endearing names, and repeating again and again that he loved me, <u>loved</u> me.

Aug. 10.

Aunt Harriet and Mr. Hamilton both talked to Jamie some about having the "marriage spirit" toward me. He acknowledged that he loved me very much, but explained to them some of Mr. Noyes's directions to me, which seemed to justify more or less specialty between us. They were both very good-natured, and only wanted to talk with us as friends without offering any criticism.

Aug. 20.

A pleasant ride to the Cascades with Alfred, Helen, Mr. Bradley, and Paul. I ought to mention here the constant and growing friendship there has been between me and Alfred for more than a year. He is very confidential with me—more so than any man ever was who was not a lover—and I have enjoyed very much my companionship with him.

Aug. 24.

Found a sealed envelope in my P.O. box; opened it, and took from within a square piece of white birch bark, freshly cut from the tree, on which were cut some initials almost obliterated by time. In an instant I tho't I knew who put it there, where it came from, and what it meant. Seven years ago the 23rd of September Homer and I walked to a beautiful wood near Sconondoan, and he cut our monogram on a tree under which we romanced.[64] I guessed that this was that cutting.

Aug. 25.

Met Homer this noon, and he gave me a conscious smile, so I said: "Did you go to ride yesterday?" "Yes," laughing. "Did you go over there?" pointing. "Yes." "What made you cut it out?" "I thought perhaps you would like to see it." We agreed to walk there next month on the anniversary of that day.

There is a continual romance between Jamie and me, and I grow larger-hearted about him too all the while. For one thing, I feel as though I perfectly understand him now, and trust him implicitly.

Aug. 26.

A proposition read from Mr. Noyes tonight in meeting, which was like the explosion of a bomb-shell. It was that we give up complex marriage, and live as celibates, with freedom to marry for the same reasons given by Paul in the 7th of 1st Cor. It was decided that this proposal should take effect Thursday morning at 10 o'clock. Fortunately I am just through.

Aug. 27.

Slept with Jamie. A pleasant visit with E.H.H. at 2 o'clock. He had such a beautiful spirit that I told Jamie afterward that I would rather have had this meeting with him (E.H.H.) than to have had a romantic reunion with Homer—pleasant as that would be. I of course could not help thinking about Homer a little, now that complex marriage is ended perhaps forever, and I thought more of it just now because, as things have progressed lately between us, it was not unlikely that we might some-time—sometime—come together again. Well, we met in a friendly way several times in the afternoon and evening, chatting confidentially about his plans with others. Just before meeting I ran down-stairs to get a lemon for Jamie, and of course started in search of the steward. Passing by the outside bath-room I caught a glimpse of Homer, and so asked him. He had not quite finished dressing, but said he would go in a minute. I can hardly tell how it happened, but there seemed to be a subtle fire between us, and before we barely knew it he hurried me into the inside bath-room, where we—

Thursday, [Aug.] 28.

A "good-bye" with Jamie in my room between 9 and 10.

Sept. 10.

There has been considerable agitation on the subject of marriage during the last week. Jamie said to me this afternoon with tears in his eyes and voice: "O, darling! Don't you go and leave me, and marry Edward Inslee. If you want to break my heart right in two, you will do that. It will tear a great piece of me away; as much as a hundred pounds of me will go with you. I would be willing to share you with him, if he should come back, and I would let you make the division between us; but I can't have you go." I begged him not to talk so.

Sept. 20.

The excitement about marriage has somewhat subsided. There seemed to be an anxiety and impatience on the part of many to get their relations of that kind settled. Although there has been great magnetism and attraction between J. and me, we would not think of marrying with-out Mr. Noyes's approval and desire to have us; yet it was pleasant to have him say the other day: "If I only thought of what I would *like* to do, I would marry you tomorrow. I should deliciously like to marry you." He said also that he did not think there was another couple better, and few as well, adapted to derive happiness from the relation as are we.

I ought to mention that Frank and I have been practising with all our youthful ardor for about two months, and are making good progress. We play some thing every Sunday evening after meeting. Last Sunday was the fifth week since we began.

I was made melancholy by fearing that Edward is likely to marry. They say he is courting a young lady. I should feel now comparatively well about his marrying (considering the situation) if I could have one talk with him.

Helen went to Wallingford about two weeks ago to spend two months, and I am taking her place in the office. Homer came to me the other day in the dining room, with one of his peculiar smiles on his face, and said: "I think if you would work somewhere else than in the office, the amount of human suffering among the clerks there would be very much reduced." Jamie thought that was pretty smart.

Sept. 30.

We think sometimes we are not first-rate celibates. We don't transgress, but we get very much wrought up, and go very near the edge of the abyss.

Oct. 5.

George Henry has been here on a visit of three days.[65] He left yesterday noon. I had two short talks with him, and he seemed just like his old self. He looked and acted as though his affection for me was still unchanged, although all that he said was perfectly decorous. He told some very favorable things about Edward, whom he saw a week ago today. He said he was the most of a communist of any one he met, and that he would give worlds to come here. I did not ask him any questions about him, but stopped his telling me about him by saying: "There is a great deal I should like to ask you about Edward, but I have promised myself I will not." He reported to others that there was not a particle of truth in the rumor that Edward thought of marrying. I was very glad to hear that. Yesterday morning I received a very insulting note from Mr. Burnham, ordering me to keep out of George Henry's way, and not to speak to him again. I showed it to Edwin, who was very indignant, and advised me to not mind a word about it. The only feeling I had was one of contempt. I did speak to G. again, cautioning him not to place entire credit in anything which was told him about me, and was interrupted by his mother, who fairly took hold of his coat to get him away, and said to me: "I wish you would let him alone." I did not answer her. I was greatly puzzled by her anxiety, and supposed she was afraid that I would influence him favorably toward Mr. Noyes. The idea that she could be afraid that he would love me seemed too absurd to think of, considering the difference in our ages, and also the fact that I have children by two other men whom I should of course have an interest in prior to any that I might feel in him. But I have learned since G. went away that he felt very badly about me, and had a talk with his mother in which he cried bitterly, and said that his getting in love with me seemed to have burnt out his capacity for loving any one else; that there was a girl in Baltimore who thought everything of him, but he couldn't love her; and that he knew he was a fool to think of marrying a woman with children by three different men, but he couldn't get over his feeling about it.

Oct. 10.

Edward has been to Cozicot, and was pleasantly received by Mr. Woolworth and others. Glad.

Oct. 13.

Jamie left for W.C. and New York.

Oct. 16.

Letters from Wallingford tell that Edward has been there on a visit of several hours this week (on the 14th) by George Killer's invitation. The first man he met was Mr. Herrick, and as the family were about starting off on a nutting expedition they invited him to go. The wagon being crowded Edward held Mr. Herrick in his lap. What a situation for a novelist to work up! Everybody spoke well of him; said he was soft-hearted, and wanted to come back to the Community.

Oct. 18.

Jamie returned this afternoon. I ran up-stairs and hid behind the door, and when he came in a moment after we met in the most affectionate manner. He embraced me rapturously, calling me his precious darling, and said I was a hundred times the nicest thing he had seen all the while he was gone. We had a charming evening with the baby, and he said he wanted very much to marry me while he was in New York. "Would you like to be Mrs. Herrick?" he asked. I told him I should consider it a great honor to be his wife.

I ought to mention that Homer, who also went to N.Y. and W.C., returned last evening, and came up-stairs, and talked with me for an hour very affectionately.

Oct. 19.

Jamie spent two hours this afternoon with me in a lawyer's office, investigating the question of his own freedom, a number having expressed doubts about his divorce having left him [at] liberty to marry. Sophie's plea for divorce was desertion, and in cases of absolute divorce we found that the defendant can remarry, except under the charge of adultery.[66]

Oct. 24.

We had quite a solemn talk last evening about withdrawing more from each other. We have been so swept forward by the power of the attraction between us that we have hardly known what to do, but we made up our minds that we would stand a little farther apart, in order that we might see more clearly what God wishes us to do about marrying. We, of course, felt pretty sober this morning, and I did not go to the office. I was sitting in my room writing at 10 o'clock when in Jamie came holding out a letter which he received by the morning mail from J.H.N. I had not the slightest idea what it could be about, and my heart almost stood still when I read these words: "No shade of doubt as to your faith and faithfulness to Christ and to me has place in my thoughts of you. As to your intimacy with Tirzah, I am not afraid of its running into the marriage spirit. You and she both are called with an effectual calling to a higher marriage, and he that called you will take care of you. I should not care if you were ceremonially yoked."

We were very joyful over it—it was such a quick and unexpected answer to our quandary of last night. Jamie wrote to Mr. Noyes about two weeks ago (without telling me) that he was very intimate with Tirzah—perhaps more than he would like, if here, and asked him to advise him, expecting he would perhaps tell him to go to Wallingford; when, instead, he made him free to marry! Altho' we had such an enthusiastic talk over the matter, I didn't suppose we should do anything about it for a long time.

Mr. Kinsley came to me yesterday, and said an irresistible impulse had come upon him to ask me not to marry; he felt peculiarly about it. "Do you feel differently about me marrying," said I, "than you did about George or Frank, or than you would about Helen?" "Yes, there is no one else in the Community that I have the same feeling about."

Oct 25.

Jamie and I were standing by the stairs at 1/2 past 4 this afternoon near the Council door, and a number of people passing in there in quick succession he asked what was up. "An extra meeting of the Council," I answered. "What!" he exclaimed. "Let's put in our application." "Why, would you?" I demurred. "Yes," he answered vehemently: "I would by all means." And off he went for a paper. He could not find one, so I went and got one for him. Then we sat down up-stairs, and talked and acted in a kind of whirlwind of excitement. He was for putting the matter right through; but I said at first it seemed as tho' I could not do anything till I had either seen Edward or written to him. Meanwhile we both signed the paper. Then he started up and said: "I'll run down and put in this application, and then we can talk afterward." I assented, scarcely thinking of the consequences. He came back in a moment, and said he marched right in before them all, and handed it to the Secretary. We talked for some time, and he says he sympathizes with my writing to Edward, and seeing him too, after we were married. Our application made a great sensation in the Council, but a greater one still in the family meeting, where it was read in the evening. Nobody dreamed of such a thing. Those like Frank, who knew the most about it, had no idea we should act so precipitately. The announcement was like a bomb-shell in their midst. Some said they were thunderstruck. People generally have supposed that Jamie would be one of the last to marry. Mrs. Ackley felt pretty badly about it on Edward's account. I cannot, of course, help having a good deal of feeling and thought with reference to him about this move; but so long as it is so hopeless that Mr. Noyes will ever sympathize with my marrying Edward, I believe I shall be a happier woman to have the heart-bleeding which I have had in that direction forever stopped. Jamie and I are wonderfully mated. He says he believes I am the best mate for him in the whole world. I cannot tell what wrenchings my heart would be subjected to if I saw Edward; but as things are now I feel I should do more cruel wrong to leave Jamie for Edward, than to marry him and cut myself off from Edward. It would perhaps be hard to choose between these two men if they both had Mr. Noyes's approval, and both wished to marry me. I should probably take the one who, I thought, wanted me the most. But there are many reasons why, as things are, I should choose to be Jamie's wife. My conscience toward Mr. Noyes, and my faithfulness to communism, are in that direction; and then, really, I have had so much freedom with him that he has got deeper into my life than E. did —and yet, and yet—I had hoped—hoped, that sometime I might once more be folded in those strong, tender arms which I remember so well. If he still loves me any, he must wish that he had stayed by the Community.

Oct. 27.

The opposition has already begun. Frank advised Mr. Herrick to fortify himself by getting a copy of the divorce decree, as Towner, W.A.H.,

Mr. Burnham and others are bound to obstruct, casting doubt on the validity of his divorce. Jamie wrote to Baltimore this morning for a copy of the decree <u>at once</u> enclosing $5.00.

Oct. 28.

Helen returned from W.C. this evening, and feels well about this proposition. She is comforted in Homer's love for her, which is immense. It seems a little queer to me sometimes to have him speak to me about her in the way I used to know of his speaking about me to others. We three had a very pretty meeting in her room this evening, he putting his arms around both of us, and acknowledging there was not left a trace of bad feeling toward me in his heart. In the Council yesterday W.A.H. proposed putting a committee of lawyers over Mr. Herrick to see that his divorce was all straight. Frank stood up for Jamie, and said he did not think such a course would be delicate or brotherly toward Mr. H. I never saw Jamie more roused than he was today. He said if they snatched me away from him he should growl as he never growled before—he felt like a lion, &c. Once he stepped over to my desk and said very earnestly: "You won't go and marry Edward till you know whether I can marry or not, will you? Promise me, promise me."

Oct. 29.

Mr. Inslee went to Frank to entreat that Edward's feelings be considered tenderly in regard to my marriage, and Frank brought up the matter in the Council today. They appointed Frank and Helen to confer with Mr. Herrick, Mr. Inslee, and me about it, with power to do what we agreed on. I assured Mr. Inslee that I had not thought of being married without first writing to Edward.

Oct. 30.

My thoughts were on Edward a great deal today, and I felt very heavy-hearted. Mr. Herrick tried to find out what the matter was, and about 6 o'clock in the evening I tried to tell him the trouble, attributing it to my feelings about Edward. "There," I said, "I've told you like a dutiful wife." "And like a dutiful husband," he replied, "I will tell you that Edward Inslee has been over at the W.P. factory all the afternoon." Of course I immediately understood my day's emotions. Mr. Herrick told me that Edward came to the shop about 2 in the afternoon, and sent word over to know if he could come here. Mr. Hamilton sent Mr. Inslee back to advise him to go back to New York without coming here. Edward was docile, and allowed Charles Marks to take him to Oneida [Depot] at 6 o'clock. I felt quite hurt and somewhat indignant at his being sent away so without a word being sent to me, and I told Mr. Herrick and Frank. I said that I thought I ought to have seen him, and I still thought I ought to do so before I married. They sympathized with the way I felt, and Aunt Harriet said she thought I ought to have seen him by all means, and she believed John would have had us under the circumstances.

Oct. 31.

Between 9 and 10 word came from Theodore at W.P. that Edward remained at Oneida over night, feeling pretty sore about being sent away. He still asked permission to come, but promised to go if there were serious objections. Theodore thought Mr. Herrick and I ought to take the responsibility of dealing with him. I said I wished him to come. Everybody else that was consulted said that was the only humane course. Mr. Hamilton agreed, and so Frank went for him. He arrived a little after 12, and I met him alone in my room with Paul. I found him the same tender and true lover that he always was, and as faithful to me in thought and act as ever man was to woman. He said he came by one of those sudden impressions which he used to have that I wanted to see him. We talked over the past and the present in a free and loving manner. Although the thought of my marrying another is distressing to him, he behaves in a noble and manly spirit about it. He says it has been his one object in life to be reunited to me, and that now that object is gone he cannot tell what he shall do. I played with him awhile at the Cottage in the afternoon, he having brought his beautiful cornet. He would never have known Paul, but they seemed to take to each other as though they had always been together.

Nov. 1.

I have talked with Edward a great deal yesterday and today. He asked me if I married only from duty, and I told him, No, that I loved Mr. H.; that he had won my heart by his kindness and goodness. "Then you are choosing between us two men, and if you love him more than you do me, I have no right to say anything." I told him that I still loved him as I always had, but that I loved Mr. H. too, and if they both wished to marry me, and had equally Mr. Noyes's approval, it would be very hard for me to choose between them, and that I should probably take the one who, I thought, wanted me the most; but that he knew me well enough to believe that I could never be happy to marry with Mr. Noyes's disapproval, and I had little hope that he would ever feel the same sympathy with my marrying Edward that he would with my marrying Mr. H. I asked him if it would not be possible for him to marry someone else in the Community, and so live here with me, and take care of the boy. He answered that his love for others here was so weak compared to his love for me, that he hardly believed it possible for him to do so. Then I said if he married outside I hoped he would stipulate for freedom to come and see his boy. He said he thought he should never marry. It seemed to him now that he could never love anyone as he had me. "Tirzah, you have been my guiding star, and the thought of you has kept me from falling in places of temptation. I have done nothing during these three years that I should not have been willing that you should see." I could fill a volume with what we said, but perhaps it would not be profitable. He left at 1/2 past 12, Paul going to Oneida with him. In the last words we had together he said: "I give you up. It is a bitter trial, but if this is the way it must be, I am resigned." I wish to be faithful to Mr. Noyes and Mr. Herrick in my dealings with him, and above all to my inner sense of what God wished me to do. I believe God helped me; for I was wonderfully sustained while he was here, having no heart-ache or temptation, but when he was fairly gone the tears would come.

The copy of Mr. Herrick's decree of divorce came this morning, and the Council met in the afternoon. Frank came and reported to us a stormy time. Had to compromise the disagreement by allowing Mr. Towner to go to Syracuse and investigate the matter. Mr. Herrick never expressed so much love for me as he did this evening. He said he should remember this day as long as he lived. It was marvelous that I could remain faithful to him when under the magnetic influence of that handsome, attractive man, and yet he trusted me perfectly.

Nov. 2.

Jamie in speaking of Edward's coming said if things had turned the other way it would have ruined all his prospects of future happiness. "Oh, no," I said, "not so bad as that." "Yes," he answered earnestly, "it would have been by far the greatest sorrow of my life if Edward had taken your heart away from me."

Homer told me the other day that one of those times when he used to be so "crazy" about me, he planned that he should enter the large hall after meeting had begun by one door, while I came in by the other, and that we should walk quickly toward the center of the room, meet, and join hands while he said: "I take this woman to be my wife," and I answered: "I take this man to be my husband." He thought we would act so quickly, and take people so thoroughly by surprise, that it would be all over with before anyone could interfere.

Nov. 3.

Mr. Towner went to Syracuse, and returned with a written opinion that there was no legal obstruction to Mr. Herrick's marrying—none whatever.

Nov. 4.

The Council met to read Mr. Towner's opinion on our case, and also to consider a proposition from us to go to Wallingford to be married, as, if Mr. Herrick married in New York, it will be under the slur of the divorce having been obtained on the charge of adultery, whereas it was for desertion. The law in Connecticut is different. A new act also in that state gives us some hope that we may be able to legitimate Hilda. We received a license from the Council to marry, and also permission to go to Connecticut for the reasons stated. We are glad to have authority from the Council to act in this matter, but Mr. Herrick had fully made up his mind that if they withheld their sanction he should act without reference to them. We neither of us acknowledge the authority of the Council to dictate to us, and only submit to it for the sake of peace.

Mr. Kinsley gives his sympathy to my marriage with Mr. Herrick. He says the night that our application was announced he awoke with a clear view of it, and saw that the previous impression he had had that I must not marry was with reference to Edward.

Nov. 5.

Jamie and I started this morning at 1/2 past 7 for W.C., leaving Hilda in charge of Miss Pomeroy. A little misunderstanding with Helen just the last thing, which made the going away rather painful; but I sent her back a postal at Utica, in order to put my mind at rest about my part of it. We found on reaching Springfield that the steamboat train was off, so we had to stay overnight there. We were glad to do so. We experienced a sensation of cumulative relief every mile that was put between us and O.C.

Nov. 6.

Heartily welcomed at W.C. at 9 o'clock this morning. Brother George and his wife, and Myron, Annie H., Beulah, Mrs. Leonard, Mrs.

Kelly, and other good friends are here, and make us thoroughly at home.
Mr. Herrick went to town and bought a license, and engaged Mr. Ira
Martin, Justice of the Peace, to come over at 4 o'clock and join us in wed-
lock. This functionary arrived promptly at the hour appointed, and performed the ceremony in the parlor in the presence of all who chose to
come, George and Annie standing up with us. The ceremony seemed
quite a solemn one to me, and I suppose it will take me a long time to
realize that I am Mrs. Herrick. They treated us to an elegant wedding
supper. George E. arrived from N.Y. in the evening, and just before I
went to bed Mrs. Ackley came and told me that she saw Edward in
N.Y. this morning, and he inquired about my marriage, and said he had
hoped to have had a chance himself. This made my heart ache some.
Edward asked me when at Oneida to write to him before I took the final
step, and I promised to do so. I wrote a letter to him the evening before
I left O.C., and it was mailed the next forenoon.

Nov. 7.

I draw a veil over last night's passionate reunion. I wonder if anything will come of this morning's suffering.

Nov. 8.

Jamie and I took leave of the Wallingford friends this morning, taking the 9 o'clock train for New York City. We got off at the New Haven
depot to find a notary before whom to make acknowledgment of Hilda.
We found him, [Charles] Ives, Jr., Justice of the Peace for New Haven
County, who was going on the same train to Bridgeport. So he certified
the document and then got aboard, and after some conversation with
Jamie, had us both swear to him concerning it. We thought we were very
fortunate to get through the matter so easily. Reached New York at noon.
Visited Astor Library and the Historical Society in the afternoon. Went
to a French hair-dresser's, and had my hair done up. Pleasant time there.
Went to Wallach's in the evening, and saw "Our Girls."

Nov. 9.

A delightful night. Changed hotels today from Grand Union to St.
Stephen's, and like this better. Went to Central Park in the afternoon. We
have a pleasant room with a bright fire in the grate. Jamie is lying on the
sofa half asleep, and I am sitting under the light with my writing. I am
very thankful for such a good, kind, loving husband, and yet there has

been a gloom over us ever since we came to the city. I suppose it is something about Edward.

Nov. 10.

Went to hear Edwin Booth in the evening in "Hamlet." Wonderful! Wonderful! I enjoyed it more than anything since we left W.C.

Nov. 11.

Started for home this morning, reaching O.C. a little before 7 in the evening. A short time after our arrival I went to Helen's room to see if there were any letters from Edward. I found two. One came the day after I left, and the other today. They were rather hard letters, although they expressed a great deal of love for me. He had consulted two lawyers in New York, who give it as their opinion that I am married to Edward. He urges me very strongly to consider this fact before moving, and says I must take the consequences if I do not.

Nov. 12.

Answered Edward that I am married, but that if I had received his letters before I left I should have waited till after more correspondence with him. I told him that if I loved him ten times more than I ever did, and felt only friendship for Mr. Herrick, I should marry Mr. H., because the idea of foresaking [*sic*] Mr. Noyes was one of the possibilities I could not contemplate, and I thought his letters plainly showed that he did not feel very friendly toward Mr. H. I felt distressed after sending this, and was afraid it was not kind enough; but what can I do?

Nov. 15.

Geo. W. returned from W.C. today. He left there the same day we did, going by way of New York. I was in the office with my husband, and he came up to us and said he thought he wouldn't spoil our honeymoon in Wallingford; but the fact was Edward met him, in New York, and told him how he had been consulting lawyers, and asked him to lay the matter before me at W.C. George promised to do so if I were not already married, but said he should probably say nothing about it if I were. He got there just an hour after the ceremony was performed, and so said nothing. He said Edward (whom he saw again on his way back) was wandering about the city, out of employment, and in a rather disheartened condition on account of having to give up this object in his life which he had had so long before him of coming back to the Community and getting me. It is heart-breaking to think of him, but it is all right and best as it is.

Nov. 16.

A letter from Edward this morning directed to "Tirzah." He says he still thinks the opinion of the lawyers correct, and that I am illegally joined to Mr. H.; but as I "prefer" another man, he shall never force me to live with him, and I need not be afraid that he shall do anything to disturb my "felicity." He has done that already. His letters have hurt my heart, all the time. He also said [several words unreadable] "<u>Mr. Noyes is a fiend.</u>" This is the [several words unreadable] that will divide us forever, unless [several words unreadable] of reading this letter I felt relieved, and think I [several words unreadable] darling Jamie.

Dec. 14.

We have been having an almost uninterrupted honeymoon for about a month. No lover ever expressed more affection for me than my beloved husband does. He said this evening, "I was never more bewitched by anyone in all my life than I am with you." He said the idea of death seemed [illegible] to him since he married me than it ever did, "It should be the greatest shock of my life if you should die," said he.

Dec. 27.

A letter from Edward directed to "T. Miller." Mr. Herrick sent it back unopened, saying that if E. wished to correspond with his wife he should address her as Mrs. Herrick.

Dec 31.

Another letter from E. to Mrs. Herrick, enclosing the one sent to me. I answered, according to Mr. Herrick's directions:

"Dear E.: I cannot correspond with you while you refuse to acknowledge the legality of my marriage with Mr. Herrick. Your treatment of him and of me is unworthy of you, and not [several words unreadable]. Tirzah C. Herrick."

This letter pleased Jamie very much. I tried several times [several words unreadable] various ways, but finally hit on this, which just suited Jamie. I was very unhappy while I had the matter in suspense and could not work out of that till I dispatched this letter. Then he was all joyous again. He said he was so glad, so <u>glad</u> he had married me and that he would rather have lived alone in the whole world, . . .

1880

Jan. 7, 1880—

A letter from [unreadable] directed to Mrs. H. C. . . . a pleasant letter, and I shall answer it, . . . Jamie. . . .

Notes

1. "Uncle George" is George Wallingford Noyes (1822–1970) who had gone to England and France with Charles Josyln (1832–1906) after Josyln had passed the New York State bar exam. Josyln attended the Columbia University School of Law. They were both sent by the community as "missionaries" to the "Old World" and on their departure an ode was composed to celebrate their journey.

2. Psalm 127:1.

3. Between 1834 and 1879 Noyes either edited or published a series of periodicals that set forth his theological and social views. They were: *The Perfectionist, The Witness, The Perfectionist and Theocratic Watchman, Spiritual Watchman, Spiritual Magazine, Free Church Circular, The Circular, The Oneida Circular,* and *The American Socialist.* See Lester G. Wells, *The Oneida Community Collection in the Syracuse University Library* (Syracuse: Syracuse University Library, 1961) and Robert S. Fogarty, "A Utopian Literary Canon," *New England Quarterly* 20, no. 1 (March 1964) for a discussion of the role of the press at Oneida.

4. The Wallingford Community (W.C.) was established in the winter of 1851 as a branch of the Oneida Community on land donated by two Perfectionists, Henry and Emily Allen. It was three hundred miles east and a hundred miles south of Oneida, and members shuttled back and forth between the two communities. Wallingford was also used as a "penal colony" for members who had established "special love" relationships at Oneida.

5. This neologism was coined by Noyes to describe the "pre-eminence mania," or the "who-shall-be-the-greatest mania." It was associated with any member who had an excessive ego and who showed a desire to be important. The term was taken from the biblical character Diotrephes, mentioned in III John 9–10, who wanted to have preeminence in the church.

6. George Cragin (1808–1884) was a member of Charles Finney's church in New York City and the publisher of the *Advocate of Moral Reform.* With his wife, Mary, he joined the Putney Community in 1840. Mary Cragin and John

H. Noyes were the first partners in the complex marriage arrangement, and she had twins by Noyes in 1847. George Cragin and Harriet Noyes were also intimate. See Constance Noyes Robertson, *Oneida Community Profiles* (Syracuse: Syracuse University Press, 1977), 27–45.

7. "Amativeness" was a phrenological term that connoted both a section of the brain ("just above and on each side of the nape of the neck") and an emotional center. According to Orson Fowler, the doyen of phrenologists, it was "The Progenitor; sexuality; gender; the love element; that which attracts the opposite sex and is attracted to it, admires and awakens admiration, creates and endows offspring; desires to love, be loved and marry; the conjugal instincts and talent; gallantry; ladyism; manliness in men; and womanliness in woman; passion. It is adapted to Nature; male, female, sexual, blending, affiliating and creative ordinances. . . . Those in whom it is large are splendidly sexed, and well nigh perfect as males and females; literally idolized the opposite sex; love almost to insanity; cherish for them the most exalted feelings of regard and esteem, as if they were a superior race of beings; love with inexpressible tenderness; and cannot live without sexual sympathy; must love and be loved; are remarkably magnetic and captivating." O. S. Fowler, *Sexual Science* (Philadelphia, 1879), 71–72. For an extended discussion of the language of sexuality, see Jesse F. Battin, "'The Word Made Flesh': Language, Authority, and Sexual Desire in Late Nineteenth-Century America," *Journal of the History of Sexuality* 3, no. 2 (1992): 223–44.

8. The Crolys were a remarkable pair. David G. Croly coined the term "miscegenation" in a political pamphlet published as part of a Democratic dirty trick in 1863 that was intended to allow the editor of the *New York World*, George Wakeman, to attack the Republicans for their supposed support of such practices. See Sidney Kaplan, "The Miscegenation Issue in the Election of 1864," *Journal of Negro History* 34, no. 3 (July 1949): 274–343 and Werner Sollors's brilliant *Neither Black Nor White Yet Both: Thematic Explorations of Interracial Literature* (New York: Oxford University Press, 1997). I am indebted to Werner Sollors for pointing out this reference. Jane Cunningham Croly was born in England and came to the United States with her family when she was twelve. Her father was a Unitarian clergyman and she was educated at home. In 1855, when she was twenty-six, her first article was accepted by the *New York Tribune*; she contributed pieces on the theater and women's issues under the pseudonym "Jennie June." She met and married another journalist, David Goodman Croly, in 1856 and in the same year she called for the first Women's Parliament. In 1862 David Croly became managing editor of the *New York World* and his wife wrote for that paper and others. In David Croly's *Glimpses of the Future: Suggestions As to the Drift of Things* (New York: G. P. Putnam's, 1888), chapters on "Improving the Race" and "The Secrets of the Jewish Race" contain references to Oneida.

9. During the 1860s Noyes developed a chronic throat infection that left him speechless for extended periods.

10. "Among the Autochthons" is a sketch of the Oneida Indians who came to the community to beg food. The term "autochthons," taken from the Greek, means "natives of the place." Tirzah describes how she visited their homes, watched them grind corn, and noticed that they enjoyed drawing on slates. She ended the piece, however, by commenting on their unruliness and the effects of miscegenation on them: "It is a striking fact that there are few straight-haired children in that school. Coarse, straight black hair has been one of the representative features of the race, everybody knows; but here, finely waving locks, far from black and complexions scarcely more than tan brown plainly betoken that miscegenation is fast extinguishing the Oneida tribe of Indians." *The Circular* 5, no. 33 (November 2, 1868).

11. "Miss Peabody" is Elizabeth Palmer Peabody (1804–1894), an educator and a friend of both Edward Ellery Channing and Ralph Waldo Emerson. As Bronson Alcott's assistant at the famous "Temple School" in 1834, she initiated a series of "conferences" to introduce women to history and literature. She was an important member of the Transcendental movement, wrote essays for *The Dial,* and ran a bookshop. Margaret Fuller (1810–1850) was a formidable intellectual and the founding editor of the Transcendentalist journal *The Dial.* She was the author of *Women in the Nineteenth Century* and her tragic death with her husband and infant son in a shipwreck off the coast of New York in 1850 sent ripples through the literary and social world.

12. Harriet Skinner (1817–1893) was John H. Noyes's sister and she joined the Putney Association with him. According to one source "she contributed more to the community publications than any other woman." See John B. Teeple, *The Oneida Family* (Oneida: Oneida Community Historical Committee, 1984).

13. Willow Place, built in 1862, was the trap factory at Oneida, located a mile and a half from the Mansion House. It was named after the street in Brooklyn on which Noyes and other members had lived during the early 1850s. The property consisted of a sawmill, a stone quarry, an iron foundry, and a farmhouse where members of the community who worked in the trap shop lived.

14. "L.W." is Susan Leona Worden (1844–1923), who Tirzah thought was too "coarse" for Edward Inslee.

15. The symbolic marriage ceremony between Charlotte Miller and James Herrick, which took place in 1873 when he received a divorce from his wife, formally ushered him into the community. Tirzah's mother died in 1874 of malaria at age 55. It was, of course, ironic that Tirzah would later marry the man with whom her mother had symbolically entered into a covenant.

16. "O.T.T." may have been a pet name for Homer Barron. Leonard Dunn was the community dentist at the time.

17. Luke 18:1. Phonography was a form of shorthand popularized by the reformer Stephen Pearl Andrews. At Oneida they used a system called "Munson," developed in the 1860s as a court stenographic system.

18. Joppa, a cottage on Oneida Lake purchased by the colony in 1872, was

used by members for swimming, boating, and fishing. It was twelve miles from
the Mansion House, and parties often went there in the summer months. It was
an hour's train ride from the community. See *The Circular*, July 21, 1873.

19. "Waist" probably meant in this context a bodice or blouse, although it
could mean an undergarment. In the United States, the term was usually reserved for a child's undergarment.

20. "Baby talk" was associated with the community's attitudes toward dolls.
In October 1874 *The Circular* recounted the history of doll keeping and doll
burning, beginning with an incident in Brooklyn in 1851 when dolls were
burned to drive away "idolatry" among the children.

21. The scenic Perryville Falls are located near Chittenago, about 15 miles
from Oneida.

22. Julia Inslee may have been Edward's mother or sister, since his father,
William, came alone to the colony in 1856 from the Newark "family."

23. Acts 9:5.

24. Sugaring-off was the process of boiling down syrup in preparation for
granulation.

25. The "lying-in" room was probably an apartment set aside for pregnant
women in the 1870s, when there were so many births. Its exact location at the
Mansion House is unknown.

26. George Sand's popular novel *Mauprat*, set in Italy, is about a musical
couple, Esmee and Bernard. He is driven by a devouring physical passion while
his cousin Esmee is consumed by a platonic love. Bernard is a savage; she is a
saint. At one point in the novel Bernard proclaims his possessive love for her: "I
understand that I love you madly and will claw out the heart of any man who
tries to take you from me. I know that I shall force you to love me and that if I
don't succeed I will at any rate not let you belong to anyone else while I am alive.
He will have to walk over my wounded body, bleeding from every pore, to put
the wedding ring on your finger and with my last breath I shall dishonour you
by saying you are my mistress, in order to mar the joy of the man who has tri-
umphed over me; and if, as I die, I can stab you I will, so that in the tomb at least
you will be my wife." Quoted in Patricia Thomson, *George Sand and the Vic-
torians: Her Influence and Reputation in Nineteenth-Century England* (New
York: Macmillan, 1977), 254.

27. Dr. Carpenter was a physician from Oneida who often attended at
births.

28. Women at Oneida were encouraged to wean their babies at an early age
in order to forestall the dangers of "philoprogenitiveness" (another phrenological term), or excessive love of children.

29. The laws of divorce and custody were in flux in the 1870s. Under
common law, the father's right to custody was superior, but in U.S. courts the
interests of the child were considered. "Whatever a child's good demands, therefore, is its rights" was the position taken by Joel Prentiss Bishop in his authori-
tative *Commentaries on the Law of Marriage and Divorce, with the Evidence,*

Practice, Pleading, and Forms: Also of Separations without Divorce, and of Evidence of Marriage in All Issues (Boston: Little, Brown, 1881). The father of a bastard child had no rights, and Haydn was, technically, a bastard. However, New York State had passed an adoption law in 1873, and social workers were keen to apply "moral" standards when placing a child in care. The "immoral" character of Oneida might have led a court to place a child in a "healthier" atmosphere. See Stephen B. Presser, "The Historical Background of the American Law of Adoption," in Whythe Holt, ed., *Essays in Nineteenth-Century American Legal History* (Westport, Conn.: Greenwood Press, 1976), 443–516 and Hendrik Hartog, "Lawyering, Husband's Rights, and 'the Unwritten Law' in Nineteenth-Century America," *Journal of American History* 84, no. 1 (June 1997): 67–96.

30. The Noyes stock was thought to be superior by virtue of J. H. Noyes's prophetic status, since he was in the line of authority that ran from Jesus to Paul and because of the New England stock the family came from. See Robert S. Fogarty, *Special Love/Special Sex* (Syracuse: Syracuse University Press, 1994) for a discussion of Noyes's views about breeding. The literature surrounding the "incest" question is voluminous. A synopsis of the biological, psychological, and sociological approaches about incest can be found in an appendix to James Twitchell's *Forbidden Partners: The Incest Taboo in Modern Culture* (New York: Columbia University Press, 1987), 243–59. Also valuable is Marc Shell's *The End of Kinship: "Measure for Measure", Incest, and the Idea of Universal Siblinghood* (Stanford, Calif.: Stanford University Press, 1988), particularly the opening chapter.

31. "Love's Embrace" may have been a reference to a poem, a short story, or a musical piece that thrilled Tirzah.

32. Possibly this section was eliminated from the typescript because it contained material damaging to Tirzah. Given the inflammatory nature of other material included in this memoir, however, it seems unlikely that any descendants would have decided to excise any passages. Tirzah seems to have been spirited out of the community to avoid any possible action by Inslee against her, and she and Charles Cragin doubtless traveled under assumed names to avoid detection or scandal.

33. *The Socialist* replaced the *Oneida Circular* in 1876 as the colony's voice to the world. It carried less religious reporting and more news about other communal experiments as part of an effort to produce a "faithful record of facts relating to the progress of Socialism everywhere."

34. In fact, Paul Inslee inherited his father's musical ability. He played cornet, conducted the Oneida Community Ltd. band, and directed a choir. He was in charge of the hardware department at Oneida Ltd. See Teeple, *The Oneida Family*, 229.

35. Luke 13:24.

36. George Kellogg (1838–1906) played the violin and held several positions within the colony, including postmaster. The initials "A.B." suggest several

individuals: Abram Burt, Arthur Bloom, or Ann Hobart Bailey. The "affair" in question may have been a discussion or a criticism.

37. Cozicot was a cottage on Long Island Sound that community members visited.

38. "Aunt Harriet" is Harriet Noyes (1817–1893), J. H. Noyes's younger sister.

39. II Corinthians 12:10.

40. "Hayes hypo" refers to the "instability" that afflicted Polly Hayes, John H. Noyes's mother. She suffered from melancholia and bouts of depression. See Robert David Thomas, *The Man Who Would Be Perfect: John Humphrey Noyes and the Utopian Impulse* (Philadelphia: University of Pennsylvania Press, 1977) for a close reading of the psychological forces that formed young man Noyes.

41. Here Noyes suggests that his breeding days are over, but in fact, three children were attributed to him after 1875, including one by Helen Miller, his niece. Clearly Noyes kept up his interest in consanguineous stirpiculture. Just after this discussion, there is further talk about Tirzah's having a child with Theodore, her cousin.

42. The conflict between J. H. N. and W. A. H. (William Hinds) continued until the breakup of the community. Hinds's opposition to Noyes came when the elder Noyes imposed Theodore on the community as leader in 1875. Hinds was joined by James Towner in leading the opposition party, called "Townerites" in the community literature.

43. Virginia Hinds (1864–1931) was the daughter of William A. Hinds and Charlotte Reid.

44. "Gilpin Commentary" was a popular Bible commentary by William Gilpin (1724–1804) titled *An Exposition of the New Testament; Intended as an Introduction to the Study of the Scriptures.* It was first published in 1790.

45 "Enceinte" means pregnant.

46. Tirzah has had her period; hence, she is not pregnant by Homer Barron.

47. Temple Noyes (1862–1949) was the son of George Washington Noyes (who died in 1870) and Fidelia Dunn (1838–1908) and, in this case, was probably taken to see John H. Noyes and Harriet Holton Noyes.

48. Maria Barron (1842–1913) and Sarah Minerva Barron (1843–1939). Minerva and John Norton (1835–1900) married at the breakup of the community.

49. "Centennial Views" was probably a viewbook that portrayed the exhibitions and buildings of the Philadelphia Exposition of 1876 that several community members had expressed a desire to see.

50. The swift response by both J. H. Noyes and Harriet Skinner suggests that there was little tolerance for "domestic violence" at Oneida. Few cases were reported in published community criticisms.

51. The term "afflatus" means a spiritual inspiration, but to members of the

community it often had a negative connotation, suggesting a cloud that hung over an individual.

52. The women at Oneida wore their hair short in obedience to Paul's dictum. In an undated letter to John H. Noyes, Tirzah wrote: "In obedience to Paul, I want to dress and wear my hair & do all such things in just the spirit and manner you would have me. This life is so short, what matter is it how we look?"

53. Ella Underwood (1849–1950). She never had any children and did not marry at the breakup of the community.

54. *Merriam Webster's Collegiate Dictionary* (10th ed.) defines cassimere as "a closely woven smooth twilled usu. wool fabric (as for suits)."

55. Richard D. Ely.

56. The "fruit house," originally a dairy barn, had been converted to house the community's many minor industries, including the canning of fruits and vegetables.

57. Lorenzo Bolles III (1854–1944) entered the community with his family in 1865.

58. Harley Hamilton (1861–1933) was a talented musician who eventually founded the Los Angeles Symphony and the Los Angeles Women's Orchestra. See Hector Alliot, "Harley Hamilton," *The Quadrangle* 4, no. 3 (March 1913): 2–3.

59. Rosamond Underwood (1853–1917). Theodore Noyes and Ann Hobart became avid spiritualists in the 1870s.

60. The "minister raid" refers to a meeting held in January 1879 to rally support against the community. Both the Episcopal Bishop of central New York and the president of Syracuse University were outspoken in their criticisms. See "Crusade of the Clergy against the Oneida Community," *The American Socialist* 4, no. 8 (February 20, 1879).

61. William Dean Howells published *The Lady of the Aroostook* in 1879.

62. Involuntary ejaculations did occur, even among experienced practitioners of male continence like James Herrick. Reportedly the community kept a supply of douches on hand for such "accidents." See Louis Kern's *An Ordered Love: Sex Roles and Sexuality in Victorian Utopias: The Shakers, the Mormons, and the Oneida Community* (Chapel Hill: University of North Carolina Press, 1981) for a highly nuanced and sensitive look at the sexual regime at Oneida. Material relevant to this part of the Oneida sexual regime can also be found at the Kinsey Institute Archives, Indiana University, Bloomington, Indiana.

63. *Signor Monaldini's Choice* by Mary Agnes Tincker (1831–1907) was published in 1879. Tincker had an interesting career as a Catholic writer, a volunteer nurse in the Civil War, and a regular contributor to such publications as *Harper's Magazine* and *Putnam's Monthly Magazine*. She published eleven novels and books, including the popular *Signor Monaldini's Choice*. Set in Rome, the novel has a provocative set of characters, including the beautiful

Camilla, with whom Tirzah identified. A *Nation* review in 1879 outlined the "actors" in this novelistic drama: "One girl with wonderful beauty and an ignorance of the world which transcends naiveté; one mysterious man of rank, who, being specially a man of the world, yet behaves with a simplicity fit for a boy; one coarse-natured family wrapped in an ignoble prosperity; one rather vague and cold-blooded artist. . . . We take it to be the writer's intention to protest against the usual conventional restrictions on women's freedom of action." In this romance Camilla (whose father is French) is befriended by a German baroness, is approached by a rejected lover (an Italian count), and meets a poor American woman who has had a liaison with the count. Camilla is murdered, then suddenly comes to life (literally from her coffin) when her lover embraces her after learning of the death of his wife. This improbable plot centers on the beautiful and magnetic Camilla, and it is little wonder that Tirzah identified with this romantic heroine and all her sexual intrigues.

64. Sconondoan was an area adjacent to the Willow Place Community on Sconondoan Creek. Skenadoak was the chief of the Oneida Indians who died in 1816 and is buried in a cemetery at Hamilton College in nearby Clinton.

65. George Henry Burnham (1854–1899) had seceded from the community in 1875. His mother, Abby Scott Burnham (1821–1900), was married to Henry Burnham (1820–1897), a Perfectionist. They joined the Putney Association in 1847 and Oneida in 1848. She had a child—George Henry—by Leander Worden in 1854.

66. Because Herrick's wife had divorced him in Maryland on the grounds of desertion he and Tirzah could legally marry in New York. If, however, she had charged him with adultery it would have been a bar to the marriage in 1879.

INDEX

Croly, David G., 16, 192
Croly, Jane Cunningham, 16, 58, 192n8

Daily Journal, 13
Darwin, Charles, 19
"Daughter of the Regiment" allusion, 24, 44n51
Deleuze, Joseph, 25
"diotrephians," 55, 151, 191n5
Dixon, William Hepworth, 17
dogma, 5

Ely, Reverend D., 145
Emerson, Ralph Waldo, 4
Enlightenment, 5
eugenics, 4, 25, 26, 29, 116–117. *See also* stirpiculture

faithfulness, 62, 99, 113, 182
family, 4, 8
"Father Noyes." *See* Noyes, John Humphrey
Finney, Charles, 5, 6, 27
Foster, Lawrence, 9
Foucault, Michel, 25, 31, 45n58
Fourier, Charles, 4–5
Fowler, Orson S., 26, 43n37, 192n7
free love, 3, 7, 11, 16; Henry James Sr. on, 12; masturbation and, 19. *See also* complex marriage
Fruitlands, 3
Fuller, Margaret, 60, 193n11

Galton, Frances, 19
generational conflict, 28–29, 56–57, 106, 107
Glimpses of the Future (Croly), 16
Goodman, David, 16
Guiteau, Charles, 16
"Gynecological Study of the Oneida Community" (Van de Warker), 22

Hamilton, Augusta, 47, 97, 155
Hamilton, Erastus, 14, 49, 115, 123, 164; relationship with T.M., 35; sexual liaisons with T.M., 19, 24
Hamilton, George W., 42n21
Hatch, James, 66
Hawley, Victor, 4
Hayes, Rutherford B., 42n21
Henry, George, 100–101, 180
Herrick, Hilda (daughter of T.M.), 39, 169, 171, 187, 188; birth of, 159

Herrick, James B., 34, 96, 109, 117; clerical standing of, 24–25; emotional breakdown of, 40; love for T.M., 171–172, 177–178; marriage to Charlotte N. Miller, 65, 193n15; marriage to T.M., 18, 98, 181–191, 198n66; relationship with Harriet Worden, 49; relationship with Helen C. Miller, 168; relationship with T.M., 17, 36, 37–39, 75, 140, 143–147, 161, 164–168, 174–175; "rover's license" and, 173; sexual liaison with T.M., 24
Hinds, Virginia, 35, 119, 120
Hinds, William, 17, 117, 136, 169
Hobart, Ann, 35, 37, 96, 102, 112, 141, 150; as community leader, 36; leaves Oneida Community, 153; relationship with Theodore Noyes, 49; relationship with T.M., 107, 129, 131, 139; Spiritualism and, 158, 197n59; status of in Oneida Community, 150; stirpiculture and, 117, 121–122
Hobart, Lily, *91*
Holton, Harriet, 7, 8, 29
home schools, 11
"home talks," 19, 23
horticulture, 11
Hunter, Henry, 49, 121, 122–123, 132, 147, 151; relationship with T.M., 35, 122–126, 133–134

"I spirit," 42n26
idolatry, 61, 68, 69, 131, 194n20
incest, 4, 20–21, 195n30. *See also* consanguinity
individualism, 4, 15
Inslee, Edward, 12, 65–66, 92, 136, 149, 159–160, 179; John H. Noyes's view of, 33, 35; leadership campaign against, 35–36, 153, 154, 156; marriage outside Oneida Community, 138, 180; rebellion against John H. Noyes, 31–32, 103–105, 163, 190; relationship with T.M., 27, 31, 32–34, 37, 39–40, 48, 66–67, 69, 79, 99–101, 113, 119; son Paul (Haydn) and, 103–106, 111, 112–113, 145, 150; T.M.'s dreams about, 142–143, 151; T.M.'s marriage to James B. Herrick and, 184–186, 188, 189–190
Inslee, Haydn. *See* Inslee, Paul
Inslee, Paul (son of T.M.), 39, 92, 109, 111, 128, 134; birth of, 33; change of

Peabody, Elizabeth Palmer, 193n11
penal reform, 5
Perfectionism, 3, 5, 6, 48; biblical ethics
    and, 8; in Brooklyn, 11–12; defined,
    41n7; millennialism and, 7; rejection
    of Calvinism, 6–7
phrenology, 25, 26, 192n7
Pitt, Theodore, 18
"platonic" relationships, 35
Pomeroy, Miss, 68, 102, 187
power relations, 4
*Practical Instruction in Animal Magne-
    tism* (Deleuze), 25
Presbyterianism, 6, 12
Prindle, Mary, 39, 120, 156
property: common ownership of, 8, 11,
    53; music as, 15; women as, 10
prophecy, 8, 195n30
prosecution, fear of, 17, 24, 173
proselytism, 11, 27
Protestant Episcopal Church, 25
public sex, 60
Puritanism, 5
Putney (Vermont) community, 6, 7, 47

Realf, Richard, 16
religion, 3, 4, 21, 26
Religion and Sexuality (Foster), 9
revivalist movements, 5, 6
Reynolds, Mr., 66
romance, 171–172, 178
"rovers' licenses," 24, 173

salvation, 57
sanctification, 7
Sand, George, 99, 194n26
science, 4, 19, 21, 59, 116–118, 145. *See
    also* eugenics; stirpiculture
self, expression of, 27
self-control, 18
selfishness, 10, 11
Seward, William H., 16
sexuality: Foucault's view of, 45n58;
    magnetism and, 26; music and,
    42n26; mutual criticism and, 13–14;
    public intercourse, 22–23, 60; sexual
    liberation, 4
Shakers, 23
sin, 9–10, 11, 21, 41n7, 57
Skinner, Charles, 37
Skinner, Harriet Noyes (aunt of T.M.), 8,
    18, 47, 55, 90, 112, 113, 114, 128;
    community publications and,

193n12; relationship with T.M., 126–
    127, 135, 139–140, 155
Skinner, John L., 19
Skinner, Joseph, 33, 49
"special love" relationships: John H.
    Noyes's view of, 73; marriage and, 11;
    T.M. and, 29, 32, 37, 48, 175;
    Wallingford community and, 191n4.
    See also love
Spiritual Wives (Dixon), 17
Spiritualism, 5, 9, 25, 158
stirpiculture, 3, 20, 25, 26, 70; goals of,
    22; introduction of, 28–29; social
    duty in service of, 23–24; T.M.'s role
    in, 35, 63, 72, 132–133, 196;
    "Weighing the Babies" ceremony,
    15–16, 88; women's rights and,
    45n62. *See also* eugenics
Stoehr, Taylor, 25
Stowe, Harriet Beecher, 21

Taylor, Nathaniel, 6
temperance movement, 4
Thacker, Mr., 66
theater, 14–15
theology, 8
Thumb, Tom, 16
Towner, James, 17, 32
Towner, Lillian, 32, 76
Towner, William, 34, 114, 115, 136, 157,
    187; as Paul Inslee's "father," 160,
    167, 168–169; rebellion against John
    H. Noyes, 167
Transcendentalism, 5–6, 193n11

"Uncle George." *See* Noyes, George
    Washington
Underwood, Charlotte E., 14
unfaithfulness, 62
Union Colony (Colorado), 16
Unitarianism, 5–6
utopian communities, 3, 5

Van, James, 156
Van de Warker, Ely, 22

Wallingford (Connecticut) community,
    42n21, 105, 108, 133, 180, 181;
    establishment of, 191n4; Oneida
    journals and, 13; T.M. at, 112, 142
Wayland-Smith, Frank, 15, 17, 48–49,
    81, 86, 89, 111, 134; music and,
    172, 179–180; relationship with

Robert S. Fogarty is Professor of History at Antioch College and Editor of the *Antioch Review*. A leading authority on American communes, he has been a Visiting Fellow at All Souls College, Oxford, and the N.Y.U. Humanities Institute and was a Lloyd Lewis Fellow at the Newberry Library. He is the author of *Special Love/Special Sex* (Syracuse: Syracuse University Press, 1994), *All Things New: Communal and Utopian Movements 1865–1914* (Chicago: University of Chicago Press, 1990), *The Righteous Remnant: The House of David* (Kent, Ohio: Kent State University Press, 1981), and *Dictionary of American Communal and Utopian History* (Westport, Conn.: Greenwood Press, 1980). His essays have appeared in the *Times Literary Supplement* and *The Nation*.